Policing for London

Policing for London

Report of an independent study
funded by the Nuffield Foundation,
the Esmée Fairbairn Foundation and
the Paul Hamlyn Foundation

Marian FitzGerald
Mike Hough
Ian Joseph
Tarek Qureshi

WILLAN
PUBLISHING

Published by

Willan Publishing
Culmcott House
Mill Street, Uffculme
Cullompton, Devon
EX15 3AT, UK
Tel: +44(0)1884 840337
Fax: +44(0)1884 840251
e-mail: info@willanpublishing.co.uk
Website: www.willanpublishing.co.uk

Published simultaneously in the USA and Canada by

Willan Publishing
c/o ISBS, 5824 N.E. Hassalo St
Portland, Oregon 97213-3644, USA
Tel: +001(0)503 287 3093
Fax: +001(0)503 280 8832
Website: www.isbs.com

First published 2002

ISBN 1-903240-93-X

British Library Cataloguing-in-Publication Data
A catalogue record for this book is available from the British Library.

Typeset by PDQ Typesetting, Newcastle-under-Lyme, Staffs.
Printed in Great Britain by Ashford Colour Press

Contents

List of figures and tables   vii

Foreword   ix

Acknowledgements   xi

Summary   xiii

PART 1   BACKGROUND

1   *Introduction*   3
     The origins of the study   3
     Aims   3
     Research strategy   4
     The structure of the report   6

2   *The Policing Environment*   8
     Demographic trends   8
     Technology and consumption   12
     Demands on the police   13
     Crime, disorder and other 'police business'   15
     Institutional change   18
     Summary   25

PART II   THE RESEARCH FINDINGS

3   *Public Concerns, Needs and Wants*   29
     Measuring concerns and priorities about crime and disorder   29
     Anxieties about crime and disorder   30
     Priority problems   38
     Policing solutions   41
     Key findings   48

4   *Londoners' Experience of the Police*   49
     Contact as police 'users'   50
     Police-initiated contacts in London   54
     Who do the police target as suspects?   59
     Vicarious experience   63
     Key findings   64

5   *Reactions to Police Contact*   65
     Satisfaction amongst victims of crime   65
     Ratings of contact as suspect   70
     Visiting the police station   71
     Sources of serious annoyance   72
     Complaints against the police   74
     Key findings   75

6 *Confidence in the Police*   77
   Measuring confidence in the police   77
   Sources of information about the police   77
   The police and other occupational groups   79
   Trends in ratings of effectiveness over time   80
   Who thinks the police do a good job?   82
   Views on fairness and integrity   84
   Willingness to help the police   88
   Considering joining the police   89
   Key findings   91

7 *Group Perceptions and Area Differences*   92
   Focus groups with the public   92
   Focus groups and interviews with the police   94
   Conclusions   101
   Key findings   102

PART III DISCUSSION AND CONCLUSIONS

8 *External Constraints on Responsive Policing*   105
   Does the MPS have more work to do than previously?   105
   Have MPS resources shrunk?   108
   Do priorities imposed on the MPS impede responsive policing?   110
   Growing public expectations   112
   Conflicting demands   113
   Summary of chapter   114

9 *Internal Organisation and Responsive Policing*   115
   Centralised decision-making   115
   Impact of quantitative performance management   118
   Specialisation and diffusion of responsibility   118
   Poor management   121
   Staff morale   123
   The same old story?   126
   Summary of chapter   128

10 *Conclusions*   129
   Change and continuity over 20 years   129
   Delivering more responsive policing: the issues   131
   Delivering more responsive policing: the mechanisms   137
   Conclusion   146

Appendix 1: The Advisory Group   149
Appendix 2: Methodology   150
Appendix 3: Logistic and Ordinal Regression Models   158

References   163

Tables and figures

Figures

2.1   Average crimes and searches in London boroughs (1998–99)   17
3.1   Trends in anxiety: per cent of respondents 'feeling very safe'
        out alone at night   31
3.2   Anxiety about crime, by area – per cent feeling 'very worried'   33
3.3   Anxieties about specific crimes – per cent feeling 'very worried'   35
3.4   Anxiety about crime, by ethnicity – per cent feeling 'very worried'   36
3.5   How much of a problem? How common? Perceptions of incivilities   37
3.6   Incivilities as a 'very' or 'fairly' big problem 1992–2000   39
3.7   Contrasting crime priorities in affluent and deprived boroughs   40
3.8   Activities the police should spend more time on   41
3.9   Activities the police should spend less time on   42
4.1   Reasons for seeking police help   50
4.2   Trends in police usage (1991–99, per cent using the police last year)   53
4.3   Telephone calls for police assistance, in 000's, 1996–2000   53
4.4   Reasons for police-initiated contact in 1999–2000   54
4.5   Contacts with the police as suspect, 1999–2000, by area   55
4.6   Trends in stops on foot or in cars, 1981–99 (per cent stopped)   56
4.7   Percentage of population with direct or vicarious knowledge of foot stops   63
5.1   Trends in annoyance with the police   73
5.2   Reasons for annoyance with police in the last 5 years   73
6.1   Londoners' sources of information about the police (%)   78
6.2   Londoners' ratings of performance of criminal justice agencies (%)   80
6.3   Trends in ratings of local police performance in London (%)   81
6.4   Area differences in confidence – per cent saying local police do 'very
        good job'   81
6.5   Ethnic differences over time in ratings: per cent saying 'very good job'   84
8.1   Expenditure (£ millions) in the MPS, 1980–81 onward, at 1980 prices   108

Tables

2.1   Average population of London boroughs by deprivation and ethnic
        origin, 1998 (%)   10
2.2   Average population of state primary schoolchildren in London
        boroughs by deprivation and ethnic origin, 1998 (%)   11
2.3   Experience of crime: people victimised once or more, 1981 and 2000 (%)   15
2.4   Police resources in the case-study areas (1998) in relation to population,
        deprivation and crime   22
3.1   Trends in worry about racial attack, by ethnicity (per cent 'very worried')   32
3.2   The top ten priorities (%)   39
3.3   The top six 'non-priorities' (%)   41
4.1   Demographic profile of those seeking contact with the police: per cent
        contacting the police in the previous year   51
4.2   Stops per 1,000 people, and number of stops per suspect, 1999–2000   55
4.3   Trends in stops (1981–1999/2000)   57
4.4   Foot and car stops: number of times stopped in 1981 and 1999–2000 (%)   57
4.5   Reasons given for vehicle stops (%)   58
4.6   Demographic breakdown of people stopped in their cars by the police:
        per cent stopped in previous year   59

4.7	Demographic breakdown of those stopped on foot by the police: per cent stopped in previous year	60
4.8	Trends in proportions stopped by the police (%)	61
4.9	Variables affecting car stops 1999–2000	62
4.10	Variables affecting foot stops 1999–2000	62
5.1	Levels of satisfaction with the police amongst victims who reported (%)	65
5.2	Trends in satisfaction amongst victims: PSI and PFLS surveys (%)	66
5.3	Reasons for dissatisfaction by crime types, PFLS (%)	67
5.4	Victim dissatisfaction in London compared to other forces (%)	67
5.5	Reasons for satisfaction, by crime types, PFLS (%)	68
5.6	Demographic differences in victim satisfaction (%)	69
5.7	Demographic differences in satisfaction amongst those stopped in cars (%)	70
5.8	Demographic differences in perceived helpfulness of desk staff (%)	71
6.1	The police and other occupational groups – percentage of Londoners saying they do a 'very good job' or a 'good job'	79
6.2	Demographic breakdown of rating of local police performance (%)	82
6.3	Beliefs about police malpractice: per cent saying it 'often happens' and 'never happens'	86
6.4	Per cent saying the police treat different groups unfairly	87
6.5	Per cent saying the police treat ethnic minorities unfairly	88
6.6	Preparedness to help the police, by ethnic group (per cent prepared to help)	88
6.7	Per cent of under 45s who had ever considered joining the police, by ethnic group	89
A2.1	Achieved sample size	149
A2.2	Demographic breakdown of PFLS and 2000 BCS subsample: weighted sample (%)	151
A2.3	Demographic breakdown of PFLS and 2000 BCS subsample: unweighted numbers	151
A2.4	Demographic breakdown of PFLS and merged datasets: unweighted numbers by ethnic group	152
A2.5	Public focus groups in case-study areas	154
A3.1	Logistic regression model for demographic predictors of police usage	157
A3.2	Logistic regression model for demographic and experiential predictors of police usage	157
A3.3	Ordinal regression model for predictors of being stopped in cars	158
A3.4	Ordinal regression model for predictors of being stopped on foot	158
A3.5	Logistic regression model for demographic predictors of annoyance with the police in the last five years	159
A3.6	Logistic regression model for demographic predictors of thinking the police do a bad job	159
A3.7	Logistic regression model for demographic and experiential predictors of thinking the police do a bad job	160

Foreword

This study was initiated shortly after publication of the report of the Macpherson Inquiry into the death of Stephen Lawrence. That report has undoubtedly been regarded as an important landmark in the development of the Metropolitan Police, leading to a period of intensive organisational self-scrutiny and reform. This study, ably carried out by researchers from the London School of Economics and South Bank University, provides us with an important benchmark against which to assess improvements. The research was planned as a sequel to the seminal study carried out by the Policy Studies Institute 20 years ago. Both the similarities and the differences between policing then and now are striking.

In September 2001, after the fieldwork for the study was completed, the World Trade Center was destroyed. For a time it seemed the event marked a complete discontinuity in the way public safety would be policed in the major cities of the developed world. Six months on it is clear that while September 11th has added a new and unwelcome dimension to the policing of civil society, the long-term challenges of policing diverse communities will remain – and may become even more central to police work. One of the strengths of this report is that it allows us to step back for a moment and take a longer view of these policing issues.

An important theme in this report is the way in which an understandable sense of urgency on the part of governments to achieve reform has led to a style of performance management with perverse effects. Perhaps the most important of these is the way in which political choices about policing style and policing philosophy have become submerged by the apparatus of performance measurement. This report is being published at a time of intense debate, both in London and nationally, about the future conduct of policing. I am sure the wealth of sound evidence and thoughtful reflection it contains will make an important contribution to a wiser debate.

I would like to take this opportunity to offer my personal thanks to the project's Advisory Group for their very substantial contribution to the study's success.

Lord Dholakia

Acknowledgements

We owe an enormous debt of gratitude to our funders, the Nuffield Foundation, the Esmée Fairbairn Foundation and the Paul Hamlyn Foundation. Without their generosity this study would not have been possible. We are also very grateful to our Advisory Group, and in particular to Lord Dholakia, who chaired it, for their help and support.

The Metropolitan Police Service was generous in its support of the study, and for the research access it provided in our three case-study sites. We would like to thank Denis O'Connor, now Chief Constable of Surrey Constabulary, who provided much of the impetus for getting the study off the ground. We are especially grateful to DCI Colette Paul and Inspector Cheryl Burden, who were consistently supportive of the enterprise and opened many doors to us. The staff of the MPS Communication User Support Unit have also been very helpful.

A great many people have given us time to discuss our emerging ideas over the last 18 months. Special thanks are due to Margaret Hyde, Patricia Lankester, Graham Lancaster, Anthony Tomei and Sharon Witherspoon. Richard Berthoud and David Smith have provided invaluable comments and suggestions about the analysis of the findings. Many others provided helpful drafting comments, including Roger Graef, Barrie Irving and Bob Morris. We are also very grateful to Lorna Whyte for her help and support throughout the project.

We are also grateful to the Home Office for making the 2000 British Crime Survey available to us, and would like to thank Chris Kershaw and his team for providing us with various BCS datasets and for their advice about analysis. We would also like to thank several colleagues within our institutions: Kate Steward at the LSE for her contribution to the qualitative analysis, and Anna Clancy and Natalie Aye Maung for their work on the British Crime Survey.

Finally, the study depended above all on the people we interviewed and who participated in our survey and focus groups, and we are especially grateful to the police officers and the school students for the frankness of their views and the insights they gave us.

Marian FitzGerald
Mike Hough
Ian Joseph
Tarek Qureshi

March 2002

Summary

The Policing for London Study (PFLS) set out to assess what Londoners wanted of their police at the start of the twenty-first century, to examine sources of satisfaction and dissatisfaction, and to consider ways of bridging the gap between expectations and reality. The initial idea for the study came from the Metropolitan Police (MPS) but it was eventually funded completely independently of the police by three charitable trusts: the Nuffield Foundation, the Esmée Fairbairn Foundation and the Paul Hamlyn Foundation. The MPS, however, gave it their full co-operation.

The main elements of the study were:

- A survey of Londoners. This comprised 2,800 people aged 15 or over and included a booster sample of black and Asian respondents. The survey had a probability sample, with oversampling of black and Asian minority groups. Appropriately weighted, the sample is representative of adult Londoners. Where possible, the survey database was combined with the London sub-sample of the 2000 British Crime Survey (BCS), which asked many of the same questions. The combined sample comprised 1,579 black respondents, 1,190 Indians, 1,005 Pakistanis and Bangladeshis, and 1,969 white or other respondents.

- Detailed case studies in three contrasting London boroughs. These involved focus groups with members of the public and with school students; in-depth interviews with key local informants and senior police officers; focus groups with police constables and sergeants and inspectors; and observation of the police at work. The case-study sites were selected to be illustrative of different sorts of London borough, with different levels of affluence and different ethnic mixes.

- Secondary analysis of borough, force-wide and other statistics, including crime figures, the computerised records of calls for police assistance, MPS data on the views of staff and socio-economic data.

Background

The MPS is unique among British police forces in at least three respects: its sheer size, its particular position and responsibilities in serving the capital city, and the fact that it is home to the majority of Britain's visible minority ethnic groups (with the exception of those of Pakistani origin).

The study was commissioned in the immediate aftermath of the Macpherson Inquiry into the murder of Stephen Lawrence. It was designed as a sequel to a similar study by the Policy Studies Institute (PSI) that was published two years after the Scarman inquiry into the Brixton riots of 1981. Both inquiries highlighted concerns about relations between the police and people of minority ethnic origin, but both studies set out to place these concerns in the context of the relationship between the MPS and the people of London more generally.

The period between the two studies has seen major changes in society, crime and policing. In particular:

- Society has become more economically polarised and, in London in particular, very much more ethnically diverse. There is increasing diversity between and within the minority ethnic groups, but the poorer groups tend to live in the most deprived boroughs where crime is highest. In many of these areas no one group accounts for a majority of the youth population. Rather, the citizens of the future in many areas will be drawn from multiple communities – both white and non-white.

- Some – but not all – types of crime have increased since 1981 and there have been changes in opportunities for and patterns of crime.

- The role of the police and the context in which they operate have significantly altered in the last 20 years. They are now far more accountable and they are expected to work in partnership with others within a framework that is defined at national level in increasing detail. A key influence on the way they now work has been the growth of quantitative performance management systems, involving the centralised setting of targets and the widespread use of statistical performance indicators.

At the time of this research, the MPS had just undergone major reorganisation and the main responsibility for day-to-day policing was now at borough level. It was also responding to the Macpherson Inquiry which found the service guilty of 'institutional racism' – despite numerous initiatives to address tensions in police relations with minorities since 1981 and the MPS's leading role in this.

Public concerns about crime

The survey results showed that Londoners were no more fearful of crime than 20 years ago and that the position in London had improved, relative to that of other police force areas. But anxiety was greatest among those living in poorer areas, and those living in poor inner-city areas in particular tended to be far more concerned than others about their personal safety. Londoners of minority ethnic origin experience more anxiety about crime, largely because of the sorts of areas they live in and, although they are more concerned than white people about racist attack, the level seems to have been falling. However, concerns about 'incivilities' – for example, problems associated with disorderly teenagers, street drug dealing and use, litter, rubbish and graffiti – *have* increased in recent years, and rises were particularly marked with regard to vandalism, followed by drug use/dealing and teenage nuisance.

Public priorities for the police

People wanted reassurance that the police would protect them from the threat of crime and disorder. Although they worried about some types of crime more than others, their anxieties were interconnected and were often triggered by incivilities.

The most frequently identified priority problems were burglary (mentioned by 57%), mugging (54%), dealing in hard drugs (47%), violence (38%) sexual crime (31%) and racial attacks (27%). People from deprived boroughs were more likely than others to identify robbery, racial attack and drug dealing, whilst those in affluent boroughs were more likely than others to prioritise property crimes.

The most favoured solutions to problems of crime and disorder were more – and more visible – police officers on the beat and more 'community policing'. There were differences between groups: white respondents and older people were more likely to favour foot patrols than younger ones or those from ethnic minorities, for example. However, the desire for local policing that was engaged with local communities was a theme that emerged in our focus groups as clearly amongst the young as the old.

It was clear that people were not simply calling for more visible deterrent patrolling but for a style of policing that was more *responsive* to local problems and local needs. This is reflected in their attitude to police stops. The vast majority (92%) of Londoners thought the police should have powers to stop and search suspects, but most of these referred implicitly – or explicitly – to the need for reasonable suspicion. Black respondents had more reservations than other ethnic groups about the use of the powers. Young people in particular resented the fact of being stopped in this way by the police – even where the police behave well. Instead, many wanted more opportunities to engage with the police in non-adversarial situations, not least in order to pass on their concerns and information with confidence.

More ambivalently, members of the public wanted the police to exercise their powers *less* in situations that may affect themselves – but still to use them to target the 'other' people whom they hold responsible for crime and disorder. In this sense young people are prime targets but they, in turn, tend to want police attention focused on 'other' young people. These are defined mainly in terms of territory (i.e. where people live or belong) but, in some areas, they see 'otherness' in terms of ethnicity also.

People in focus groups did not believe the police could be effective in isolation, though. They were often aware the police have little or no control over the *causes* of crime and disorder, and young people often referred to the lack of leisure facilities as well as poor employment prospects as two such causes. However, they tended to be sceptical about the part played by local authorities in particular; and few survey respondents had heard of the Crime and Disorder Reduction Partnerships (CDRPs) set up under the Crime and Disorder Act 1998.

Using the police

Over a third of Londoners (38%) sought some sort of help from the police during 1999–2000. More than half of these (21% of the sample) did so in order to report crime but nearly as many (18 %) had done so for other reasons – in particular to report nuisance or disturbances as well as suspicious persons. The extent of 'sought contact' rose from the early 1980s until the mid-1990s but fell quite steeply thereafter, reflecting falls in many types of crime in the late 1990s.

Police users were more likely to be from middle-class backgrounds than others, more likely to be under 40, to be a car owner, to live in inner or central London, to be affluent and to be single. After taking into account these other factors, there were no ethnic differences in usage rates.

Majorities of crime victims who notified the police in 1999–2000 were satisfied with the response – 66% saying they were very or fairly satisfied. Women were more likely to be satisfied than men, and those who lived in affluent boroughs more than those in poorer ones. Middle-class victims were less likely to be dissatisfied.

The proportion of 'very satisfied' victims was much lower than in 1980 – 32% compared with 45% – and the proportion who were dissatisfied had grown from 23% in 1980 to 34% in 1999–2000. However, victims in London were less likely than those elsewhere to be critical of the level of effort or interest shown by the police. The main reasons for dissatisfaction tended to be perceptions of lack of effort or lack of interest on the part of the police, and these considerations seemed more important than getting a 'result'. That is, victims often had fairly realistic expectations about the chances the police would actually *solve* the crime. However, they *did* want the police to respond when they call them, to listen to what they have to say and to keep them informed of what happens subsequently. The victims least likely to be satisfied tend to be those living in more deprived areas, as well as men, young people and minority ethnic groups.

Experience as suspect

A quarter of Londoners (24%) were approached by the police in 1999–2000. This group partially overlaps with the 38% who sought police help over this period. In fact, over a half (55%) of those who had been approached as suspects had also themselves sought help from the police over the same period. Only a third of non-suspects had done so.

The most common form of experience of the police as suspect was being stopped in a car. Some 10% of Londoners reported being stopped in a vehicle in 1999–2000, and 2% said they had been stopped on foot. Although foot stops are much rarer than car stops, 42% of men under 35 had either been stopped on foot at some time or had close friends who had this experience. For black young men the figure rose to two thirds. Just over a third of foot stops and just over a fifth of car stops resulted in searches. Young suspects were more likely to be searched than older ones, and working-class ones more than middle-class ones.

The best demographic predictors of being stopped by the police were being young, being male, being black, being working class and being single. Part of the explanation for this is to be found in differential exposure to risk. For example, young men without access to cars who frequently go out after dark are 'available' for foot stops for much longer periods of time than those who have cars or who go out infrequently. Surveys are unable to take account of all the relevant factors that may determine patterns of police activity.

Since the mid-1990s the proportion of people subject to police stops fell sharply, from a peak of 21% in 1993 to 12% in 1999–2000. Although a smaller proportion of the population is now stopped by the police, the minority within this who are stopped more than once has increased. Taking a longer view, a smaller proportion of the London population were stopped in 1999–2000 than in 1981. However, this trend masks large differences between ethnic groups. Fewer black and white Londoners were stopped in 1999–2000 and substantially more Asians and people from other minority ethnic groups.

Overall, a majority of those stopped by the police rated their professionalism highly. Some 71% of those who were stopped in vehicles were satisfied with the way they were treated, and 37% said they were very satisfied. However, there were large differences between groups. The young, those living in poorer boroughs and those from ethnic minorities were more likely to be dissatisfied than others. Similar patterns of findings emerged for foot stops, though overall levels of satisfaction were lower.

Sources of annoyance

A third of Londoners said they had been really annoyed by the way the police had behaved towards themselves or someone they knew; a fifth (21%) said this had happened in the last five years. The main reasons for annoyance in the last five years were unfriendly manner, unreasonable behaviour and failure to do enough.

There were large differences between groups. Young people were more likely to report annoyance than older people, and ethnic minority respondents more than white ones. A third (34%) of black respondents reported annoyance compared with 19% of whites. The best statistical predictors of reporting annoyance in the last five years were: being young, being black, earning more than £15,000 a year, being middle class and having access to a car.

Four out of ten of those who had felt really annoyed – or 9% of the total sample – felt like complaining; 2% of the sample actually did so; and the majority of these (around two thirds) were dissatisfied with the outcome.

Confidence in police effectiveness and integrity

Londoners said that the news media, rather than personal experience, were their main source of information about the police, and this was true especially for people over 45. Among some members of our focus groups, their reliance on these sources had become a cause for concern. Individuals of different ethnic origins thought that what they learned from the media might be distorted because there was no interest in reporting good news. Word of mouth was also an important source of information. (Many more of our younger respondents had friends who had been stopped on foot than had themselves been stopped.) Our focus groups suggested that bad experiences had far more currency than good ones, and these tended to over-ride the impact of good experiences.

Overall, people had less confidence in the police than in many other public services. Asked to rate the quality of the MPS's work, Londoners rank the police below firemen, nurses, teachers and doctors and on a par with social workers. However, the police are ranked higher than all other criminal justice agencies.

In assessing confidence in the police it is important to distinguish between views about effectiveness and those about integrity and impartiality. People may trust the police to be fair without believing them to be effective, and vice versa. The proportion of Londoners saying the police do a 'very good job' fell from 32% in 1982 to 20% in 2000. The proportion thinking the police do a bad job doubled, from 9% to 18%. This decline was not specific to the MPS, however: other police forces have fallen from a higher starting point to the same level.

Young people, poor people those in deprived areas and ethnic minorities rated the effectiveness of police work lower than others. The best predictors of dissatisfaction included being stopped on foot and being stopped in a car. Neither of these is surprising. However, seeking police help was also a predictor, after taking other factors into account, such as experience of the police as a suspect and being a victim of crime. Our focus groups brought out the intensity with which many young people – of all ethnic origins and in different areas – see police activity as biased against them and based on negative stereotypes of youth. There was less consensus on the question of other types of bias. Some respondents in our focus groups believed they and people like them received a poorer service when they called on the police for help and/or that they were more likely to be targeted for suspicion than other groups. But the 'other' groups in question were as likely to be people who lived in other areas and/or who were more middle class as to be members of other ethnic groups. We also had examples of white people believing the police were biased in favour of minorities, as well as the reverse, while several respondents of minority ethnic origin also believed the notion of 'institutional racism' was exploited on occasion. These tended to agree that the police had recently become more reluctant to engage with minorities. By contrast, some older members of minorities claimed they had become more aware of police prejudice as a result of media exposure in the last couple of year although, for others, it simply confirmed what they had always known. Corruption was an issue that rarely surfaced in the focus groups with members of the public.

The survey data on police integrity suggest two conflicting trends. Extreme views – whether positive or negative – appear to have tempered over time. On the one hand, the proportions believing the police *never* act illegally or improperly fell significantly between 1981 and 2000. In 2000 they were much less likely to say the police never use threats or force, or that they never fabricate evidence. On the other hand, the proportion believing this sort of illegal behaviour was *common* had either remained the same or declined, and the proportion thinking the police corruptly accepted bribes or favours had fallen.

A third of the sample (36%) thought the police treated ethnic minorities unfairly, and this proportion was much higher than in 1981 (22%). The increase was largely amongst white respondents; there were only small increases amongst minority ethnic groups.

Survey trends on preparedness to help the police are encouraging. According to the PFLS, Londoners in 2000 were more likely to say they would report a pub fight and identify an offender who had vandalised a bus shelter than in 1981. In 2000 more black and Asian respondents under 45 said they had considered joining the police than in 1981 – though figures for white respondents showed no change.

In our focus groups – and among young people in particular – few respondents said they would actively *discourage* someone they knew from joining the service, and only one (white) boy said the person would be ostracised within his community. But few would actively encourage anyone to join. Most cited the dangers attached to the job and the lack of respect as against a salary they could earn as easily doing something else. In addition, several minority respondents assumed that minority entrants would encounter racism – both inside the service and from the public. The only exceptions to this generally negative picture were several girls and young women of minority origin in different areas who argued it was important for members of minorities to join the service in order to lead by example and to help reform it from within.

Group perceptions and area differences

People regularly mentioned in focus groups that the police treated different groups differently – and often at the expense of their own group. Young people in particular saw themselves as labelled negatively by the police, but people also thought this applied to some ethnic groups, poorer people and men. In focus groups with the police it was clear that their views of the public were strongly conditioned by their perception of who was most willing to co-operate with them. Clearly there can be a dynamic quality to the relationships between the police and the frequently policed: if mutual suspicion and distrust are the starting point for an interaction between the police and public, there is a greater than average chance that the end result will be mutual dissatisfaction.

To a large degree, the police's 'usual suspects' tend to come from the groups who are also perceived to hold more negative views of the police. A higher proportion of these live in highly deprived, high-crime areas, and this lends itself to labelling by area. The problem is compounded by police deployment. In particular, officers on response teams encounter the public almost exclusively in adverse circumstances, and these encounters have greater potential for confrontation in higher-crime areas that are also more ethnically diverse.

Police perceptions

Police officers in our focus groups were asked about the main issues in policing their local area, how they thought the police were perceived locally and the main issues facing the service for the future.

Many were very frustrated at their inability to respond to people's needs and, in particular, to deliver the quality of service they expected. They felt victims frequently had to wait too long for the police and that they were not able to spend enough time with them when they did arrive.

They blamed the limited capacity of response teams on a number of factors. There was the pressure to meet targets for a narrow range of crimes, relatively few of which featured in the calls they had to answer. There were the demands of paperwork (including management information in relation to targets) and inadequate IT systems. Response teams were also thought to be short-staffed because of the demand for personnel in specialist units, and because of the temporary transfer of response staff from normal duties to cover for emergencies and shortages elsewhere.

They also thought their ability to do their job properly was limited by recruitment difficulties in the MPS and by the increasing loss of experienced officers who were retiring early or moving to forces where the stress was less and the quality of life better. They were sceptical about the quality of their management, and thought the public was increasingly reluctant to give information about crime to the police and, in particular, to be prepared to give the evidence needed to charge and prosecute offenders.

Many officers had worked in different parts of London and they tended broadly to divide the capital into three types of area:

1. Middle-class residential areas, where people tended to be well disposed towards the police generally and were more likely to co-operate with them, whether as victims or suspects.

2. More-deprived areas where crime rates – and especially violent crime rates – were high and support from the public low. People here were seen as generally hostile

to the police – including victims of crime, many of whom were also 'known' to the police.

3. Areas of central London that were intensively policed because they were high-crime areas. Crime in these areas was characteristic of city centre areas and had little to do with the nature of the resident population. Support for the police in these areas was generally high, though areas where drug markets or sex markets operated tended to be exceptions.

Some officers were aware that the way in which they thought about different areas could lend itself to the stereotyping of local people. They also recognised that the nature of their job could give them a distorted view of the public because it brought them into contact with an unrepresentative cross-section in atypical circumstances. They said that policing styles tended to vary between different types of area, in part reflecting the prevailing norms of the environment, including public attitudes towards the police. Policing styles were also reinforced by officer deployment, though. The relative paucity of officers to deal with incidents in low-crime areas placed a premium on negotiation and mediation skills. By contrast, in high-crime areas where interpersonal conflict was greatest, officers were more likely to arrive at incidents when levels of aggression were highest; and they could rely on calling backup rather than needing to defuse the situation.

The high-crime areas where policing styles tended to be most confrontational were the most ethnically mixed. The main concerns articulated by officers with regard to ethnicity were as follows:

- They felt they were in a no-win situation in which different sections of the local community (including white people) saw them as biased in favour of other ethnic groups.

- They felt some members of minority ethnic groups automatically assumed that any approach from the police was racially motivated, and thus they said it was safer for officers to disengage from contact with these groups rather than risk a complaint.

- They believed the sheer diversity of the population of the capital made it difficult to be adequately informed about all the different groups. Especially when they moved boroughs, many officers felt they lacked the knowledge to avoid unwittingly giving offence and were poorly placed to secure the co-operation of all sections of the community in tackling crime.

Our individual interviews with officers on senior management teams locally tended to confirm many of the views expressed in the focus groups. The more senior officers, though, were particularly exercised by the tensions between the central demands they were required to meet, the needs expressed by local residents and the conflicting interests of different sections of the population within this. It was impossible to meet the range of priorities imposed on them, especially when reorganisation had made it more difficult to get to know their staff and, thereby, to keep up morale and performance.

Obstacles to responsive police

The broad thrust of our findings about Londoners' views of the police is that in 2000 they found the police less responsive, less visible, less accessible and less engaged with the community than they would like. The material from the case studies sheds light on some of the reasons for this.

External constraints on responsive policing

There was no conclusive evidence that increases in workload lay behind the falls in public ratings. Whether measured by police statistics or the BCS, crime had fallen since the mid-1990s, although some relatively rare categories of crime (such as street robbery) were beginning to show rapid increases at the time of fieldwork. Demand on the police as measured by the statistics recording telephone calls for police help showed a level trend. Some demands on the police are likely to have increased, however, particularly those from other local agencies.

At the same time, MPS resources shrank in real terms between the mid-1990s and 2000, and this has been exacerbated by problems of recruitment and retention of police officers and, in particular, of support staff. These problems were particularly acute at the time of our study. Whilst the overall reduction in resources was not large, its effects will have been felt heavily at borough level by constables in response teams. It also seems likely that public expectations of the service will have grown, given that various government initiatives in the 1990s (such as the Citizen's Charter and the Victim's Charter) fostered a greater sense of public sector consumerism.

One important factor has been the unintended consequences of performance management systems that were imposed on the police throughout the 1990s. Quantitative performance targets were set by successive Home Secretaries and by the Audit Commission which gave primacy to crime-fighting objectives at the expense of order maintenance. They also imposed uniform objectives across areas, limiting the capacity of local police to prioritise according to local need.

Finally, the intrinsic nature of the police role sets limits to the extent to which satisfaction levels can be raised. In so far as policing involves the resolution of conflict, it is often a 'zero-sum game'. Different groups have different expectations of the police – most notably the young and the old – and it can be difficult to accommodate the wishes of all.

Internal organisation and responsive policing

If the flexibility of the MPS to respond to local problems was constrained by central government initiatives, the problem was compounded by the high degree of centralisation in MPS decision-making. At the time of the fieldwork, borough commanders had limited scope to use their own discretion to tailor their resource allocation to local need.

The crime-fighting focus had also brought growing specialisation, with the establishment of teams to tackle, for example, burglary, robbery, drugs, auto-crime and hate crime. Specialised units can work well in their own terms. However, there is also a risk that they may be set up in a way that strips the uniformed patrol strength of its officers and erodes their job satisfaction and skills. Our findings suggest this happened.

Our focus groups and interviews with officers also suggest that the highly centralised management system with a heavy emphasis on compliance with numerical targets tended to disempower middle managers and to demoralise their staff. The targets local managers had to deliver did not match with the workforce's understanding of what the job was actually about. This compounded the cynicism about management which is, in any case, inherent in 'cop culture' and undermined the workforce's sense of purpose.

Concerns about staff management and staff development were numerous, and echoed those charted by the PSI study 20 years earlier. Initial training and in-service training were both felt to be inadequate, and it was felt staff appraisal and career-planning systems operated patchily. These problems were compounded by the rapid turnover of senior staff at borough level, which made it hard to ensure sufficient continuity to provide for effective leadership. Senior staff also felt their ability to provide this leadership was hampered by the plethora of demands relating to performance management and by other demands on their time.

Cumulatively, these factors appeared to have a serious impact on the morale of the staff who carry the main burden of responsibility for day-to-day contact with the public. We had expected to encounter a degree of disaffection within the organisation but were surprised by its extent. Staff in focus groups felt unsupported by their senior managers, under-rewarded and under-resourced.

Pointers for policy

The main conclusions of the study and their key policy implications are discussed in Chapter 10. Their starting point is that developments over the last 20 years have obscured the importance of the police's role as peace-keepers. Yet this becomes ever more important in securing social cohesion as the capital becomes increasingly diverse. At the same time, the experiences and perceptions of the police which young people from different ethnic groups take with them into adulthood will be critical in determining whether, in the future, the MPS polices London with the consent of the majority of its citizens.

The study concludes there is a need to develop policies that:

- Offset the perverse effects of the current quantitative performance management regime by developing an alternative paradigm which emphasises the development of professional standards.

- Improve approaches to local consultation to ensure this is better informed and more realistic.

- Improve the policing of incivilities in ways which avoid causing unnecessary damage to police-community relations.

- Ensure a more visible and more accessible police presence on the streets – but deploying patrol officers with a clear sense of purpose rather than simply to reassure the public;

- Strengthen the capacity of uniformed officers to respond to calls from the public, for example by better integration of specialist and generalist work and by better management.

- Ensure that local managers have sufficient autonomy and flexibility to respond to local needs.

- Sustain and strengthen support for inter-agency work by the police, especially in the context of the local partnerships established under the 1998 Crime and Disorder Act.

The study has two main conclusions.

The legacy of discrimination and over-policing continues to overshadow the service's relations with black people, and the danger persists of replicating similar problems with other groups. But improving police relations with individual minorities cannot be achieved in isolation.

The minority ethnic groups most at risk are those who, on average, are much poorer than whites and more likely to live in high crime areas. Areas of high deprivation have always been high crime areas; and their residents have always been subjected to policing which has been both more intensive and more adversarial. So, as long as this tradition persists, it will continue to have a disproportionate impact on these groups – even if they were not also discriminated against on the grounds of race.

The police cannot ultimately be effective in tackling crime unless they re-engage with the public.

The use of quantitative performance management regimes has resulted in an increasingly narrow focus of resources on a small number of discrete targets which have to be met in the short-term, ignoring the inter-relatedness of crime, disorder and incivilities. This has meant withdrawing resources from policing activities that win the trust of local people. Yet the police ultimately depend on this trust if they are to be fully informed about local patterns of crime and disorder in the first place. And they can only effectively tackle crime and disorder if local people are willing to play an active part in the identification and prosecution of those who are responsible.

Part I

Background

Chapter One: Introduction

This report presents key findings from the 'Policing for London' project, a research study funded by the Nuffield Foundation, the Esmée Fairbairn Foundation and the Paul Hamlyn Foundation. It provides a snapshot of policing in 2000, seen from the viewpoints of both the public and the police.

The origins of the study

The Metropolitan Police (MPS) initiated the study in the wake of the inquiry into the death of Stephen Lawrence (the Macpherson Report, published in 1999). When the report was published, Sir Paul Condon, then Commissioner, announced that the MPS would commission an independent study along the lines of that carried out by David Smith and others at the Policy Studies Institute (PSI) in the early 1980s (Small 1983; Smith 1983a, 1983b; Smith and Gray 1983) which was published in the wake of the Scarman report into the Brixton riots of 1981. The challenges of policing an ethnically diverse community and of building confidence in the police especially within minority ethnic groups remained key concerns for MPS managers nearly 20 years on. They were looking for an authoritative study to help them assess the position at the end of the twentieth century and to provide a baseline against which to measure improvement as the MPS moved into the new millennium.

The MPS initially put the work out to competitive tender with a view to funding it by themselves or in partnership with another funder. It then became clear that the study would benefit from being carried out on a larger scale than originally envisaged. The MPS contacted a number of funders, and three of these, the Nuffield Foundation, the Paul Hamlyn Foundation and the Esmée Fairbairn Foundation, expressed interest. But their conditions were clear: they were willing to fund the work on the condition that it be funded wholly independently of the MPS. The funders were mindful of the importance of the MPS's continuing support for the study. But in the context of the new London-wide Metropolitan Police Authority (MPA) they thought it would be important to establish that the work had been funded wholly independently of the MPS. The revised proposal went through full peer review and was revised to take into account reviewers' comments. A wide-ranging advisory committee was established, of which the MPS and the MPA were prominent members. We have regarded both the MPS and the MPA[1] as primary audiences for the work.

Aims

The study had four related aims:

- to identify the diverse range of interests and concerns which the police need to consider if they are to deliver an equitable service to the population of London into the new century;

- to identify systematically current causes of satisfaction and dissatisfaction, along with the gap between service delivery and people's concerns and expectations;

---

[1] The MPA came into existence in July 2000 and thus had no input into the shape of the study.

- to identify the main reasons for the dissatisfaction and the obstacles to bridging the gap;

- to make practical recommendations for the necessary change.

Its starting point was that the population of London is richly diverse, and is becoming more so. Given that the impetus for the study was provided by the Stephen Lawrence inquiry, ethnicity has been an important focus of our analysis, and far more data are available in this field than on other aspects of diversity. However, we are very conscious that the population is diverse in many other ways which have implications for any study of policing. Socioeconomic differences as well as differences in lifestyles and sexual orientation may be especially relevant. As far as our methods allow, we have tried to accommodate these in our analysis and we are conscious of them in framing our conclusions.

Research strategy

A study of this complexity must of necessity use a variety of research methods. We took as given that a follow-up to the PSI study would need to examine trends since 1981, when the PSI fieldwork took place, including any changes in the views and experiences of Londoners. So we were committed to a structured sample survey. However, we also wanted to set these trends in the context of wider developments in both society and policing and to get a sense of the underlying dynamics which shaped these views and experiences, as well as the reasons for any change over time. This required a qualitative dimension to the work and, in particular, one that would enable us to explore local variations in the London-wide picture and differences in the ways in which the issues are viewed by different stakeholders.

To meet these different requirements we settled on a research strategy that combined a representative sample survey of Londoners with detailed case studies in three London boroughs, involving focus groups, interviews and observation.

The survey

Further details of the methodology are in Appendix 2, and a full account can be found in the survey's technical report (Brown and Whitfield, 2002). In brief, the Policing for London Survey (PFLS) was undertaken for us by the National Centre for Social Research. It was designed to provide a random sample of about 2,750 people aged 15 or over within the Metropolitan Police area. The bulk of the fieldwork took place from July to November 2000, with a few interviews in December. In total 2,800 interviews were achieved. Ethnic minority respondents were over-sampled using a technique known as focused enumeration. In analysis data were weighted to restore representativeness.

Calculating response rates for a focused enumeration sample is complex. Our best estimate is an overall response rate of 49%, with a slightly higher rate for the core sample (see Appendix 2 for details). This is low against the benchmark of a straightforward national probability sample, where response rates of 65–75% are still achievable.[2] London response rates have always been lower than national ones, and focused enumeration samples pose particular challenges. The implications of the low response rate are considered in Appendix 2.

---

[2] Office for National Statistics (ONS) (2001b) provides response rates for major British cross-sectional surveys. Eight out of 20 achieved 65% or less across the country as a whole; three achieved 75% or more.

It is not possible to present response rates by ethnic group, as it was often impossible to establish the ethnic group of 'non-responders'. Where such information was available, refusal rates were highest amongst white households, and non-contact rates highest amongst black ones. Language problems resulted in unproductive outcomes most frequently in Asian households. The technical report has full details.

The PFLS shares many questions with the original PSI survey. The surveys were broadly similar in design and size. The PSI one was also carried out by the National Centre for Social Research (under its previous name, Social and Community Planning Research). Interviewing took place in the second half of 1981. The PSI response rate was higher than PFLS's, at 70%, reflecting the generally higher response rates that could be achieved 20 years ago.

In designing our survey we took advantage of the fact that we could get access to the 2000 British Crime Survey (BCS), a large-scale survey designed primarily to provide a national index of crime (Kershaw *et al* 2001). This had a London subsample of 2,943 respondents who answered detailed questions on their experience of, and attitudes towards, the police. The BCS sample design was similar to that of PFLS, although differences in over-sampling yielded fewer Asians and more black and white respondents than PFLS. Where we needed precise estimates – for example, in measuring experience of the police – we pooled the two samples, using identical wording in the questionnaires. Appendix Tables A2.2 and A2.3 provide a demographic breakdown of the two samples, separately and in combination, benchmarked against ONS population estimates. The samples appear to reflect the London population well, but young people are slightly under-represented, as are males.

Like any survey, our estimates are imprecise because they are subject to sampling error. Wherever we comment in the text on differences between groups, it can be assumed that the difference is statistically significant – that is, the chances of the difference occurring by chance are less than five in a hundred.[3]

The case studies
In selecting the sites for our detailed case studies, the natural unit of analysis was the borough, especially since the MPS had recently moved to borough-based policing. In preparation for the study, we had compiled socioeconomic, demographic and crime statistics for each borough to allow us to draw up profiles for each (for full details see the PFLS website, www.policingforlondon.org). This enabled us to group the 32 boroughs into four clusters based on average levels of deprivation, as calculated by the Department of Environment Transport and the Regions in 1998.[4] For our case studies, we chose three boroughs that were ethnically diverse in different ways. Borough A came from the affluent group, Borough B from the

---

[3] i.e. p<.05, with an assumed design effect of 1.5 throughout. As a very rough guide, if 56% of men in the PFLS have a given attribute and 50% of women do, this difference is statistically significant; for the larger, merged PFLS/BCS sample a difference of four percentage points would be significant. If 3% of men in the PFLS had an attribute and 6% of women, this would be significant; a difference of two percentage points would be significant for the merged sample.
[4] The 1998 data were the most recent available when this work was undertaken. Individual boroughs' scores have varied in subsequent years, producing slightly different groupings. A handful have shifted up or down into the next group; but the core pattern has remained the same.

average and relatively deprived groups combined, and Borough C from the most deprived group of London boroughs.

In each of the case-study areas, we conducted four public focus groups in the summer of 2000. These comprised 106 local residents, selected on the basis of age, class and ethnicity (see Appendix 2). They were recruited by an agency specialising in this work, but the research team facilitated the groups. We also conducted a further nine focus groups with a sample of Year 11 students (young people aged 15 and 16, who were selected for us by their teachers) spread across the three sites. Their ethnic origins were very varied, but white pupils formed only a minority of the total.[5] In each of the boroughs we also interviewed 'key informants': people from non-statutory organisations who had contact with the police on behalf of particular sections of the local population; local authority staff responsible for partnership working in each authority; and five of the local MPs.

We carried out a range of interviews and focus groups with the police in each area. Semi-structured in-depth interviews were conducted with all three local commanders, with their deputies in Boroughs A and C and with several other officers at Chief Inspector level holding general operational or management responsibilities. All heads of Community Safety Units (CSUs) were interviewed, as were heads of Management Information Units as well as officers with responsibility for partnership working and for schools liaison. Nineteen police focus groups were held in all, including three with civilian staff. A total of 130 officers participated in the focus groups, the majority of whom were of constable rank and covered a range of responsibilities.

In each area, at least one period of observation was undertaken in a custody suite and another of a car patrol. We also accompanied officers on foot patrol in two of our boroughs and on a drugs raid in a third. The fieldwork also offered numerous opportunities for observation of police–public interaction at the front counters of several police stations.

We promised all our respondents that we would preserve their anonymity and that we would endeavour to anonymise the boroughs also. Each was unique in some respects; but our main aim in studying them was to capture the likely differences in experience and perspective associated with living in different *types* of area. Throughout this study, therefore, we have tried to avoid providing details which would allow them easily to be identified.

The structure of the report

Chapter 2 describes the 'operating context' within which the MPS works. It considers changes in the population of the capital, as well as trends in crime, disorder and other demands on the police. It discusses changes in the legal and managerial framework within which the police work and developments in the policing of diverse communities.

Chapter 3 presents findings on public concerns, needs and wants. It covers anxiety about crime and people's views on policing priorities. Chapter 4 describes Londoners' experience of the police both as 'users' and as suspects. Chapter 5

---

[5] Unfortunately we only had a single period with each class, so there was no opportunity to get pupils to fill in a questionnaire including this information.

summarises levels of satisfaction amongst those with police experience, and aims to tease out the determinants of satisfaction and dissatisfaction. Chapter 6 discusses public confidence in the effectiveness and integrity of the MPS, and covers sources of information about policing and views about competence, fairness and accountability. Chapter 7 focuses on the group dimension to perceptions held by different sections of the public and the police and the different ways these play out in different areas.

Chapters 8 and 9 explore some of the reasons for variations in satisfaction with police performance: Chapter 8 considers the external constraints on responsive policing while Chapter 9 examines some of the organisational obstacles.

The final chapter offers our conclusions.

Chapter Two: The Policing Environment

The role of the police service has never been legally defined, but its purpose was originally described as 'the prevention of crime … the protection of life and property [and] the preservation of public tranquillity' (Mayne 1829). Although the balance between these functions has shifted at different times, each tends to set police officers in actual or potential conflict with members of the public. They may either use their powers proactively to prevent or detect crime or they may be called on to intervene in disputes between individuals or groups. The circumstances in which the service is expected to fulfil this role, though, have altered beyond recognition since its inception, and significant changes have taken place since the Policy Studies Institute (PSI) study was conducted in 1981. There have been large demographic changes in London. There have been economic and cultural shifts with particularly rapid developments in technology and communication (including international communication), and the political environment has also altered, nationally and internationally.

In particular, the social strains arising from the recession in the late 1980s affected policing as much as other social institutions at a time when many of those institutions were also undergoing change. Along with restructuring, private ownership and choice were increasingly being introduced into services which had mainly been provided by the state in the postwar period. They were also increasingly required to model themselves on businesses, in particular by demonstrating 'cost effectiveness' (more recently referred to as 'value for money') and their ability to meet set targets.

This chapter first examines the more general changes in the policing environment before looking at trends in crime and disorder over the same period. It then goes on to consider the institutional context within which the police have responded to these issues generally and to the policing of diversity in particular.

Demographic trends

The London population, which had declined from the 1960s until the early 1980s, has been growing again and looks set to continue (Matheson and Edwards 2000). According to the 1981 census the figure was 6.8 million; it now stands 10% higher at 7.4 million. The average age of Londoners is lower than the rest of the country, and this trend is likely to continue. Whilst nationally the number of pensioners will grow, in London it is projected to fall.

Economic disparities

Londoners' incomes are a fifth higher than the national average; however, the high cost of housing means that London has not only the highest proportion of affluent households, but also the largest proportion of those with a low standard of living (Matheson and Edwards 2000). In other words, there is greater economic disparity than elsewhere and, while local figures are not available, it seems likely that economic polarisation in London has increased over the last 20 years in line with national trends: the 1970s saw little change nationally in the distribution of income, but from

1981 onward the rich became a lot richer, and the real disposable income of the poor grew only slightly.

Under-supply of London housing has ensured that the affluent and the poor continue to live in close proximity. Given the associations between poverty and offending, the consequence is that in the 1980s and 1990s crime problems are more evenly distributed across the population than in North American cities, which have much greater economic segregation, and increasingly by comparison with deindustrialised northern cities in this country, where *over-supply* of housing is encouraging economic segregation. Rather, a recent phenomenon has been the increasing development of very affluent areas *within* parts of cities which had previously been in serious decline, an example of which has been the transformation of London Docklands. Nonetheless, there are important differences in the average levels of deprivation between the 32 boroughs served by the Metropolitan Police (MPS). Levels of affluence vary sharply *within* many boroughs, though, and the contrasts were greater in Borough B than in Borough A but they were most marked in Borough C, where the average level of deprivation was the highest.

Ethnicity

The MPS has a higher proportion of residents from visible ethnic minority groups than any other police force area. According to Office for National Statistics (ONS) figures for 1999, enumerated minorities made up 22% of the London population aged 16 or over, compared with 4% for the rest of the country. Within London, the population classified as Indian formed the largest single group (5%), followed by black Caribbeans (4%), black Africans (3.5%), Pakistanis (1.5%) and Bangladeshis (1.5%). The London population is substantially more diverse in ethnic terms than 20 years ago. Equivalent figures for 1981 quoted in Smith (1983) suggest that 11% of Londoners were from minority ethnic groups, that 3% were of West Indian and 4.5% of south Asian origin (i.e. from India, Pakistan or Bangladesh).

There are considerable variations between these groups, though, in terms of their income, age structure and distribution across the capital; and these are reflected in our survey sample, where different groups tended to be drawn from different types of London boroughs (Table 2.1). Studies of the income of visible minorities have consistently shown very high levels of poverty among Pakistanis and Bangladeshis, with the black groups also much poorer on average than whites. The picture for the Indians is more mixed, with the effect of relatively high average levels of individual income mitigated somewhat by the larger numbers of households with dependent children (Modood *et al* 1997, Berthoud 1998).

All the minority groups tend, on average, to be younger than whites, but this is especially true of the 'other' groups (many of whom are of mixed ethnic origins) and the Bangladeshis. These groups therefore tend to have higher than average rates of growth. Also, immigration to London has been rising in pace with globalisation (Home Office 2001b) and has a differential impact of the size of the various groups. It seems to account in particular for the increase in the black African population shown in published tables from the government's *Labour Force Surveys*.

Table 2.1: Average population of London boroughs by deprivation and ethnic origin, 1998 (%).

	Affluent	Average	Relatively deprived	Very deprived
White	86	75	72	67
Black Caribbean	1	4	6	8
Black African	1	3	4	7
Black other	1	1	2	3
Indian	5	7	6	4
Pakistani	1	2	3	2
Bangladeshi	0	1	1	5
Chinese	1	1	1	1
Other	4	6	6	3

Source: London Research Centre (tables provided on request)

London is the main centre of residence of all these visible minorities *except* for the Pakistani group, most of whom live in certain areas of the north east and north west. The extent to which they are concentrated in the capital, though, varies and their distribution across the boroughs broadly reflects their economic position. Thus, there are relatively few people from minority ethnic groups in the most affluent boroughs and the predominant group here is of Indian origin. Minorities form about 40% of the population on average in the most deprived boroughs, and the largest groups here are the black African and black Caribbean groups, along with the Bangladeshis.

Figures for the school population are collected annually by the Department for Education and Skills (DFES),[1] and these give some idea of the rate and direction of change for the future. It is not possible to take account of pupils in private education. However, nationally these account for only about 7% of all pupils and their inclusion would probably only marginally alter the picture in Table 2.2.

By the time this study was being undertaken, around half the population in state primary schools both in the 'average' group of London boroughs and in those which were relatively deprived came from a range of different minority groups. The most marked change, though, was in the very deprived boroughs where white children accounted for less than 40% of primary school pupils (albeit they remain the largest single group in most). Black Africans now form the second largest group in the very deprived boroughs, followed by Bangladeshis.

In each of our case-study areas, the white population was somewhat smaller than average, with minority groups forming between a quarter and a third of the total within each. The extent to which the profile of the population at large contrasted with that in state primary schools, though, varied markedly between them. In

---

[1] The DFES classification is slightly different from that used by the 1991 census. It includes some white minorities (such as Greeks) in its 'Other' category.

Table 2.2: Average population of state primary schoolchildren in London boroughs by deprivation and ethnic origin, 1998 (%).

	Affluent	Average	Relatively deprived	Very deprived
White	81	57	53	44
Black Caribbean	2	6	10	12
Black African	2	6	9	15
Black other	2	4	5	4
Indian	6	9	7	4
Pakistani	1	3	5	2
Bangladeshi	1	3	3	10
Chinese	1	1	1	1
Other	4	11	7	8

Source: DFES

Borough A, the figure for white primary school pupils was 10% lower than for the population as a whole; in Borough B, the figure was 20% lower; but in Borough C, it was nearly 40% lower.[2]

However, figures for the visible minority ethnic groups enumerated by government surveys do not fully describe the extent of ethnic diversity in the resident population of London, and the picture is further complicated by the large numbers of foreign visitors to the capital at any one time. Many white ethnic minorities also have well established communities in certain boroughs (in particular, the Irish, Turks, Greeks, Poles and the Jewish community), including Boroughs A and B. But reference has also been made to the impact of immigration. Most of those who enter legally come as spouses and dependants; but a growing proportion of the total in recent years have come as refugees and asylum seekers. Many of these do not belong to the main visible minorities. The largest numbers have come from countries of eastern Europe and would be described as 'white' in the classification used in most official statistics at the time of the study. But a significant minority have also come from countries of the Middle East, in particular Iraq, Iran and Afghanistan. Most of these are young men (Home Office 2001b), and thus form a much larger proportion of the 'frequently policed' population.

London Research Centre figures (Storkey and Bardsley 1999) suggest that refugees and asylum seekers, while they formed only a very small proportion of the total population, were also unevenly distributed across the boroughs. Like the poorer groups among the visible minorities, they too were most likely to be found in the most deprived boroughs which are already the most ethnically diverse. Again, though, there were variations between individual boroughs. Borough A had received

---

[2] These contrasts may be slightly exaggerated by two factors. Boroughs A and B both had significant white minorities who will have been counted as 'white' in the overall population figures but as 'others' in the school statistics. It also seems likely that a higher proportion of white parents in Borough C had their children privately educated.

far more than average for an affluent borough (although, where it had responsibility for some of the most recent arrivals, it housed many of these outside the borough). The overall numbers were higher in Borough C but they were highest of all in Borough B, which was more central than the other two and whose ethnic make-up was more diverse.

Technology and consumption

The mobile phone and the personal computer did not exist as part of everyday life two decades ago. They are also just two examples of new technology which have simultaneously created opportunities for crime, as well as new possibilities for responding to crime. Four out of five offences recorded by the police involve theft; the British Crime Survey (BCS) figure is two thirds. Patterns of crime are shaped significantly by the pool of available targets for theft.

Technology and new crime targets
The 1980s saw a rapid growth in London (and elsewhere) in burglary and vehicle crime. This was driven at least in part by in the increased availability of desirable, portable, valuable goods. When the PSI survey was conducted, there was an unsaturated licit market for televisions, audio systems and in-car audio systems, all of which were expensive. Videos were still a rarity (one in seven London households had one); camcorders had not been invented. In the 1980s and early 1990s these commodities commanded some value in illicit markets. More recently technological innovation has reduced the cost of these items, to the point where the illicit market for them is almost saturated. This could partly explain why burglary rates have been falling since the mid-1990s. There has very probably been a fall in demand for the sorts of stolen goods yielded from burglaries but this is less likely to be the case for the stolen goods from robberies. A high proportion of these involve cash and credit cards but the large increases in recent years have in large measure reflected the increase in mobile phone ownership (see below).[3]

A similar trend on much shorter timescales has emerged for personal computers. These – and their component parts – were scarce, desirable and expensive in the late 1980s and early 1990s, and thefts, especially from offices, were commonplace. Now, nearly half London homes have PCs (ONS, 2001b); their licit price, and that of component parts, has fallen rapidly, which has therefore severely disrupted the illicit market for them.

The latest 'hot product' to emerge (cf. Clarke 2000) is, of course, the mobile phone. In the mid-1990s they were still a rarity and a status symbol; ownership is now totally unremarkable – even if their running costs are significant and some models have much more *cachet* than others, especially with the young.

Consumption
The availability of goods that were unthought of in the early 1980s is one aspect of the wider, significant changes which have taken place in patterns of consumption since that time and which, in turn, have produced changes in lifestyle. One other specific aspect of these changes has been in the consumption of illicit drugs. Several completely new forms of illicit drugs have emerged since 1981, whilst patterns of consumption of other more established drugs have changed. The reports of the PSI

---

[3] It is difficult to offer evidence, as our knowledge of stolen markets is rudimentary. Nor do we rule out other contributory factors such as improved security technology and more effective policing.

study are almost totally silent on drug issues – reflecting the relative lack of concern about drugs of dependence then. Cannabis use was well established among some subgroups of the young adult population, but levels of consumption were clearly lower than today.[4] Heroin use was rare. Whilst some people smoked cocaine in its freebase form, crack had not arrived in Britain, nor had ecstasy.

Whilst reliable long-term trend data for London are not available, cannabis use is now widespread, with a quarter of Londoners under 35 admitting use in 1999–2000 (Aye Maung 2001). Just under a tenth of Londoners in this age group used cocaine in this period, and 5% reported ecstasy use. Use of all three drugs was highest among people in their early 20s.

Drugs of dependence – largely crack and heroin – are now reckoned to be a significant driver of property crime, even though a very small minority of illicit drug users can be regarded as problem users (Hough *et al* 2001). The number of problem drug users in London has been estimated at around 50,000 (Childs *et al* 2000) with an average weekly spend of £200 or more (Edmunds *et al* 1998, 1999; Bennett, 2000). By no means all these will fund their drug use through acquisitive crime, and by no means all of those who did so would stop offending if they were no longer dependent on opiates or crack. But it can safely be assumed that if around 25,000 criminally active Londoners had to support drug habits of this order in 1981, levels of shoplifting and to a lesser degree burglary would have been very much higher. And 20 years ago London was relatively free of the systematic violence associated with some forms of drug distribution (Dorn *et al* 1992).

It is apparent, though, that very large numbers of people using illicit drugs are *not* involved in acquisitive crime. Rather, their 'recreational' use of drugs highlights a further much wider development in patterns of consumption over the last 20 years, with a significant expansion in a diverse leisure industry which symbolises major changes in traditional patterns of employment. Large numbers of young people in particular are now involved in a 'night-time economy' which also poses new challenges in policing – both in terms of opportunities for crime and the potential for disorder (Hobbs *et al* 2001).

Meanwhile, changes in technology have also increased the speed of international communication and the numbers of people involved, whether electronically or physically. The pace of 'globalisation' over the period has also been accelerated by international political developments – not least the collapse of communism in Europe. And these developments too have provided new opportunities for crime, including the smuggling of goods and people, as well as increasing the threat of international terrorist activity.

Demands on the police
The MPS, like other police forces in Britain, remains substantially a demand-led organisation. A large proportion of its resources is involved in responding to the calls made on it not only by individuals but by other agencies and businesses, and these demands are not evenly distributed across the capital.

---

[4] The BCS offers national trend data that indicate a tripling in 'last year' cannabis use from 6 or 7% in the early 1980s to 19% in 2000 amongst the under 35s – though comparisons are not straightforward (see Mott and Mirrlees-Black 1995; Ramsay and Partridge 1999).

In the case of demand from individuals, people make choices about whether or not to call the police in a range of situations which go much wider than the unequivocally criminal (as classically described by Bittner[5]); these include situations in which it may or may not make sense to apply the criminal law, such as disputes and disturbances where arrest may be an option but where the police may still be able to resolve the situation without resort to the law. In other dimensions of police business such as the handling of accidents and natural disasters, the use of the criminal law is largely irrelevant. Both instances, though, may involve conflict, if only in the sense of interposing the police between different parties.

Anyone faced with a situation in which the police *could* be involved first will decide whether or not to involve the police. Once they *are* involved, the police then decide whether the demand is a legitimate one to which they *should* respond. There are subsequent decisions relating to the most effective way of handling the incident – whether to define it as a criminal incident and whether to use powers of arrest. Other considerations may then come into play about how (and whether) the incident is recorded.

This analysis may simply state the obvious; however, it needs stating because it points to the difficulty of using police workload statistics (such as recorded crime figures and data on 'calls for service') as indices of real changes in levels of crime and disorder. As with any agency offering free public services, one can assume that, other things being equal:

- demands on the police will rise in line with their capacity to deliver; and

- police preparedness to take work on will be inversely related to levels of demand.

This is not to suggest that the police are powerless in their ability to shape or control demand. They can explicitly or implicitly convey to their users what is, and what is not, 'police business'. However, the elasticity of demand for police services means that they, in common with other public sector services such as the NHS, have a tendency to experience an endemic workload crisis, always operating at that uncomfortable point where demand slightly exceeds capacity to deliver. For many decades police researchers throughout the industrialised world have documented the sense that pervades police occupational culture of a 'thin blue line' strained to breaking point (see Reiner 1978, 2000, for discussions).

Other factors besides capacity to deliver will also affect demand. Thus over the last 20 years the public have had progressive ease of access to the police, with the growth in phone ownership and, especially, the recent growth in the number of mobile phones. The growth of home insurance (at least in the 1980s) also provided a stimulus to report crimes. On top of these factors, the police are under various pressures both to inflate and to depress their workload statistics. In the early 1990s the performance management pressures on them encouraged under-recording of crime; in the late 1990s there have been countervailing pressures to record crime as fully as possible.

---

[5] Bittner (1970) characterises demands on the police as deriving from situations involving 'something that ought not to be happening and about which someone had better do something *now!*'

All these factors mean that official figures will not fully reflect the levels of crime and disorder in society and the picture they give may to some degree distort their underlying pattern, including the pattern of change over time. This makes it essential to compare the official figures as far as possible with measures that are independent of police administrative statistics. The most readily available source are surveys which focus on individuals' experience of crime and disorder and, for these reasons, these too have grown in importance over the last 20 years. As we saw in the last chapter, however, response rates to surveys have been falling and the drop has been especially marked in high-crime areas. Also, those which rely on contacting people in their homes tend to miss out on the experience of those sections of the population who are most likely to be out – in particular young people. Yet their lifestyle may both increase their risk of certain types of crime and the likelihood of their coming into contact with the police.

Crime, disorder and other 'police business'

The PSI survey (in combination with the Policing for London Survey – PFLS) offers a simple comparison of crime levels in 1980–81 and in 1999–2000. In interpreting the findings one must bear in mind that the later survey had lower response rates than the earlier one, and that both may be affected by sampling error. Table 2.3 presents a picture that is in some ways consistent with the media image of an ever-rising tide of crime, and in some ways at odds with this. Burglary, car theft and assault show very little change. By contrast, robbery and theft from the person, vandalism and other forms of crime (largely thefts from home and the workplace) show large increases.

The British Crime Survey (BCS) paints a similar but fuller picture, as it can say what happened in the intervening period. According to the BCS, most categories of crime in London rose from 1981 until the mid-1990s, and then fell steeply back to the levels seen in the early 1980s.

Table 2.3: Experience of crime: people victimised once or more, 1981 and 2000 (%)

Crime type	PSI (1981)	PFLS (2000)
Burglary (including attempts)	6	5
Theft of vehicle (including attempts)	6	7
Theft from pocket, briefcase or bag	3	8
Other theft	7	8
Deliberate damage to property	4	15
Physical attack or assault	4	5
Other incidents	2	7

Although crime survey statistics provide an essential benchmark against which to measure recorded crime overall, even those with relatively large samples are inevitably limited in their ability to measure some numerically small categories of crime. They tell us little about incidents of crime and disorder in which teenagers are the victims. And the data are not amenable to analysis on a borough-by-borough basis. For these purposes, we are thrown back on police statistics which overall show a fall in crime throughout the 1990s with a slight upturn at the end of the decade (albeit this was in part driven by changes in recording introduced by the Home Office in 1998).

Like survey data, the police statistics indicate that 'volume crimes' of burglary and vehicle crime appear to be falling steadily. However, there has a very steep increase in street robbery from 1998 which continued up to the point of writing (albeit the rate of increase had dropped slightly). Although bullying and violence between teenagers go largely unreported and unrecorded in police statistics, the street robbery figures provide strong evidence of new patterns of crime among young people. They appear largely to be driven by the theft of mobile phones by teenagers, and the victims have also increasingly come from the school-age population (FitzGerald 2000; Harrington and Mayhew 2001; Home Office 2001).

While the increase in street crime has taken place across most boroughs, the problem is greatest in boroughs that have traditionally suffered from high levels of crime. The precise ranking of individual boroughs in the spectrum of low to high crime areas varies from year to year but the overall pattern remains broadly constant.

The pattern of crime across any area is determined by the number of motivated offenders, the availability of attractive crime targets and the extent to which these targets are protected against crime (Felson 1998). These factors are often in tension. Thus, in London, persistent offenders tend to live disproportionately in deprived inner-city areas. Attractive targets, by contrast, are to be found in greater profusion in city centre areas and in affluent areas, even if these are sometimes less accessible to offenders. Targets in affluent areas also tend to be better defended against crime. What this means in practice is that levels of crime are highest in two types of area: central London boroughs – where there is a good supply of targets; and in deprived London boroughs – where offenders are plentiful.

If one considers recorded crime rates per 1,000 population, recorded crime rates were highest in mid-2001 in the central London Boroughs of Westminster, Camden, and Kensington and Chelsea. However, a large proportion of these crimes would have been committed against non-residents. Shoplifting, for example, tends to be high in these areas, as are many car thefts and crimes are committed against office workers and tourists – so a rate per resident population is somewhat inappropriate. Westminster, in particular, has a crime rate more than double the London average.

If Westminster is removed, Figure 2.1 broadly illustrates the relationship between levels of recorded crime and levels of deprivation. Using recorded police searches as a surrogate measure for police activity, it also illustrates the higher levels of proactive policing in the higher-crime areas.

Of our three case-study areas, our intermediate borough (Borough B) had by far the highest number of crimes per thousand population, but this was because it included part of the central area where crime was high but there was only a small resident population. Borough C, though, illustrated the extent to which policing tactics may vary even between boroughs that are apparently similar. Its recorded searches were far higher than other comparable boroughs, reflecting the extent to which the use of the power has always tended to vary between policing areas. In terms of overall

Figure 2.1: Average crimes and searches in London boroughs (1998–9).

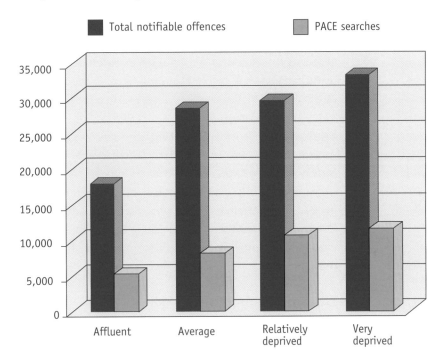

Note: PACE searches are those carried out under powers set out in Section 1 of the Police and Criminal Evidence Act 1984.

trends in crime, though, it was Borough A that was the exception. Despite being high-crime boroughs, the figures in Borough B and Borough C had tended to track the pattern for the capital as a whole and both had succeeded in containing the rise from the mid-1990s to below the London average. In our low-crime borough, by contrast, there had been a steady increase over the whole of the decade.

Non-crime work

Independent measures of the extent of non-criminal or near-criminal disorder are harder to assemble. We have both survey data and police statistics on *demands* for police service. As is shown in Chapter 4, the survey data indicate a decline in both crime and non-crime demands on the police. The trend in non-crime demands is consistent with the picture emerging from the MPS's records of telephone calls to the service.

Public order policing

Capital cities face atypical problems of public order policing. They inevitably provide the focal point for political demonstrations but they are also magnets for leisure activity on a large scale. The size, concentration and heterogeneity of their resident and transient populations further increase the likelihood of large-scale public disturbances in capital cities.

Reference has already been made to the serious riots in Brixton, in April 1981 during the course of the PSI study. There were further disturbances in the mid-1980s (notably in Tottenham in 1985 which resulted in loss of life) and both sets of events were precipitated by conflict between parts of the black community and the police. Since then, there have been other occasions of large-scale disturbances, though few have taken place over a number of days in residential areas. And, in sharp contrast to those of the early and mid-1980s, their origins are to be found more in political dissent than in hostility to the police.[6] Nor have those in London been specifically associated with minority ethnic groups, by contrast with recent events in some northern forces. From the mid-1990s some of these provincial forces began to see disturbances involving certain groups of young Asians which had echoes of London in the 1980s.

More than other forces, the MPS also has to deal with the policing of large-scale sporting events and mass entertainment events such as the Notting Hill Carnival. Meanwhile, the large diplomatic presence in the capital, major ceremonial occasions (including visits by heads of state) and the fact of its being the seat of government all impose further demands and pose particular additional threats – including the threat of terrorism. Together with the sheer size of the population living in, working in and visiting the capital each year, these make the challenge of policing London in some sense unique.

Institutional change

The last two decades have seen a number of institutional changes in the MPS, relating to:

- systems of accountability
- partnership work
- priorities
- organisational structure.

Accountability

It was a commonplace observation in studies of policing in the 1970s and early 1980s that the police were a paradoxical organisation, having the trappings of a militaristic command structure, which masked the reality of very extensive low-level discretion (Skolnick 1966; Reiss 1971; Banton 1973). Since then, it has generally become accepted that the legal and administrative frameworks within which the police operate are significant determinants of police action. It seems likely that the shift is not one in academic fashion but in the realities of policing in late industrial societies. Patrol officers still exercise their powers largely unsupervised (except by each other) but they almost certainly *are* more accountable now than they were two decades ago.

One of the major catalysts for this change in England and Wales was the Police and Criminal Evidence Act 1984 (PACE), which derived in large measure from the Scarman report. Among its key provisions were the following:

- The introduction of custody suites and custody sergeants in police stations.

- Much more rigorous procedures for handling suspects in police stations.

- The introduction of a system of lay visitors who could monitor practice in police stations.

---

[6] The clearest examples are the poll tax demonstrations in the late 1980s and, more recently, the May Day 'anti-capitalist' marches in 2000 and 2001.

- The extension of the MPS's powers for stopping and searching suspects to other forces but with the requirement to record any searches under this provision.

- Fuller record-keeping relating to detention in police stations.

- A greater degree of independence in the complaints procedure.

- Provision for fuller local consultation with the public over policing issues.

A further restriction on police autonomy came in 1986, when their prosecutorial function was transferred to the newly established Crown Prosecution Service (CPS).

PACE and the CPS increased the extent to which the police were legally accountable and exposed day-to-day police work to independent review. Trailing these developments were growing systems of administrative or managerial accountability. Whilst the criminal justice system had somehow managed to evade the first wave of public sector managerialism imposed by government in the 1980s, this increasingly made itself felt on the police in the 1990s. Important staging posts in this process include publication of the Sheehy report (1993) and two reports by the Audit Commission (1993, 1996). Although a Home Office review (1994) found it difficult to identify any core or ancillary tasks that could readily be removed from the police, the Police and Magistrates Courts Act 1994 was of particular importance in shifting the balance of power away from police authorities towards the Home Secretary, who gained new powers to set national policing objectives, supported by measurable performance indicators. It also required more explicit articulation of local policing plans, with local objective setting. This new performance management regime was embraced by many forces, including the MPS. By the end of the decade it had imported from New York a 'compstat' process whereby senior management held local commanders responsible in person for their performance against statistical performance indicators such as crime levels and clear-up rates.

More recently – and since the time when fieldwork was conducted – accountability for policing in London has passed from the Home Secretary to the Metropolitan Police Authority (MPA). This body was set up through the Greater London Act 1999 to create a police authority for the capital which came into being in July 2001.

Partnership working
On top of this growth in legal and administrative accountability has come the broadening of responsibility for crime control. The concept of multi-agency working which originated mainly in the 1980s extended to crime, and Child Protection Committees provide an early example of police, probation, social services and others working in harness. In the mid-1980s there were various central government initiatives to get agencies other than the police to take crime prevention seriously, followed by the Morgan report's (1991) recommendation that responsibility for crime prevention should actually be placed with local authorities.

After a few years' lull, reflecting the then Conservative government's distaste for this idea, the new Labour administration implemented them in the Crime and Disorder Act 1998 (CDA). The CDA placed a statutory responsibility on the police, local authorities, the probation service and the health service to set up local crime-reduction partnerships. They had a responsibility for developing and implementing crime-reduction strategies that were specific to local need (as determined both from statistical evidence and through consultation). The police also play a central role in two other multi-agency bodies: the Youth Offending Teams set up in 1999 under provisions of the CDA by the Youth Justice Board, and the (non-statutory) Drug Action Teams (DATs).[7]

At the time of the study, all these partnerships were in their early days; and there were wide variations between boroughs. It was apparent that arrangements for CDA working were much further advanced in Boroughs B and C than in Borough A, largely due to their longer experience of multi-agency working prior to the CDA. But the difference in their approaches also appeared in part to reflect local differences within and between the relevant partners. In Borough B one of the deputies to the local commander was given full-time responsibility for integrating police activity into partnership working, in close liaison with an exceptionally dynamic partnership unit in the local authority chief executive's department. In Borough C, the commander took the lead (along with his other responsibilities) but the police had funded a relatively large unit dedicated to partnership working. In Borough A, however, responsibility in the local authority had been given to a single, part-time very junior member of staff who left the post early in the fieldwork period and had not been replaced by the end of it. The local commander, meanwhile, had obtained agreement to locate a middle-ranking officer in the town hall; but the remit of the officer and his working relationship with their local authority counterparts were by no means certain. Both Boroughs B and C had been very successful in submitting joint bids with their partners for money from a range of government programmes (see further below). By contrast, the local authority in Borough A appeared reluctant to engage in the process and, in any case, the low level of overall borough deprivation put it in a relatively weak position to lay claim to special funding.

Priorities
In the period after the Brixton riots – followed by the publication of the Scarman report and the PSI study – the debate turned yet again to the best balance to strike between maintaining order and enforcing the law. The last Royal Commission on the Police in 1960 had decided that the service's core role was the maintenance of the 'Queen's peace', and the riots were taken as a prime example of the way in which insensitive crack-downs on crime could trigger disproportionate disorder. The MPS's view in the mid-1980s was that primacy should be given to the maintenance of order. The then Commissioner, Sir Kenneth Newman, published a paper (MPS 1984) setting policing principles that included the following passage:

> Where a conflict arises between the duty of the police to maintain order
> and their duty to enforce the law, priority will, but only in the last resort,
> be given to the maintenance of public order through the commonsense
> exercise of police discretion.

Sir Kenneth and his successor, Sir Peter Imbert, pursued a series of strategies designed to regain public trust through more responsive styles of policing which had a great deal in common with the community policing methods already advocated by

---

[7] Increasingly, local partnerships are finding ways of integrating these bodies into a single administrative structure. Some DATs embrace issues relating to alcohol.

John Alderson (1979, 1984). By the early 1990s a holistic approach was being developed to align the internal culture of the organisation better with external changes through Imbert's 'Plus Programme'.

However, the tide had already begun to turn again by this stage. We have already discussed how new 'managerialist' systems of performance management began to emerge from the late 1980s. In parallel with these there were some important changes in the definition of police function. In the white paper on police reform (Home Office 1993), as well as other reports already referred to, one can detect a significant narrowing of the focus of policing over this period to crime fighting (see Morgan and Newburn 1997 for a discussion).The Audit Commission work, in particular, took it for granted that the police should have a crime-fighting focus; it also rekindled optimism that crime could be substantially reduced if police resources were *targeted* more effectively.

As discussed above, some of these initiatives were significant in introducing the current legal and administrative framework of current police management – with an emphasis on priorities, objective setting and performance management using statistical indicators. An important consequence of these and other pressures for 'value for money' is the way in which debate about the police function has become increasingly framed through the managerialist 'lens'. The requirement on police forces to set out publicly in their policing plans what they intend to do, and to demonstrate thereafter that they have done it, has led inevitably to a simplification of public statements about policing. The police have been under pressure to formalise their organisational aims and objectives, and to state them publicly in a way that allows quantitative targets to be set. This has led to an emphasis on crime-fighting goals. These have the appearance, at least, of being readily quantifiable while they are also capable of commanding public assent because they are simple, comprehensible and appear to offer the public protection from specific, identifiable threats. The fact that these managerialist pressures were at work until the mid-1990s against a backdrop of rising crime and an increasingly populist political debate about 'law and order' also limited senior officers' room for manoeuvre in proposing a more subtle balance of policing goals.

Structural change

Many of these developments have been reflected in significant changes in the framework of police relations with outside bodies and in the internal organisation of the service itself. The forms this has taken have often varied considerably by area (as reflected in arrangements for partnership working under the CDA). Key developments have included changes in the funding for the service, largely as the result of a new national formula for the allocation of central government funding to different forces. But increasing government funding has also become available in recent years for specific purposes, often via a competitive bidding process. Another development was the change in mechanisms for local police accountability with the new constitution of police authorities introduced by the Police and Magistrates' Courts Act 1994. Within the service in turn much of the work that would have been undertaken 20 years ago by middle and junior ranking police officers is now undertaken by civilians, while some police functions have now passed to other agencies.

Another key development was the restructuring of the MPS along borough lines, which began in 1998. Previously there were two or, in some cases, three operational command units in each London borough; the partnership provisions of the 1998 CDA made rationalisation inevitable. Thirty-two local commanders became responsible for the delivery of policing in areas which, in terms of their size of population, were often as large as small provincial forces.

Resource allocation to the new borough units was based on a formula in which crime levels and deprivation were the key factors (as Table 2.4 illustrates). Policing structures and the deployment of resources within these units, though, varied – in part – reflecting differences in the pre-existing arrangements which had to be accommodated within the new, larger units. A common feature, though, was that, in trying to maximise the use of the available resources, areas generating fewer demands tended to lose out to high-crime neighbourhoods or 'hotspots'. The closure of a number of police stations was symbolic of this. Meanwhile local commanders also had to juggle the new demands generated by partnership working (including the secondment of staff to the Youth Offender Teams) and the need to improve specialist provision – whether in setting up teams to tackle priority crimes to which targets attached or in resourcing Community Safety Units (see below).

Table 2.4 also shows the staffing provision in each of our case-study areas in relation to population, deprivation and crime levels at the time of reorganisation, as well as the number of officers available in principle for response policing. In order to preserve the anonymity of sites, we have presented rounded rather than precise figures. Thus Borough A has by far the lowest deprivation score and the lowest level of crime per thousand residents. So, despite serving a resident population larger than that of Borough B by about 70%, it has fewer staff. Borough B, however, has the smallest population but by far the highest levels of crime in relation to this, but is not as deprived overall as Borough C. Borough C is the best resourced of the three, and it also appears to have by far the largest number of officers available for responding to calls from the public. Despite its lower rates of crime per thousand population than Borough B, rates of violence against the person account for a higher proportion of the total.

Table 2.4: Police resources in the case-study areas (1998)
in relation to population, deprivation and crime

	Borough A	*Borough B*	*Borough C*
Size of resident population	324,000	190,000	231,000
Deprivation score	7	28	34
Crimes per thousand population	81	220	174
Crimes of violence against the person per thousand population	11	27	25
Total number of police staff (including civilian staff)	838	850	899
Staff per thousand population	2.6	4.5	3.9

The policing of diverse communities

Concerns about police relations with the black community in particular had been raised since the 1960s (Rose *et al* 1969; Humphry 1972), and the previous PSI report had been commissioned by the MPS in response to these concerns *before* the Brixton riots and the subsequent report of Lord Scarman's inquiry put them so squarely under the political spotlight. Scarman identified the immediate problems underlying the Brixton riots as an interaction between intense levels of social deprivation and a history of unlawful policing methods, racially prejudiced police conduct and lack of community consultation. However, he also recognised the wider dilemmas facing the police in striking a balance between enforcing the law in a high-crime area and the risk of alienating sections of the community who would inevitably find themselves disproportionately targeted. His was an authoritative voice in reiterating the primacy of preserving 'public tranquillity'.

With regard to racial prejudice among the police, he saw this as individual rather than institutional, but with widespread consequences. The PSI study, however, painted a slightly different picture. The researchers found that prejudiced attitudes and expressions of prejudice were normal and regarded as natural within the force; however, they judged that this had less influence on policing on the ground than might be expected.

The government of the day took up few of Scarman's recommendations but the service itself was naturally anxious to avoid repeating the experience of the disturbances and the collective trauma of a further public inquiry. Smith (1983a) reports that they had already begun to make important changes before even the Scarman report was published as well as in immediate response to it. At around the same time, the police had also come under increasing critical scrutiny over their response to racial violence and harassment. Especially in areas with relatively large and increasing minority ethnic populations, these developments created a growing momentum for change within the service. Against this background, the rioting in 1985 was a setback but one which also reinforced the momentum. A number of wider developments in the early 1990s gave new impetus to this and the focus also broadened in two ways. Equality of treatment *within* the service began to receive attention in parallel with developments concerned with service delivery, and wider aspects of diversity also began to be recognised, in particular issues of sexual orientation (for an overview of these developments, see FitzGerald 1997; HMIC 1997).

When Her Majesty's Inspectorate of Constabulary (HMIC) undertook the first major national review of initiatives in this field, the Home Secretary's foreword to the report recognised that the police had done as much – if not more – to improve equality of service delivery than any other public body. The HMIC report itself, though, found that the response had been uneven and, despite the significant progress made in many areas, *integrating* a community relations approach into the mainstream of police activity remained a major challenge (HMIC 1997).

The HMIC report *Winning the Race* was published as the Macpherson inquiry into the racist murder of Stephen Lawrence was starting its work. As Lord Scarman's inquiry had done, the Macpherson Inquiry broadened its terms of reference to examine not only the specifics of the murder investigation (and into subsequent police enquiries) but also the factors which underlay the evident tensions between police and minority ethnic groups. For, despite all that had been done in the intervening period:

It soon became apparent that a narrow interpretation of our terms of reference would have been pointless and counterproductive. Wherever we went we were met with inescapable evidence which highlighted the lack of trust which exists between the police and the minority ethnic communities. At every location there was a striking difference between the positive descriptions of policy initiatives by senior police officers, and the negative expressions of the minority communities, who clearly felt themselves to be discriminated against by the police and others. We were left in no doubt that the contrast between these views and expressions reflected a central problem which needs to be addressed (Macpherson 1999: 45.6).

In contrast to Scarman, Macpherson's report analysed the root of this problem as institutional racism, which it defined as

the collective failure of an organisation to provide an appropriate and professional service to people because of their colour, culture, or ethnic origin. It can be seen or detected in processes, attitudes and behaviour which amount to discrimination through unwitting prejudice, ignorance, thoughtlessness and racist stereotyping which disadvantage minority ethnic people (ibid.: 6.34).

It also concluded that institutional racism underlay some of the failings of the murder inquiry itself and subsequent inquiries into the handling of the case.

The service had already begun to take a series of high-profile initiatives to address areas in which they expected to be criticised before ever the Macpherson Inquiry reported. These included considerable strengthening of the resources committed to murder investigations and of the service's capacity to deal with major incidents generally as well as improving arrangements for family liaison. They also attempted to address the racial issues raised by the Lawrence case in a number of ways. One was to pioneer new approaches to stop and search and to commission an evaluation of the pilots for this which would serve as a study of their use of the power more generally (FitzGerald 1999a, 1999b). Another was to involve many of the service's critics in a panel of independent advisers with whom it would share information on future critical incidents and who would serve both as a sounding board and unofficial watchdog.

Possibly the best known of the MPS initiatives in anticipation of the Macpherson report, though, was the Race and Violent Crimes Task Force. This was set up in the summer of 1998, as the name implied, with a primary aim of improving the MPS's performance in relation to racially motivated crime (although it increasingly emphasised that it covered 'hate crime' more generally). Recorded racist incidents, in fact, cover a very wide range of activity since their definition includes any incident (whether or not a criminal offence) which is reported to the police and which any party believes to have involved an element of racial motivation. The numbers of such incidents rise gradually across our four types of borough, in line with the level of deprivation, with crime generally and with the extent of ethnic diversity in the resident population. However, the profile of victims also changes: the number of black and white victims is almost equal in the areas where the scale of problem is greatest, while Asians form the largest group of victims only in the most affluent areas which record fewest racist incidents.

At borough level, local Community Safety Units (CSUs) were set up in the wake of the Race and Violent Crimes Task Force, but their work has also varied to some degree by area. Many were based on the Vulnerable Persons Units which had already begun to develop *ad hoc* prior to the move to borough-based policing. Some of these had their origins in developing a dedicated response to domestic violence but had expanded to include work on racist incidents, although some areas had also set up units specifically for the latter purpose. The overall size of the CSUs in our case-study areas broadly reflected their level of recorded racist incidents. The largest unit was again in Borough C, where the number of incidents was nearly twice that in Borough A, but its response to homophobic incidents was also more advanced than many other boroughs – largely as a result of a well organised local lobby on these issues. In Borough A, domestic violence remained at least as important an aspect of the work of the CSU as racist incidents, but the unit also had responsibility for child protection issues. All three had increasingly had to deal with incidents where the victims came from the refugee communities and in Boroughs B and C some of these incidents had been carried out by members of their British-born visible minority population.

The Metropolitan Police Commissioner at the time of the Macpherson Inquiry, Sir Paul Condon, accepted the verdict of institutional racism only very reluctantly and after expressing considerable reservations about the consequences that could flow from popular and police misunderstanding of the term. However, the MPS responded positively to the report of the inquiry by mounting the first phase of its diversity strategy. Many of the key elements of the strategy were already in place, as described above, but a new programme of race training was also announced for staff in all boroughs. By the time our fieldwork was complete, the senior management of the MPS had changed and the second phase of the diversity strategy was launched. Its scope was wider than in the first phase, placing greater emphasis on diversity in its broader sense and on issues of equality *within* the service (including gender equality) as well as in service delivery. Meanwhile, in view of the overload on the CSUs, instructions had been issued that their remit with regard to racist incidents was to deal only with the most serious cases and/or those involving particularly vulnerable victims. Where race was an aggravating factor rather than the primary motive for the incident, the case should normally be dealt with by the mainstream of the service (in practice, officers on response teams).

Summary

- London and Londoners have changed since the time of the previous study. In part these changes reflect wider changes in society, including changes in opportunities for crime. But the ethnic make-up of the capital has also changed significantly. These changes have been most pronounced in the most deprived areas but they have important implications for the future of policing in London more generally. The MPS serves a citizenry which is increasingly ethnically diverse, mainly as a result of changes in the indigenous population but catalysed by immigration, including that of white people of minority ethnic origin.

- Crime in London rose from 1981 until the mid-1990s, and has fallen since. Some types of crime, notably robbery, show recent and significant increases however. The problems of measuring trends using official statistics, however, may have been exacerbated by pressures on the police which have affected recording practices. Meanwhile victim surveys have also become less reliable as a check on the police figures as response rates have fallen, particularly in high-crime areas. It is nonetheless evident that crime tends to be highest in two types of borough: central London boroughs and those where deprivation is highest.

- Demands on the police may have increased in other respects. Some come from other public services and from the private sector, but they also reflect the greater accountability of the service and significant institutional change, including the necessity of working in partnership with other agencies. An increasingly important driver of these changes in the 1990s has been the development of a managerialist régime which has prioritised the service's crime-fighting role and measured its performance against set targets.

- There have been sustained efforts over the whole of the period to address the problems in the police's relations with minority ethnic communities highlighted by the Scarman report in 1981. Despite this, the Macpherson Inquiry of 1999 found the service guilty of 'institutional racism' and our study was undertaken against a backdrop of new initiatives to try to tackle this. Meanwhile the service was also in the immediate aftermath of major reorganisation to align the main units of service delivery with local authority (borough) boundaries.

Part II

The Research Findings

Chapter Three: Public Concerns, Needs and Wants

At the heart of the Policing for London project was a desire to get a better grasp of what Londoners wanted from their police service. The original impetus for the study came from a desire amongst senior Metropolitan Police (MPS) managers to minimise the mismatch between the organisation's policing priorities and those of the public. In doing this, the MPS faced two sorts of challenge: deciding how to adjudicate between the conflicting priorities of different groups and, where clear priorities emerge, deciding what activities to do *less* of, to enable them to make the compensating cuts demanded by re-prioritisation.

This chapter summarises findings on Londoners' concerns about crime and disorder and about their policing priorities. We draw largely on the Policing for London Survey (PFLS) and on the focus groups conducted with adults and teenagers in the three case-study sites. However, we designed the PFLS to share measures of anxiety about crime with the British Crime Survey (BCS), and we have drawn most of our measures about incivilities and their impact on people's quality of life from the BCS.

Measuring concerns and priorities about crime and disorder

In trying to identify what priority to attach to problems of crime and disorder, politicians and police managers can assess crime problems against several different criteria, including:

- frequency (or relative frequency – e.g. benchmarking one area against other areas' frequencies);

- gravity – or the impact of incidents on people's lives and livelihoods;

- the public anxiety provoked by the risk of victimisation;

- trends (or relative trends – e.g. benchmarking the area against neighbours' trends); and

- the consequences of *not* taking action.

Some problems of crime and disorder are therefore very commonly recognised as *widespread* (riding on pavements, for example, litter and dog mess). People may regard these as a nuisance, whereas others may see them as symptoms of disorder but which are rarely reckoned in themselves to be *serious*. On the other hand, crimes such as street robbery are relatively *rare,* but can cause great distress to victims and provoke considerable public anxiety.

One could argue that those types of crime that are *rising* steeply deserve more attention than those that are falling – regardless of severity. A further issue is the balance to be struck between short- and long-term consequences of different policing policies. For example, the 'broken windows' hypothesis (Wilson and Kelling 1982; Skogan 1990; Kelling and Coles 1996) is that there may be few short-term costs in ignoring minor disorder; however, there may be considerable long-term costs, as minor incidents cumulatively lead to much larger problems of crime and social decay.

Ignoring these 'incivilities' and focusing primarily on the crimes that trigger greatest worry may therefore have its own costs.

Yet there may also be costs in 'cracking down' on incivilities, since police interventions are likely to fall very disproportionately on those sections of the population with whom they most need to improve relations (see Bowling and Phillips 2002 for a discussion). However, Borough C had significantly revised the balance of its priorities in the course of the study after analyses of local data had suggested a clear progression from rowdyism, vandalism and bullying on its poorer estates to much more serious predatory crime.

On the one hand, there is a cogent argument for focusing resources on the most serious problems and on those that create most concern. This is reinforced by managerialist considerations which place a premium on hard measures of the impact of resource allocation and results that are demonstrable in the short term. On the other hand, narrowing the focus in this way could rule out preventive strategies which might be highly effective but whose impact is less certain and may only become apparent in the medium to long term.

The unimaginative use of sample surveys and focus groups to guide priorities can compound 'short-termism'. Respondents generally identify as priorities those crimes of middling gravity where the risks are greatest for most people, but they are unlikely to identify effective long-term solutions to crime. Qualitative research methods can tap people's thinking in more subtle ways, but the value of both surveys and focus group discussions is limited by people's ignorance about crime and policing. The views captured by both methods will usually be both *uninformed* and *unreflecting*. That is, neither approach can provide a sound basis for hard choices about priorities but they *can* provide important insights into the views and opinions of the people to whom the police and policy-makers need to account for these choices. Combining our quantitative and qualitative data provides a cogent picture of Londoners'

- anxieties about crime;

- perceptions of the frequency and severity of 'incivilities';

- priorities attached to particular problems of crime and disorder;

- preferred policing solutions to these problems; and

- least-favoured policing solutions.

Anxieties about crime and disorder

There is an extensive literature on 'fear' of crime and the term itself is often contested, as are the ways of measuring it (see e.g. Hale 1995; Hough 1995; Farrall *et al* 1997, 2000). Although it is often suggested that fear of crime is a problem in its own right, previous research has suggested that there may be considerable rationality in people's worries about crime. Direct or indirect experiences of crime are good predictors of anxiety about crime, as is people's social and physical vulnerability to victimisation (see e.g. Hough 1995). Indirect 'signs of crime', such as the presence of litter and graffiti, are also associated with worry about crime. Anxieties about crime and disorder are especially relevant to this study because they are likely to shape what people want and expect of the police. Using the same survey measures over time can give some indication of trends, as well as the forms these anxieties take. Meanwhile the ways in which people talk spontaneously in focus groups about anxieties related to crime can provide important insights into *why* certain people feel anxious and in what circumstances.

Trends in anxiety about crime

People tend to presume that crime is ever rising, and with it fear of crime. In fact the PFLS and BCS show no evidence for increasing fear of crime across London. Figure 3.1 suggests that a larger proportion of Londoners feel safe out alone at night than 20 years ago, whilst the position elsewhere is a little worse.

Figure 3.1. Trends in anxiety: per cent 'feeling very safe' out alone at night

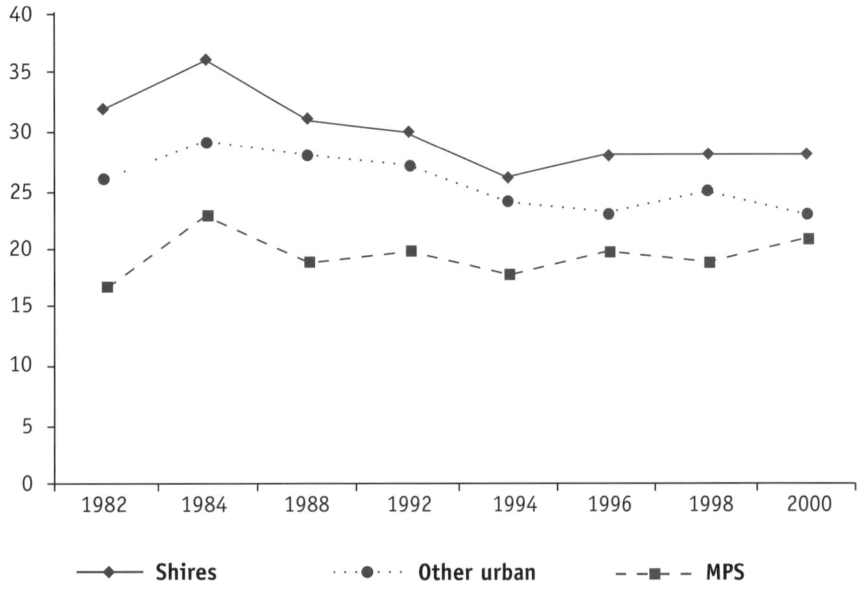

Notes: Weighted data, unweighted *n* (82–00): 10,843; 19,999; 10,353; 10,021; 14,461; 16,303; 14,903; 22,820
Source: PFLS/BCS (2000); BCS (1982–1998)

A similar picture emerges for worry about specific crimes. In 1984, when the BCS first asked such questions, 30% of Londoners were 'very worried' about burglary and 28% about robbery; 39% of women were worried about rape. By 2000, according to the PFLS/BCS, these figures had fallen to 20%, 20% and 32% respectively. In 1984 Londoners were more worried than those living in other metropolitan areas; by 2000 the difference had disappeared.

The issue of racial attacks and harassment, however, had only just begun to reach the policy agenda by 1984 (see the previous chapter). The first BCS to oversample minority ethnic respondents was in 1988, and a question on worry about racial attack was first asked in 1994. Sub-samples of minority groups in 1994 and 1996 are small, especially for Asians, which probably explains the considerable fluctuations from year to year in Table 3.1.

Table 3:1: Trends in worry about racial attack, by ethnicity
(per cent 'very worried')

	1994	*1996*	*2000*
White	10%	8%	6%
Black	30%	28%	26%
Indian	42%	31%	27%
Pakistani/Bangladeshi	45%	24%	30%

Note: Weighted data, unweighted *n* = 2,571 (94); 1,746 (96); 5,332 (00)
Source: BCS/PFLS

The BCS also asked whether racial harassment was a problem. The proportion saying that it was doubled from 9% in 1992 to 18% in 2000. This trend was consistent across ethnic groups – despite the fact that racially motivated offences have fallen (Clancy *et al* 2001). It is very probably the result of the sensitizing effects of the inquiry into the death of Stephen Lawrence.

Variation by group and across area
There are, however, important variations within the overall picture of worries about crime both by area and by group. Figure 3.2 presents findings relating to burglary, mugging, worry about racial attack and rape (the last for women only) by area. On both these and other measures, people in the deprived inner boroughs were the most anxious, followed by those in poorer outer boroughs.[1] In general, respondents who lived in central London or in affluent outer boroughs were less likely to say they were worried than those in poorer areas – though central Londoners were as likely as those in poor outer boroughs to say they were very worried about burglary.

Another important difference across area was that people in affluent areas were more likely to worry about property crime than crimes of violence. By contrast, those in more deprived areas where crime was higher were more worried about crime in general, but their main concerns were about their personal safety rather than burglary or car crime. This is not surprising since the level of crime overall tends to increase with deprivation but the rise tends to be more marked for crimes of violence.[2]

Young people in general tend to be most at risk of violence, as those in our focus groups were well aware. For many in the most deprived areas of Borough C, though, the threat of violence appeared to be almost endemic in their environment, and it affected their day-to-day lives to a much greater degree:

> *Boy:*
> Round my area though it's terrible … There's muggings, things going on and nothing happens [i.e. nothing is done about it]. Like a guy got shot round my way in bed and it's only a few minutes from the police station.

---

[1] Boroughs are grouped according to an Office for National Statistics (ONS) typology of areas. According to this, *deprived boroughs* are Hackney, Islington, Lambeth, Southwark, Newham and Tower Hamlets. *Central London boroughs* are Camden, City of London, Hammersmith & Fulham, Kensington & Chelsea, Wandsworth and Westminster. *Poor outer London boroughs* are Brent, Ealing, Greenwich, Haringey, Lewisham, Waltham Forest, and Barking and Dagenham. *Affluent outer London boroughs* are Barnet, Bexley, Bromley, Croydon, Enfield, Harrow, Havering, Hillingdon, Hounslow, Kingston-upon-Thames, Merton, Redbridge, Richmond-upon-Thames and Sutton.
[2] The average number of crimes per thousand population in the affluent group of boroughs was 81 but it was just under double that in the most deprived group (160). The figures for crimes of violence were 11 and 25 respectively.

Figure 3.2: Anxiety about crime, by area – per cent feeling 'very worried'.

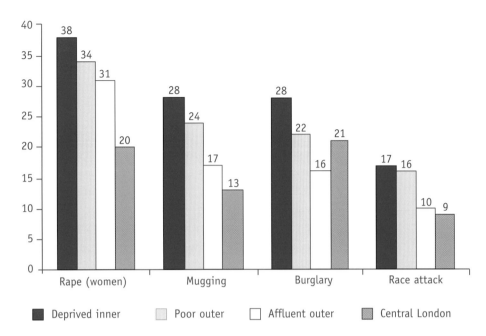

Notes: 1. Weighted data, unweighted n = 5,721 (rape 3,004)
2. Excluding 'don't knows'/ 'not applicable'
Source: PFLS and 2000 BCS

Girl:
Another time somebody got stabbed in the face with a knife because they wouldn't give up their mobile phone.

Schools in such areas have increasingly begun to engage security staff, and the young people we talked to in one school in Borough C were ambivalent about such measures. They resented, for example, not being allowed out at lunchtimes, yet they knew this protected them from groups of other young people who would congregate in the vicinity of the school to mug them or pick fights. On the other hand, the heightened security offered little protection on the journeys they still had to make to and from school.

There were area differences also in perceptions of who was responsible for the crime. All groups – including young people themselves – said that most crime tended to be committed by young people, although the girls we talked to in all areas pointed out that older people (including the police) tended to underestimate the extent of girls' involvement. Those in more affluent areas saw the people responsible as outsiders who came into the area to commit crime. However, young people in more deprived neighbourhoods said that crime here tended to be committed against people who did not 'belong', and these distinctions obtained not only between boroughs but within them also. A girl who lived on a notorious estate in Borough A explained:

Because I know a lot of the people that live there or hang around there, they all know my face, they know I live there, they know my family and my friends that live in [the estate] so they don't trouble me... I know some of the girls that go to this school, when they go to [the estate] a lot of the boys – even the girls … they'll try and take their phones, take their money… But none of that has ever happened to me there, 'cause they all know who I am.

In Borough C, though, where there were more high crime neighbourhoods, 'belonging' and not belonging had begun to be defined in terms of ethnicity:

> *Boy:*
> The whole of [Y neighbourhood] – it's terrible. If you look at someone bad, that's it: throws a knife at you … or a bottle. You can't look at anyone. It's like here. You don't get many different races except white people coming here really, but [Y neighbourhood] it's mainly black people and then [here] is mainly white people. That's just what people do, so when people move to certain areas, like white people move to [here] 'cause it's mainly white people, and that's where it all starts – you get certain areas filling up with a certain race and that starts the problems.

In sum, most people's anxieties about crime tended to focus on people 'other' than themselves. Territory was often an important marker and, in some neighbourhoods, this was also racialised.

The most direct example we came across was when we conducted a focus group with young Bangladeshis in a library in Borough B which was surrounded in the course of the evening by a gang of white youths. The police had to be called to disperse them and the young people had to be escorted home. But the young people themselves made it clear that the reverse situation could as easily have occurred only a few streets away. It was apparent also that these distinctions were not simply between minorities and whites.[3] The account of an older black man in another focus group helps illustrate the complex interaction between ethnicity and the well established phenomenon of young men vying collectively for control of the streets in certain areas. He had lived in the area for a long time but took a short-cut one day with a friend through particular streets:

> It was as if you were walking through a forbidden valley – the stares we got from people … It's been turned into a ghetto … it's like a no-go area … I was looked at in an intimidating way, by … Asian young men, 14–15, overflowing with male hormones and wanting to punch somebody. And I'm thinking: 'Don't look at me like that.' Horrible feeling!

It is important to stress that this racialised construction of 'otherness' was by no means universal, and respondents of all ethnic origins saw it as particular to a small number of neighbourhoods. They also constructed 'otherness' in a range of different ways. In addition to defining people who lived outside their area as 'other', they

---

[3] Several of the young men in this group, for example, claimed solidarity with black people but expressed overt prejudice against Somalians.

tended to fear individuals whose behaviour might be unpredictable. These too were identified collectively and were often associated with particular areas:

> I don't like going down to [Y] in the evening because there are always scary people – as in 'weirdos' (like mental...). And they often come up to you and that's quite scary and you don't know how to handle it. (Schoolgirl, Borough A).

Additionally, those who were not part of the group saw large crowds as particularly intimidating because of their perceived potential for violence. Reference was made to groups of rowdy young people hanging around, and to football crowds, but in particular to the sudden presence on the street of large numbers of people when pubs and clubs shut down. These had been drinking and possibly taking drugs, putting them in the category of people whose behaviour might be unpredictable – and on a large scale. The following comment about clubs by a man in Borough C is very similar to the observation by another man in Borough A in relation to pubs (although violence was more of a threat than a fact in Borough A).

> What amazes me is how few police on the beat there are, if you go to [X] High Street, 4 o'clock on Saturday morning, or Friday when the clubs are coming out. There's a load of drunken people getting into vehicles, there's a load of arguing and fighting, knife fights occasionally inside and outside...

In terms of the level of anxiety between different groups of people, surveys have consistently shown women to be more anxious about crime than men – whether on traditional measures of 'fear' or in relation to specific crimes. In fact, as Figure 3.3 shows, there are large differences for crimes of violence, but much smaller for burglary and vehicle theft.

Figure 3.3 Anxieties about specific crimes – per cent feeling 'very worried'.

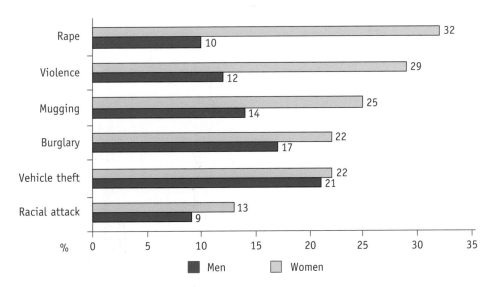

Notes: 1. Weighted data, unweighted $n = 5,719$ (vehicle theft: 3,733)
2. Excluding 'don't knows'/ 'not applicable'
Source: PFLS and 2000 BCS

**Figure 3.4: Anxiety about crime, by ethnicity
– per cent feeling 'very worried'**

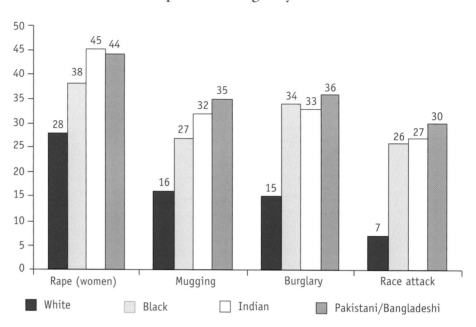

Notes: 1. Weighted data, unweighted *n* = 5,332
2. Excluding 'don't knows'/ 'not applicable'
Source: PFLS and 2000 BCS merged

It is often presumed that fear of crime is greatest amongst the elderly. On most measures of worry about crime this is not so. People aged 60 or over were no more likely than others to say they were very worried about burglary, mugging or vehicle crime – probably reflecting the fact that their lifestyles expose them to lower levels of risk than younger people. However, there were large differences on one measure, which asked how safe people felt out alone in their area at night: 19% of those aged 60 or over said they felt very unsafe, compared with 8% of the rest of the population.

There are significant differences in anxiety between ethnic groups, as Figure 3.4 shows. They arise in respect of a range of crimes, although they are most pronounced in the case of racial attack. Some, but not all, of this difference can be attributed to the fact that minority groups tend disproportionately to live in deprived areas where the level of crime adds to overall stress levels among the local population. However, large differences between white and other ethnic groups remain after area has been taken into account (see Clancy *et al* 2001 for a fuller analysis at national level).

Concerns about 'incivilities' and disorder
As well as asking about anxieties about specific crime, the 2000 BCS asked how common various 'incivilities' were, including relatively low-level problems of disorder such as adolescent rowdyism, drug use, litter and graffiti, noisy parties and other disturbances. And it asked separately how big a problem these were perceived to be. The results for London are presented in Figure 3.5. In general, the ranking of 'very big problems' matched that for 'very common'. The clear exceptions to this rule

**Figure 3.5 How much of a problem? How common?
Perceptions of incivilities**

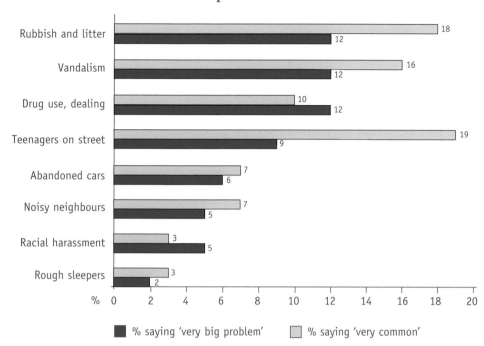

Notes: 1. Weighted data, unweighted *n*: how common? – 1,080; how big a problem? – 1,101
2. Excluding 'don't knows'/ 'not applicable'
Source: BCS (2000)

were litter, vandalism and 'teenagers hanging around': people were much less likely to say these were big problems than to say they were very common.

The survey explored this set of issues further, asking whether any of the incivilities on the list had 'had a bad effect on your quality of life since January 1999': 54% of Londoners said that none of them had had any effect; 18% mentioned rubbish and litter; 15% mentioned teenagers hanging around on the streets; 14% mentioned vandalism and graffiti;11% referred to noisy neighbours and loud parties; and 7% mentioned drug users and dealers. Less than 5% mentioned the remaining issues.

Comparing Figure 3.5 with Figure 3.3, it is apparent that even those incivilities which were perceived as a 'very big problem' exercised a much smaller proportion of respondents than did worries about specific crimes. Taken at face value, this suggests that incivilities merit less attention than crimes. However, this ignores the very 'interconnectedness' between the two in people's minds. Respondents in our focus groups often linked them spontaneously. They connected incivilities both with a sense of direct threat to personal safety and with the prevalence of crime in the area more generally. Thus two young women in Borough B associated drugs paraphernalia with the sorts of 'wierdos' who might turn violent, but they also saw them as symbols of a criminogenic environment.

Young woman 1:
It just worries me that my parents … That my mother walks down [the street] and she gets attacked. That's what bothers me – because they [the 'druggies'] don't know what they're doing, they're out of their heads.

Young woman 2:
The drugs [bother me], and the druggies basically. Because I've got a little brother and a little sister and all that, and I don't want them growing up in a society with all these drug dealers. They might turn out like that. I don't want that to happen.

For older respondents in Borough A, both vandalism and litter were associated with people who came into the area from outside; that is, they might be in the area to commit crime but, in any case, the vandalism and litter were associated with pubs and restaurants. This connoted drunkenness and, with it, the threat of violence and disorder. With this older group, though, anxiety about their own physical vulnerability was not only connected with the threat of violence:

Man 1:
It does annoy me, the people who've committed the vandalism aren't from [this area].

Woman 1:
No … you see these gangs of young people and … maybe they've been drinking up in [town centre] or somewhere up there and they come back and on the way they do this [vandalism].

Man 2:
I think that they really should not be allowed to throw any rubbish. They should be fined for that. They should be. Actually they throw banana skin, they eat the banana, the skin is thrown and we fall and break our neck.

Woman 1:
This rubbish business is really very vital.

These quotations illustrate the way in which people tend to see problems of crime and disorder as a series of interconnected *processes,* rather than discrete and unrelated *events.* This perspective is somewhat at odds with a managerialist approach which divides them into specific categories of problem and seeks to assign separate priorities to each. Structured surveys can quite readily force respondents to make such choices, by predefining the response categories available to them. Focus groups, by contrast, are much less structured, and leave participants free to express themselves in their own terms. This may go some way to explaining why few participants in our focus groups were prepared to specify what categories of crime should be prioritised by the police.

While the BCS shows no evidence of an increase in anxiety about *crime,* it does suggest an increase in people's perception of incivilities as a problem. A question on incivilities was first asked in 1992 and, as Figure 3.6 shows, the trend on a number of key measures is upward. In particular, the proportion saying that drug dealing and use is a problem has almost doubled over eight years.

Priority problems
Having established a general picture of respondents' concerns, the PFLS moved on to try to get them to identify specific problems that should be a priority *for the police*

Figure 3.6: Incivilities as a 'very' or 'fairly' big problem, 1992 –2000

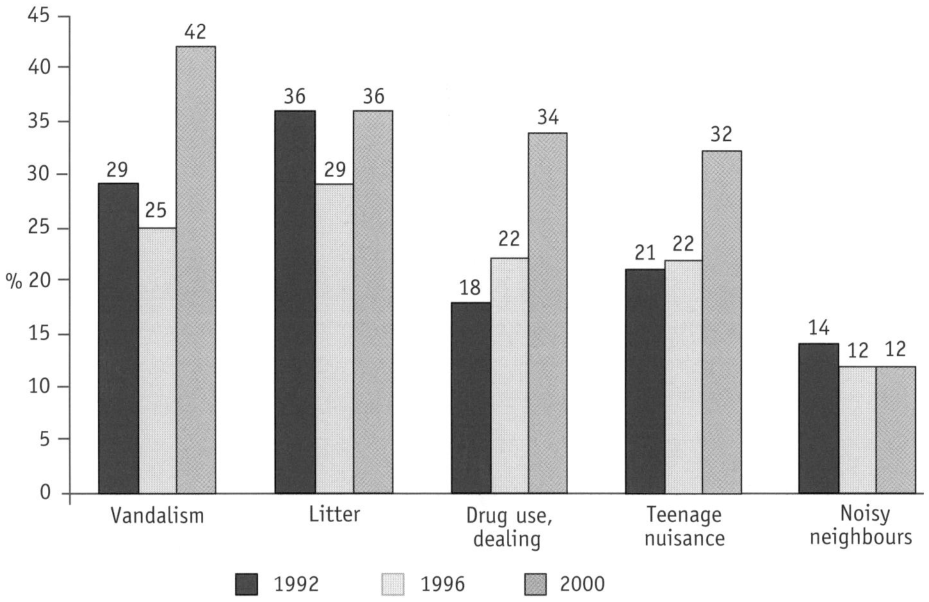

Note: Weighted data, unweighted *n* = 1,422 (92); 1,202 (96); 1,082 (00)
Source: BCS core (1992, 1996, 2000)

(as opposed to any other agency). It also asked their views on how well the police currently dealt with these problems, and what they saw as the best ways of tackling them.

Priority problems

People were asked to identify up to five priority problems from a list of 18 possible candidates. Priorities were defined as problems 'which the police in your areas should spend most time and energy trying to fight'. People's choices of priority problems are shown in Table 3.2. Burglary, mugging and dealing in hard drugs emerge as clear priorities. In each case around half the sample included the problem as a priority. The table also shows the ordering for first, second, third and fourth priorities. Many people had 'run out of steam' by the time they had nominated four.

Table 3.2: The top ten priorities (%)

	1st Priority	*2nd Priority*	*3rd Priority*	*4th Priority*	*Any priority*
1. Burglary	28	11	8	6	**57**
2. Mugging	10	16	16	13	**54**
3. Dealing hard drugs	18	10	12	9	**47**
4. Violent crime	13	8	7	10	**38**
5. Sexual crime	9	8	7	6	**31**
6. Vandalism	6	13	6	5	**31**
7. Racial attacks	3	5	10	8	**27**
8. Vehicle theft	2	4	6	8	**21**
9. Other autocrime	2	3	7	9	**20**
10. Drink driving	4	6	5	5	**20**

For each priority the selected respondents were asked to say how well they thought the police were doing at present in tackling the problem. Some 69% thought the police were already doing well in tackling burglary, but the figure for mugging was 57% and for hard drug dealing it was down to 50%.

There were geographical variations in priorities, reflecting differences in risks. In general people from affluent boroughs were more likely to mention burglary, vehicle crime and vandalism, and those in more deprived boroughs were more likely to select mugging, racial attack and drug dealing (see Figure 3.7). As with anxiety about crime, people from minority ethnic groups were much more likely to mention racial attack. For example, 48% of black respondents, 42% of Pakistanis and Bangladeshis and 39% of Indians selected this, as against 22% of white respondents.

Figure 3.7 Contrasting crime priorities in affluent and deprived boroughs

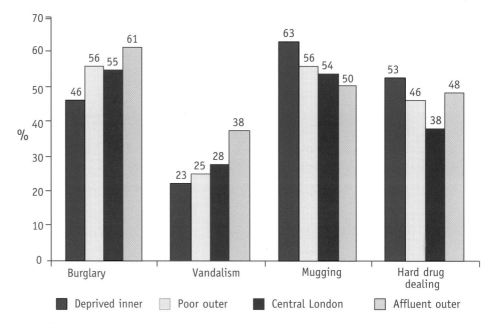

Note: Weighted data, unweighted n = 2,705
Source: PFLS

Non-priorities

The problems least often nominated as priorities tend to suggest which types of police work respondents viewed as least important in the overall scheme of things. Disputes with neighbours received fewest nominations: only 1% of the sample gave it any priority. Prostitution was chosen by 3%[4]; taking 'soft drugs' was mentioned by 4%; noisy neighbours by 8%; domestic violence by 9%; dealing in 'soft drugs' by 12%; taking 'hard drugs' by 13%; and disorderly behaviour by 17%.

However, respondents were also asked to select up to three problems on which the police should spend less time. As the final column of Table 3.3 shows, they were more reluctant to do this than to identify areas where they wanted to see more police effort. The number of respondents who were prepared to identify any item as a non-priority was much lower than the proportion who named priorities in Table 3.2, and

---

[4] For a small number of respondents this may have been a high priority, reflecting the highly localised nature of sex markets. Prostitution may have a major impact on the lives of people living and working in the vicinity but hardly impinges at all on people outside it. By contrast, drug dealing also tends to be localised but its effects are more pervasive. Street dealing probably takes place across a much larger number of sites than prostitution, but young people in particular are likely to come across a range of other outlets. Also many focus group respondents referred to drugs paraphernalia as a particular form of litter which caused them anxiety.

few named more than two items. Nonetheless, six problems were nominated as non-priorities by at least 10% of the sample and these are broadly the converse of respondents' priorities.

The two main non-priorities that emerged were neighbour disputes and noisy neighbours. Nearly half the sample suggested that the police should not be involved in dealing with these – or certainly not at the expense of other police activity. And a quarter of the sample took the same view of the policing of drugs such as cannabis. Other non-priorities, though, were selected only by small minorities.

Table 3.3: The top six 'non-priorities' (%)

	1st non-priority	2nd non-priority	Any non-priority
1. Neighbour disputes	23	20	47
2. Noisy neighbours	20	19	42
3. Taking soft drugs	14	13	27
4. Disorder/rowdyism	5	5	14
5. Dealing soft drugs	6	6	13
6. Domestic violence	4	7	12

Policing solutions

Having canvassed views on London's crime problems, we asked respondents about solutions to crime and disorder. The lead-in to this section of questions stressed that the police had limited resources and could not always cover everything. Respondents were then asked to say which activities the police 'should do more of'. They were allowed a maximum of three choices from a show-card menu with 15 items on it. Figure 3.8 summarises the results for those activities which commanded support from at least 10% of the sample.

Figure 3.8: Activities the police should spend more time on: per cent choosing each item

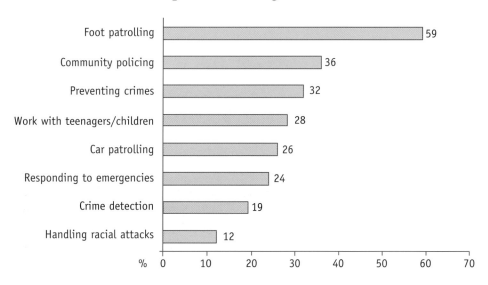

Notes: 1. Weighted data, unweighted *n* = 2,690
2. Only the 8 activities which secured more than 10% support are shown.
Source: PFLS

Figure 3.9: Activities the police should spend less time on: per cent choosing each item

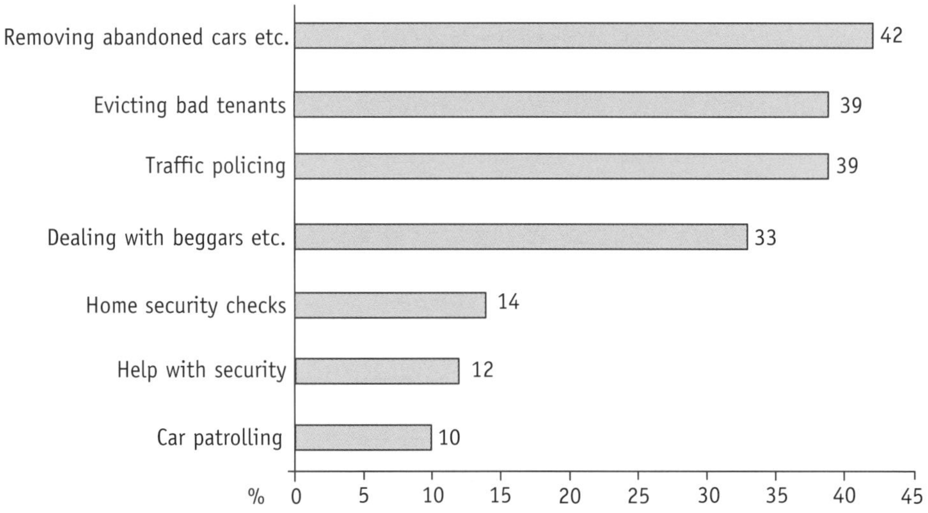

Note: 1. Weighted data, unweighted *n* = 2,384
   2. Only the 7 activities which secured at least 10% support are shown.
Source: PFLS

There was a clear preference for more foot patrol (59%). If we include those who called for more car patrols, 69% of the sample wanted the police to spend more time patrolling. There was also a clear preference for 'working with the community' (community policing), crime prevention and work with teenagers and children.

Respondents were then asked to identify functions or activities from which the police should withdraw. They were offered the same menu of options as before. Results are in Figure 3.9. Not surprisingly, the list of seven activities that were selected by at least 10% of the sample was the converse of the list of preferred activities. However, there were some striking differences across area and between groups within this. Other data from the survey as well as insights from our focus groups suggest that the choices in this list are driven by two main considerations. One is that people do not prioritise issues where they have not personally needed help from the police. Thus, we have qualitative evidence that police assistance with home security has been highly appreciated and has been important in offsetting other, more negative impressions especially among victims of crime. Yet very few people actually receive this service. The second consideration, by contrast, is that people may also give a low rating to police activities that may impact negatively on their own activities. The most obvious example is traffic policing, given that the largest number of police-initiated contacts with members of the public were car stops (see next chapter) and the increasing numbers of motorists who are now caught by police speed cameras.[5]

The fact that 26% favoured *more* car patrols in Figure 3.8 while 10% favoured *less* in Figure 3.9 also helps to illustrate some of the dilemmas in the choices which face police managers. At its simplest, meeting the demands of the larger group on this issue risks alienating the smaller group. However, as our qualitative data showed, people may also hold views that appear to be contradictory. They may want more intrusive policing directed at the 'other' people they perceive as a threat but want less

---

[5] Nationally, cameras provided evidence for 802,000 motoring offences in 2000, an increase of 46% over 1999 (see Home Office 2001c).

of the same activity if it impinges directly on them. These considerations need to be borne in mind in interpreting the differences between areas and groups.

Support for more foot patrols was spread evenly across affluent and poor boroughs but support was noticeably lower among those groups most at risk of being stopped by the police. Young people were much less likely than their elders to want more foot patrols and so too were people from minority ethnic groups.[6] However, minority ethnic groups were more in favour of closer links between police and community: Pakistani, Bangladeshi and in particular black respondents were more likely to advocate community policing methods than white Londoners.

What do people want from patrol?
The PFLS confirmed the overwhelming evidence of the public's desire to see more 'bobbies on the beat'. Few previous surveys, though, have tried to pinpoint what people actually expect from this extra patrolling. The PFLS asked all those who advocated more time on patrol to say what types of activity the patrols should engage in. The most common responses can be summarised as:

- to deter or prevent crime (65%);

- providing reassurance (49%);

- work with schools (25%);

- gathering local intelligence (24%);

- dealing with disturbances (20%); and

- providing advice on crime prevention (15%);

No other responses secured support from more than 5% of the sample.

Our case studies further reinforced how widespread was the desire for the police to be not only more visible but also more accessible. Older participants, remembering a time when it had been far more common to see officers on foot, tended to stress the reassurance argument.[7] But younger people, knowing themselves to be at risk, made more explicit connections between crime prevention generally (and their own need for protection in particular) with the reassurance provided by an increased police presence. A schoolboy in Borough C explained they wanted 'police officers at the schools making sure that everyone was going home safely and there's no-one out there looking for trouble'. They were realistic about how much difference an increased police presence could make in practice, but still, said a girl in Borough A:

> I think you'd feel a lot safer if the police were around. I think it would prevent more crimes. It wouldn't prevent them that much, but maybe if they were patrolling [people] would be more cautious to do crimes.

Importantly, a number of respondents in the focus groups – and the young people in particular – did not see the increase in patrol as an end in itself. They explicitly linked

---

[6] Forty-four per cent of the under 30s advocated more foot patrols, compared with 59% of those aged between 30 and 59, and 76% of those aged 60 or more. The figures for different ethnic groups were: white 64%; black 45%, Indian 51%; Pakistani/ Bangladeshi 46%.

[7] One officer we accompanied in Area A described how an old lady had kissed him and burst into tears because it was so long since she had seen a policeman on foot patrol.

it with the three other top items in Figure 3.8; that is, they conceived of the increase in patrols in relation to more community involvement (especially with young people) in the context of an enhanced crime *prevention* role for the police. Putting extra resources into detection was a much lower priority, that is, patrol was seen as part of a package which could help prevent crime by setting up a two-way process. On the one hand, they argued that the police needed to get to know local people better as individuals *outside* – and to some degree instead of – the normal frame of encounters which (especially with young people) tended to be potentially confrontational. This was the best hope of surmounting officers' stereotypes of young people in general and those from minority ethnic groups in particular. On the other hand, building up trust in this way might surmount young people's reluctance to become involved in helping the police. Young people had a lot of information about what was going on in their area, but they were also vulnerable and the norms against 'grassing' tended to be especially strong in high-crime areas:

> If they had more, sort of visits, like communities and all that, and then like going to the Youth Club and talking to youths and all that. They should socialise more. If the youths got to know them, and they get to know the youths, then they wouldn't pick on them. Because if they don't get to know them, they just pick out any of them on the streets, they don't really know what they do, what sort of background they're from. If they got to know them, right – next time they're driving past them, and it's put on the radio, like 'Blah blah blah – you're looking for an Asian boy: bring him in for assault' whatever … they're going to look at that kid and say: 'No. I know him. He wouldn't do something like that, let's just leave him alone and find someone else' (young Bangladeshi woman, Borough B).

> I would tell them to build up youth trust – because at the end of the day we are the ones that are always on the streets and we see everything … They need to stop seeing kids and thinking: 'There's a 15 year old girl: she must be doing something…' or 'That 15 year old boy is wearing a tracksuit and a cap so he must be doing something…' Because sometimes, it is not even about: 'She's black, so she's done something' or 'She's white…' It isn't even about what colour you are. Sometimes it's just the fact that you're a kid or you're a teenager that makes them think: 'I'm going to come and talk to you; I'm going to search you.' If they build up our trust, [if] they spent less of their time questioning us and talking to us about stupid things like vandalism and stuff like that … If they spent more of their time talking to us, getting to know us – being friendly … Then we'd trust them and we might tell them the sort of stuff that they want to know (white schoolgirl, Borough C).

Some boys in Borough C specifically envisaged police community involvement schemes as providing natural opportunities for them to pass information on to the police without the risk of being exposed as a 'grass':

> Say like … sporting schemes. And then there could be like kids against police officers and then the kids can then, like, tell the police information

but it looks like they're speaking to them. That could help them in all kind of ways.

Support for stop-and-search

One activity undertaken by patrols, though, is a perennial source of tension. Young people in particular (in all our areas) complained about being stopped and questioned by the police, whether or not they were also searched.

There is nothing to stop the police speaking to anyone they choose and ask them questions – although the individual is not formally obliged to reply. In terms of their formal powers, the Road Traffic Act allows them to stop any vehicle at their discretion. Section 1 of the Police and Criminal Evidence Act 1984 (PACE), though, gives them the power to 'detain' people in public places only where they have 'reasonable grounds' for suspecting that a search will uncover 'stolen or prohibited objects'.[8] Codes of practice have successively refined details of the circumstances in which the PACE power can (and cannot) be used.

The survey asked whether the police should have powers to stop people, and if they think they have sufficient reason, to search them. We then asked an open-ended question about the circumstances in which stops were justified, and those in which they were not. Only 8% thought the police should *not* have powers to stop and search people on foot or in cars and, although black respondents were significantly more likely to say this, the proportion objecting in principle was still under a fifth of the sample (17%). Yet very few respondents in any group were *unconditionally* in favour (4% of all who said the powers should be available). The vast majority gave answers which referred explicitly or implicitly to the need for reasonable suspicion. Those who supported the use of the powers were also asked about situations in which people should *not* be stopped. Almost half (45%) mentioned circumstances in which there was lack of suspicion, and around a third mentioned circumstances when criteria were inadequate, such as stopping people simply on the basis of their age, sex or ethnicity (grounds explicitly forbidden under the codes governing PACE stops).

Our respondents, then, were drawing a very clear distinction. They actively wanted the police to engage more with their local communities in non-adversarial ways, but they took exception to being stopped and questioned when, in their view, they were simply going about their lawful business. Even if officers handled the encounter well, they resented being treated as suspects and/or subjected to a measure of social control which was effectively an abuse of the police's authority. As schoolgirls in Borough A put it:

> *Girl 1:*
> I was just walking through [X part of Borough A] with my friends and they stopped us: 'Where are you going,? What are you doing?' The amount of times that I've been spoken to by them in [X part of Borough A] for just being there …

---

[8] The power under s. 60 does not require 'reasonable grounds', though. It can only be invoked for limited periods in circumstances where serious violence may occur and was originally conceived of in connection with football matches. Its use by some forces (including the MPS) has increased considerably in recent years.

Girl 2:

The police officers they even say to us: 'Oh, we're just patrolling the area ... We have to do it because it's getting a reputation' ... It's not so bad (but it *is* getting worse) – but they don't want to be down there obviously.

Moderator:

And how does it make you feel getting stopped like that?

Girl 2:

I'm annoyed, because they go: 'What are you doing here?' And when you're like visiting friends and they're like: 'Hurry up and go home, and don't stay down here.'

Tackling problems in partnership

When asking about priority problems, the survey asked respondents to specify who *other than the police* had a role to play in tackling the problems they mentioned. In relation to burglary a third of people said neighbourhood watch had a role, a fifth saw a greater role for the general public, and a tenth thought the council should be more involved. Those who nominated mugging as a problem saw a similar role for the same groups (23% specified a role for the general public, 17% mentioned neighbourhood watch and 14% the council). For dealing in hard drugs, a far greater range of agencies or people were mentioned (16% mentioned parents, 12% teachers, 11% members of the public and 10% health agencies).

Our focus groups also suggested that people do not believe responsibility for crime control lay solely with the police. And the local authority was most often seen, in principle, as a potential partner. However, in all three areas there was strong scepticism about their role in practice:

Moderator: What about the council?
Woman: You're having a laugh (Borough A).

Moderator: What about B council? How good is it at looking at these issues would you say?
Woman: Looking at yes, doing something about maybe not.
Man: B council is useless (Borough B).

Moderator: Which agencies do you believe should be involved in preventing crime?
Woman: Well, it should come under your local council ...
Moderator: So, in this area, that would be C Borough Council?
Woman: I find that highly unlikely.
Moderator: Why do you say that?
Woman: You've got to actually live in one of their properties – and watch how, you constantly pay your rent and poll tax and you're watching how they just allow the flats to deteriorate ... they've got people just doing their jobs and they couldn't care less, because they haven't got to live in it – so everything is deteriorating (Borough C).

Schools were also mentioned in the focus groups, as was the government – especially in relation to the causes of crime. The need for both leisure facilities and employment opportunities for young people came out strongly, as in this group of young people in Borough B:

> *Moderator*: Is it all just down to the Police, or are there other groups that ought to be involved?
> *Young man 1*: The Youth Services.
> *Moderator*: The Youth Services, what sort of things could they be doing?
> *Young man 1*: Youth Club and that – at least it should be open more often, so people, like, don't get into trouble.
> *Moderator*: Right, anybody else?
> *Young man 2*: Yes, as [I] was saying, if they were open more days right, and then people were coming off the streets into the club, so they wouldn't be around looking for trouble. Because if the Youth Club is closed, they have nothing to do – just hanging around causing trouble…
> *Moderator*: What about any other organisations locally that could be doing more to tackle crime rather than just the police?
> *Young man 1*: Employment service – find us jobs.

Despite this clear perception of the need for partnership working, few members of the public seemed to be aware of the Crime and Disorder Partnerships. Only 9% of our survey respondents, when asked, said they had heard of the crime reduction partnerships introduced in 1998, and no reference was made to them at all in our focus groups. There were few demographic or area differences in awareness, though black and white respondents were more likely to be aware of them than Asians. A third of those who had heard of partnerships, or 3% of the total sample, said they had been consulted about crime, for example through questionnaires, telephone interviews, public meetings or surveys in the local press. The whole sample was asked if the partnerships would be effective: 42% said they didn't know; 41% thought they would be successful; and the remaining 17% thought they would fail.

In our case-study areas partnerships tended to be better established and more proactive in the more deprived, high-crime areas – although many outstanding issues remained to be resolved. Even where working relationships between individuals were good, tensions had inevitably begun to surface about differences in the styles of working of different agencies (a point developed further in the concluding chapter of this volume). But local authorities too were operating under some of the same constraints as the police. Strong competing internal demands for limited resources, along with the imperative of meeting targets for the delivery of their own services meant they had limited spare capacity to pool in new, joint initiatives. Successfully bidding for funds to kick start these initiatives in the short term could rebound later. When central funding ran out, agencies might then have to choose between falling back on their own resources to sustain projects – or incurring the opprobrium of local residents by shutting them down.

Meanwhile, there was evidence also of an understandable wariness among the various agencies involved about the demarcation of responsibilities, and this was best illustrated in relation to the quasi-policing functions of the local authorities. On the one hand, agencies were wary of the partnerships being used as an excuse for any other agency to shuffle off responsibility to them. In one area a local authority respondent was unusually enthusiastic about the role of local wardens – as long as the police were required to take responsibility for them (and, by inference, to foot all or some of the bill). On the other, there was a concern about loss of control and, by extension, of political capital. A major stumbling block in another area throughout the fieldwork period was the authority's proposal to introduce a warden scheme with minimal reference to the police.[9]

Key findings

- People want reassurance that the police are protecting them from the threat of crime and disorder.

- Although they fear some types of crime more than others, their anxieties are interconnected and are often triggered by incivilities.

- The survey data provide no evidence that anxiety about crime has been increasing in London, but there *has* been an increase in concerns about incivilities.

- Different sections of the population have different levels of anxiety, and people's fears may vary by area, age, gender and ethnicity.

- Their sense of threat is often associated with people they identify as 'other' than themselves. 'Belonging' in a particular area is important in this context and in a few localities this is identified with ethnicity.

- People find it much easier to say what they want the police to do more of than to identify activities the police should do less of or drop.

- They want the police to be more visible and accessible – not because they expect this will cause an immediate fall in crime or simply as a symbolic form of reassurance. They see more bobbies on the beat as one of several measures to improve crime prevention by securing the trust and co-operation of local people.

- The use of intrusive policing tactics such as stop and search can undermine trust and co-operation, especially among young people and ethnic minorities. Yet majorities of all groups accept the need for the power in principle.

- People do not believe that the police alone can tackle crime. But they are sceptical about the role played by others, especially local authorities, and few are aware of the local partnerships set up by the Crime and Disorder Act 1998.

- Local authorities labour under similar constraints to the police, and different styles of working can create tensions even in the most effective partnerships. These problems may play out in setting up and running local warden schemes.

- In articulating their policing priorities people are likely to be uninformed. They do not naturally conceive of issues in the discrete categories required by policy-makers and they have particular difficulty in identifying non-priorities.

- This adds to the complexity of consultation and still leaves managers with hard choices between the different concerns and interests of different groups.

---

[9] In the early stages of the fieldwork, the police were finding it difficult even to obtain a copy of the job description for these posts.

Chapter Four: Londoners' Experience of the Police

Roughly half of Londoners have some sort of contact with the police in any given year, and many others will know people who have. Experience of the police can not only shape the perceptions of those who are directly involved but the accounts they give may also influence the opinions of others. Vicarious or indirect experience will shape people's expectations of the police, and may well shape their response to subsequent encounters with the police (cf. Small 1983). In addition, where there are patterns to unsatisfactory encounters – even if these represent only a minority of the total – these are important in helping us meet our aim of identifying the reasons for the gap between people's expectations and the service they receive.

Our focus groups reinforced our sense that perception in these matters may be as important as reality, and acknowledging this is essential in helping to bridge the gap. Some respondents who had had little or no recent contact still referred back to incidents that had happened to them or to people they were close to several years previously. Many, including our young people, had a range of direct and vicarious experiences to draw on and these usually tended to be very mixed. On balance, though, a single bad experience could outweigh the impact of many that were good or neutral. As some of our police officers were also only too well aware, these bad experiences had a disproportionate impact on perceptions and could, in turn, come into play in people's future encounters with the police.

This chapter describes Londoners' experience of the Metropolitan Police (MPS) while the next chapter considers in more detail their reaction to this experience. First it considers our respondents as 'users' of the police and then moves on to their experience of being approached by the police, most often as 'suspects'. Our survey database allows quite good measurement of both forms of contacts with the police.[1]

In summary, 38% of Londoners sought contact with the police in the previous year according to the combined samples of the Policing for London Survey (PFLS) and the British Crime Survey (BCS), and 24% were approached by the police. However, the two groups are not mutually exclusive. More than half (55%) of those who were stopped in the previous year by the police also had contact with the police as users, and users were more likely than others to experience police stops. A quarter (25%) of the combined sample had themselves only *sought* contact with the police; 11% were *approached* by the police without themselves having sought any contact; and 13% experienced both types of contact. People in deprived inner London boroughs were significantly more likely to experience both types of contact (19%) than others (12%).

We can provide some long-term trends by comparing the PFLS survey with the Policy Studies Institute (PSI) one, and the BCS can provide estimates of more recent trends. Using multivariate statistical techniques of logistic and ordinal regression analysis, we can also provide some estimate of how much the differences in experience between different groups are related to the simple fact of their

---

[1] The PFLS covers the 12 months before interviews – which took place mainly between August and November 2000. The 2000 BCS asked about the period from January 1999; fieldwork took place mainly in the first quarter of the year, and thus the 'recall period' was slightly longer than for the PFLS.

membership of the group. That is, it can take account of other relevant factors which may be important in determining people's experience – for example, their age and sex, the area they live in and their lifestyle. Details of these analyses are given in Appendix 3.

Contact as police 'users'

Thirty-eight per cent of Londoners sought some form of contact with the police in 1999–2000.[2] Figure 4.1 provides a breakdown of types of contact. The most common single reason for contacting the police was to *report a crime* (21% of the sample); 18% made contact with the police for other reasons. The degree of contact varied by borough. Use of the police was greatest by central London residents and those living in deprived inner boroughs: 43% of respondents in each category had sought police help in the previous year. The outer London boroughs saw less demand – 37% for the poorer boroughs and 36% for the more affluent areas.

Figure 4:1: Reasons for seeking police help

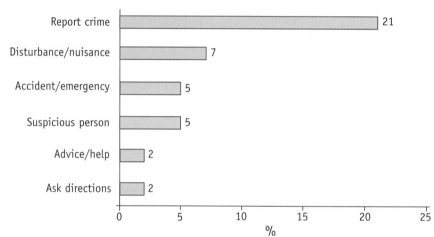

Notes: 1. Weighted data.
2. More than one response option allowed. Totals therefore exceed 100%.
Source: PFLS/BCS (2000)

The higher levels of demand in central and inner London are likely to be a function of levels of risks of crime and disorder, but they cannot entirely explain these differences. Reporting rates amongst victims of crimes such as burglary did not differ significantly across area, but central London residents appeared readier to mobilise the police than did those in deprived inner boroughs. It is possible that, in general, people in outer London made fewer demands on the police simply because the police presence tends to be lower, so it is more difficult to contact them. On the other hand, the better-off residents of inner London may be less hesitant about using the police in less serious incidents.

Who uses the police?

Table 4.1 shows that men have more 'sought' contact with the police than women, and that people under 60 have more than their elders. Middle-class respondents were

---

[2] The PFLS yields a rather higher estimate of sought contact than the BCS, reflecting differences in the structure of the questionnaires. The BCS asked respondents to *include* reported crimes discussed earlier in the 'crime counting' part of the survey; the PFLS *excluded* these contacts during the interview, but *included* them in analysis. The probability is that some BCS respondents ignored the instruction to include contacts that had already been discussed.

more likely to be police users than others, and white people more than those from minority ethnic groups.

We carried out two logistic regression analyses on the merged dataset of PFLS and BCS to try to disentangle the relationships between police usage and variables such as ethnicity, age, sex, income, marital status and class. The first simply included demographic factors, and the second included experience of crime and experience of 'unsought' police contact.

Table 4.1: Demographic profile of those seeking contact with the police: per cent contacting the police in the previous year.

Male	40
Female	36
Aged 16–29	42
Aged 30–59	41
Aged 60+	26
Social class: non-manual	42
Social class: manual	33
White	38
Black	34
Indian	34
Pakistani/Bangladeshi	32

Source: PFLS and BCS (2000), weighted data, unweighted $n = 5,700$.

The first, demographic, model identified the following variables (in order of predictiveness):[3]

1. Coming from a middle-class household.
2. Being young.
3. Living in a car-owning household.
4. Living in inner or central London.

Details of the analysis are in Appendix 3 Table A3.1. It shows that middle-class Londoners are heavier police users than others, that use decreases with age and that use is associated with car ownership and with living in inner London. Some of these relationships are simple. For example, crime risks are higher in inner London than outer London, so inner London residents are more likely to report crimes. Car ownership may increase the chances of sought contact in more complex ways: first, the car is a target for crime; secondly, there is the risk of vehicle accidents; finally, it is likely that those without cars have a more restricted lifestyle which overall exposes them to fewer of the risks that may demand police involvement. Ethnicity did not emerge as a predictor, nor did gender. The apparent underuse of the police by ethnic minorities, shown in Table 4.1, is probably best understood as a function of income, social class and car ownership. In other words, the results do not suggest that

---

[3] As indicated by the order in which the variables were selected in a stepwise regression model.

ethnicity in itself reduces the chances of people from minority ethnic groups using the police.

The next step in the analysis was to include victimisation and 'adversarial' contact with the police as predictors (see Appendix 3 Table A3.2). Hardly surprisingly, victimisation emerged as the strongest predictor of police usage. Less expected, experience of being stopped by the police, whether on foot or in a car, was a positive predictor of seeking police help. Being stopped in a car was the second strongest predictor. That is, other things being equal, those who had been stopped were more likely to have sought police help in the last year. One might expect that experience as a suspect might disincline people to use the police. This may still be so. The positive relationship between seeking police help and being an object of police suspicion could equally well be interpreted as indicating that those who attract police suspicion tend more than others also to find themselves in situations where they need police help, whether or not in relation to crimes committed against them. The model identified the following predictors:

1. Being a victim of crime.
2. Being stopped by the police in a car.
3. Coming from a middle-class household.
4. Being young.
5. Living in inner or central London.
6. Living in a car-owning household.
7. Being stopped on foot.

Trends in police usage

Figure 4.2 shows that the proportion of Londoners using the police has fallen steeply over the last decade. According to the BCS, 46% of Londoners used the police in 1991, a figure which fell slightly to 43% in 1995 and then steeply to 34%[4] in 1999. Use of the police has fallen across the country, but the fall has been steepest in London. In 1991, 42% of those in shire counties and 43% of those in other metropolitan areas used the police; the figures for 1999 were 36% and 37% respectively. The steep fall-off in the second half of the decade is largely accounted for by reductions in the number of crimes reported to the police, which in turn reflects a real fall in crime (see above and also Kershaw *et al*, 2000, 2001).

The MPS computer-aided despatch (CAD) system can shed some light on trends in demands on the police. All telephone calls going to the central control room or to local ones are recorded on the system. It is unclear whether the proportion of calls recorded has been static over time and whether changes in the rules for recording crime have affected the system.[5] Whatever the case, at the time our study was undertaken the number of calls for police assistance as recorded through the computerised system was fairly static, with some changes within categories (see Figure 4.3). The total number of calls allocated a final classification in 1996 was 2,750,710. In 2000 there were 2,728,225 such calls, a fall of 1%. Crime calls showed an increase of 17%; within this, some categories showed steeper rises (for example, calls relating to vehicle crime were up by 23%). According to both police statistics and the BCS, vehicle crime was falling over this period, so it seems possible

---

[4] This figure excludes the PFLS dataset, to ensure comparability with previous BCS sweep. See footnote 2.
[5] It seems likely, for example, that common assaults, now treated as crimes, would have been recorded as disturbances in 1996 and 1997.

Figure 4.2 Trends in police usage
(1991–1999, per cent using the police last year)

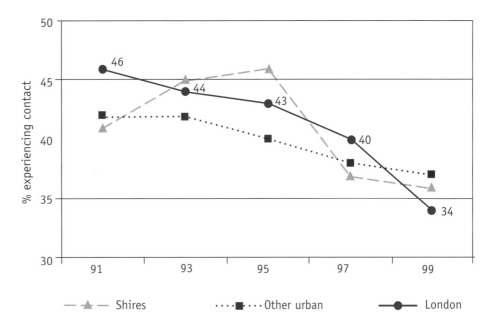

Notes: 1. Weighted data
        2. PFLS excluded, to retain comparability with earlier BCS sweeps
Source: BCS (1992–2000)

Figure 4.3: Telephone calls for police assistance, in 000's, 1996-2000

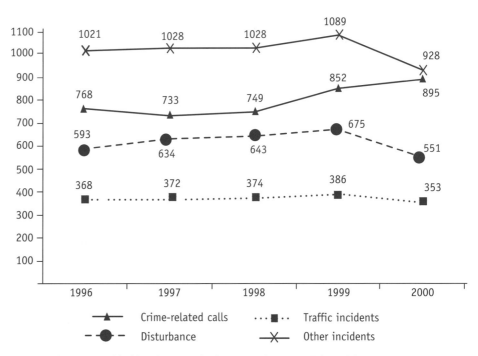

Notes: 1. Figures provided by Communication User Support Unit, MPS.
        2. Figures refer to all calls given a final classification
        3. Duplicate calls and false alarms have been removed.

that there have been changes in the way in which CAD crime calls are recorded. All other types of call fell between 1996 and 2000: traffic incidents fell by 4%; disturbance were down by 7%; and other accidents, injuries and incidents were 9% down. These falls are consistent with the survey trends described in Chapter 4. On the basis of CAD statistics there is no obvious basis for thinking that the volume of work increased over this period.

Police-initiated contacts in London

Twenty-four per cent of adult Londoners were approached or contacted by the police in 1999–2000. Figure 4.4 provides a breakdown of types of contact. The most common form of contact by far was a car stop at 10%; 3% were stopped on foot. Ten per cent of those who had been stopped in cars or on foot had experienced this more than twice in the year.

Six per cent were approached for information about a crime. In the majority of these cases respondents said they were approached as witnesses; a sixth (1% of the sample) said they were approached as suspects. Two per cent had been involved in traffic accidents or offences (split equally between witnesses and offenders), and under 1% said they had been arrested.

Figure 4:4: Reasons for police-initiated contact in 1999–2000

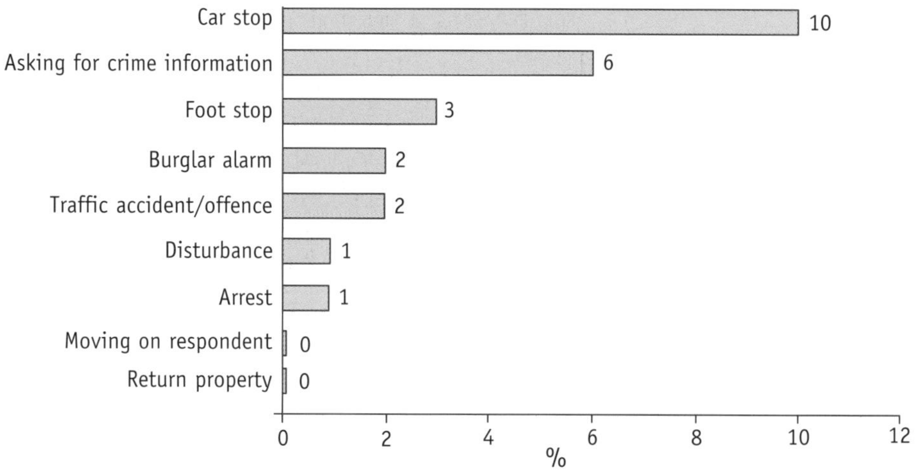

Notes: 1. Weighted data, unweighted $n = 5,709$.
2. More than one response option allowed. Totals therefore exceed 100%. 4% also cited other reasons for being contacted.
3. 12% of respondents from car-owning households were subject to car stops.
Source: PFLS and 2000 British Crime Survey.

The chances run by the overall population of being stopped were relatively small. As we have seen in the previous chapter, though, this can be a major source of friction between the police and young people in particular, including those in their early/ mid-teens, who are too young to have been included in the survey. Twelve per cent of Londoners in our sample had had this experience in the previous year; most of those who *were* stopped (64%) had only been stopped once. However, 20% were stopped twice, 7% were stopped three or four times and 10% of those stopped (around 1% of Londoners) said they had been stopped five or more times in the last year. The characteristics of those who were frequently stopped are considered in more detail later in this chapter.

Table 4.2 provides a breakdown of the proportion of people stopped, by type of stop, and of the number of stops per 1,000 population. It also shows the average number of stops per person stopped.

Table 4.2: Stops per 1,000 people, and number of stops per suspect, 1999–2000

	Foot stops	*Car stops*	*Any stops*
Percentage stopped	3	10	12
Stops per 1,000 population	7	18	25
Average number of stops of those stopped	2.5	1.8	2.1

Note: Weighted data, unweighted *n* = 5,709
Source: PFLS/BCS

Variations by area

Within London, residents of inner-city boroughs were more likely to be stopped than those who lived elsewhere. Of the former, 4.4% were stopped on foot, compared to 2.5% of the latter, a finding just reaching statistical signficance. Looking at car stops across the whole sample, there was little difference across area. However, the same pattern emerged as for foot stops when the analysis was restricted to car owners. Inner and central London residents were much less likely than others to have access to a car. However, those that did are *more* at risk than car owners in outer London, and the difference (18% versus 13%) was again statistically significant. We cannot say, of course, whether drivers were stopped in their home borough or not, or even whether they were stopped in London, but the data point to more intensive activity in inner London.

Comparing London with other police forces, differences were marginal overall. Those outside London were more likely to be stopped in cars (12% compared with

Figure 4:5: Contacts with the police as suspect, 1999/2000, by area

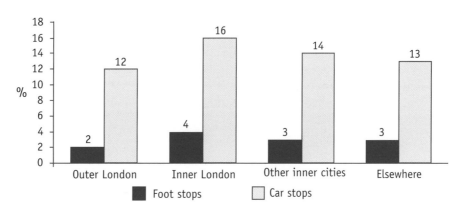

Notes: 1. Weighted data, unweighted *n* = 4,189 (outer London)
      1,532 (inner London) 2,363 (other inner) 15,481 (other outer)
    2. Car stops calculated on base of respondents from car-owning households.
Source: PFLS, 2000 BCS.

10%), but this was a function largely of more widespread access to vehicles. Figure 4.5 compares inner and outer London with comparable areas outside of the capital. The figures for car stops include only those respondents coming from car-owning households. Differences *within* types of area (inner and outer cities) are not statistically significant, nor are rates in London statistically different from those elsewhere.

Trends

Figure 4.6 shows trends for foot and car stops combined. Police-initiated contacts were fairly stable in the 1980s, but then rose sharply until 1993; they have since fallen back below the levels of the 1980s. Sixteen per cent of Londoners reported being stopped on foot or in cars in 1981, according to the PSI survey (17% according to the BCS) but the figure for 1999–2000 was only 12%. In the 1980s the MPS was stopping roughly the same proportion of people as other forces but by the mid-1990s the London rates had substantially outstripped those of other forces. However, by 1999 the MPS figure was marginally below those of other forces. Levels of foot stops were stable during the period so the fall was accounted for by reductions in the number of car stops. It seems likely that the sharper drop in London than in other forces from the mid-1990s reflects a change in policy which restricted the issue of 'producers'[6] – the forms requiring motorists to produce their documents subsequently at a police station.

Figure 4.6: Trends in stops on foot or in cars, 1981–1999 (per cent stopped)

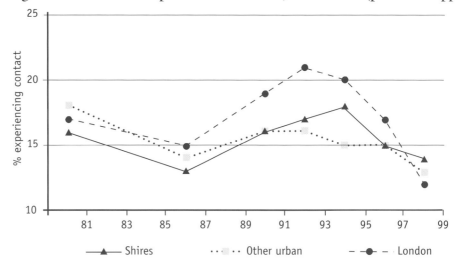

Notes 1. Weighted data
Source: BCS 1982–2000

A shorter trend line can be calculated for any form of police-initiated contact. The figure was 30% in 1993, according to the BCS; the figures for 1995, 1997 and 1999–2000 were 33%, 31% and 24% respectively, reflecting the decline in stops. The trend in *other* forms of police-initiated contact has been relatively steady since the mid-1990s – 18% in the mid-1990s falling to 15% in 1999–2000.

The PSI survey allows us to examine trends in the incidence of stops – that is, the number of stops, expressed as a rate per 1,000 population. The top row of figures in Table 4.3 shows the proportion of the population subject to different forms of stop

[6] These forms are also known by the acronym HORT 1s.

in 1981 and in 1999–2000. According to the PSI survey, 16% of Londoners were stopped on foot or in vehicles in 1981, a figure little different from the BCS estimate for 1981 of 17%. Prevalence rates have fallen over this period (and have obviously fallen more steeply since the mid-1990s). However, the average number of stops per person stopped has increased, and as a result the rate of stops per 1,000 population (in the second row of Table 4.3) has increased.

Table 4.3: Trends in stops (1981–1999/2000)

	Foot stops		Car stops		Any stops	
	1981	1999/2000	1981	1999/2000	1981	1999/2000
Percentage stopped	3	3	14	10	16	12
Stops per 1,000 population	7	7	21	18	28	25
Average number of stops among those stopped	2.0	2.5	1.5	1.8	1.7	2.1

Note: Weighted data, unweighted n = 2,420 (PSI), 5,709 (PFLS/BCS)
Sources: PSI (1981), PFLS/BCS (1999/2000)

Table 4.3 shows there has been a marked drop in the percentage stopped but the average number of stops per 1,000 population has reduced rather less sharply, i.e. car stops are more focused now on a smaller pool of suspects than in 1981 but the average number of stops experienced by suspects has risen. Another way of putting this is that in 1981 75% of respondents stopped said they had been stopped only once, but this figure had fallen to 64% in 2000 (see Table 4.4). One possible explanatory factor may be the increased access to cars by the young over the last two decades, exposing them to greater police attention.

However, it may also reflect increased 'targeting' of police attention on certain people or places. This tends to mean that fewer members of the public at large fall into the frame of police suspicion, but those who do may find their activities scrutinised more closely. This increased intensity seems to have been focused on

Table 4.4: Foot and car stops: number of times stopped in 1981 and 1999–2000(%)

Number of times stopped	1981	1999/2000
1	75	64
2	12	20
3	6	5
4	2	2
5-9	3	7
10 or more	2	3

Note: Weighted data, unweighted n = 390 approx (PSI), 742 (PFLS/BCS)
Sources: PSI (1981), PFLS/BCS (1999–2000)

young people. Whilst the prevalence of stops has declined slightly for the under 25s, the number of stops per suspect has risen from 2.4 to 3.4.

Reasons given for stops
Respondents who said they had been stopped were asked if the officer who stopped them offered a reason for the stop. Of those stopped in cars 89% had been[7] and 89% of these thought the reason good enough. Thus one in five said they were either given no reason, or no satisfactory reason. The reasons for vehicle stops are shown in Table 4.5. Of those stopped on foot 75% said they were given reasons, and just over half (58%) of those offered a reason found it acceptable. Thus under half of the whole sample (43%) were given a reason they found acceptable. Forty per cent of those stopped on foot were told that the stop was in relation to an offence.

Table 4.5: Reasons given for vehicle stops (%)

Speeding	15
Other driving	18
Parking	2
Other traffic offence	13
Vehicle defect	14
Routine vehicle check	20
Check ownership	7
Non-motoring offence	3
Other matter	9
TOTAL	100

The numbers of those stopped on foot are too small to support detailed analysis of the presence of differences between subgroups in proportions given reasons. For car stops, those in inner-city boroughs were significantly less likely to say they were given reasons than others – 78% compared with 92%. Differences between age groups and ethnicity were not significant.

Searches
In 1999–2000 37% of foot stops and 22% of vehicle stops in London resulted in searches. Out of London the proportion of both foot stops and car stops which resulted in searches was lower – 21% for foot stops and 8% for car stops. It is well established from other research (Willis 1983) and the published statistics (Home Office 2000) that, as reflected by police statistics, the risks of being searched in London are considerably higher than elsewhere. However, these findings highlight the fact that, broadly speaking, officers in the MPS are no more likely to stop people

[7] The PSI study asked a similar set of questions, but only of those who said they were 'not doing anything out of the ordinary'. The reason for this was presumably that, for example, the 30% of the total who were stopped on foot who knew they were doing something unusual (and by implication suspicious) would neither expect nor require a reason. Fifty-two per cent of all those stopped in cars were given reasons, and 51% of those stopped on foot. If one accepts the PSI rationale, and adds together those given reasons and those doing something unusual, then 81% of those stopped in cars and 75% of those stopped on foot understood why they had been stopped.

than their counterparts in other forces, including those in urban areas. But they are significantly more likely to search them when they do, whether in a car or on foot.

There were some clear demographic differences between those who had been simply stopped and those whose stop resulted in a search. Suspects under 30 were much more likely to be searched – 37% as against 10% of older suspects. Eight per cent of those in social classes I and II were searched, as against 27% of others. White suspects were less likely to be searched than those from minority ethnic groups, but the difference was not quite statistically significant (at the 5% level). The same was true for residents in deprived boroughs.

Who do the police target as suspects?

There are clear demographic patterns amongst those who are stopped by the police. Table 4.6 shows variations between groups in their experience of car stops. In interpreting Table 4.6 one must bear in mind patterns of car ownership, which obviously shape exposure to risk of car stops. It is clear that young people have a much higher risk of being stopped and that white people overall face lower risks than members of any minority ethnic groups, with black people having the highest risk, followed by Pakistanis and Bangladeshis.

Table 4.6: Demographic breakdown of people stopped in their cars by the police: per cent stopped in previous year

	1993	*1995*	*1997*	*1999–2000*
Male	20	22	20	13
Female	16	12	9	7
Aged 16 – 29	32	29	20	17
Aged 30 – 59	17	15	15	10
Aged 60+	2	5	2	3
Social class: non-manual	21	15	17	10
Social class: manual	14	18	11	11
White	16	16	14	9
Black	25	23	n.a.	15
Indian	23	14	n.a.	12
Pakistani/Bangladeshi	23	11	n.a.	13
Other	28	26	n.a.	12

Note: Weighted data, unweighted *n* = 5,709 (PFLS/BCS).
Sources: BCS (1994–1998); PFLS/BCS (1999–2000).

If one examines only those whose household owned a vehicle, the gap in stop rates between minority and white respondents opened up further: for example, 19% of black car users were stopped as against 17% of Pakistani and Bangladeshi car users, 13% of Indians and 11% of white ones. The difference between white car users and black, Pakistani and Bangladeshi car users is statistically signficant, as is the difference between Indian and black car users. The factors which determine the chances of being stopped in a car are cumulative. Of the male respondents under 30 who had access to a car 576 were from a minority ethnic group. They had a one in three

(34%) chance of being stopped in 1999–2000 while the risks for comparable young white men was 29%. For other car users the risk was only 12%. Whilst these are significant disparities in risk, the ethnic gap appears to have narrowed over time. Pooling data from the 1994 and 1996 BCS suggests that young men from minorities[8] had an almost one in two (46%) chance of being stopped in a year in the mid-1990s and young white men a 39% chance as against 17% for others. Smith's (1983) PSI survey suggests that this converging trend may have a long history. He found that 49% of West Indian car owners under 25 – including women – were subject to car stops, and he concluded that the rate for young West Indian males with cars would have been considerably higher.

Table 4.7 shows how foot stops vary by demographic group. It should be remembered that not all differences are statistically significant. For example, the difference of three percentage points between white and black respondents in 1999–2000 *is* significant, but the difference of two percentage points between Indians and other Asian respondents is nearly, but not quite, significant. The London sub-samples of the BCS between 1993 and 1998 were smaller than our merged sample and the imprecision of the survey estimates will be greater still.

As with car stops, the young are stopped more often than people over 30. Men are stopped more often than women. Those from minority ethnic groups have higher rates than white respondents, with the exception of the Indian group.

Table 4.7: Demographic breakdown of those stopped on foot by the police: per cent stopped in previous year

	1993	1995	1998	1999–2000
Male	4	8	6	5
Female	2	1	3	1
Aged 16–29	9	11	12	7
Aged 30–59	2	3	2	2
Aged 60+	1	1	–	<0.5
Social class: non-manual	2	5	5	4
Social class: manual	5	5	5	4
White	2	5	4	2
Black	5	6	n.a.	5
Indian	0.3	3	n.a.	3
Pakistani/Bangladeshi	8	4	n.a.	3
Other	9	4	n.a.	5

Note: Weighted data, unweighted *n* = 5,709 (PFLS/BCS).
Sources: BCS (1994–1998); PFLS/BCS (1999–2000).

---

[8] Of the male respondents from minorities in the pooled sample 467 were under 30 and had access to a car.

As with car stops, the factors which determine the chances of being stopped in a car are cumulative. A man under 30 from a minority ethnic group had an 18% chance of being stopped in the previous 12–15 months, compared with a 2% chance for the rest of the sample. Young white men had an 8% chance of being stopped on foot. The risks of being stopped on foot were higher in inner and central London than in outer London – 4.4% as against 2.5%; this difference was statistically significant.

There have been some striking changes in patterns of stop broken down by ethnicity. As elsewhere, we have not been able to disaggregate the PSI Asian category into more specific groups. Table 4.8 shows the proportion of people stopped in the previous year. It is clear there has been a marked fall in the proportion of white and black Londoners stopped by the police – most notably the proportion of black people stopped on foot – but there has been a marked growth in Asian and other visible minorities' experience as suspects. The growth is entirely accounted for by increased rates of car stops. Increased car ownership amongst the Asian group is likely to be one factor, but changes in the demography of the capital will also be important. A higher proportion of the Asian population of London is under 30 – and thus more at risk of being stopped – than 20 years ago.[9]

Table 4.8: Trends in proportions stopped by the police (%)

	Foot stops		Car stops		Any stops	
	1980–81	1999–2000	1980–81	1999–2000	1980–81	1999–2000
White	3	2	14	9	17	11
Black	11	5	18	15	24	18
Asian	2	2	5	12	7	14
Other	7	5	4	12	11	12

Multiple stops

Two per cent of our sample – or a sixth of those stopped – had been stopped in a car or on foot three or more times in the previous year, and this group accounted for around half of all stops carried out.[10] Eighty-four per cent of these were male. Two thirds were under 30. A quarter (26%) were black. In focusing the analysis on males under 30 alone, we run up against a problem of small numbers since only 113 white, 162 black, 165 Indian and 190 Pakistani or Bangladeshi respondents fall into this category. Nonetheless, 30% of young black men reported being stopped three or more times, as against 9% of white respondents, 8% of Indians and 9% of Pakistanis and Bangladeshis in this age group.

Factors associated with police contact as suspect

As with police users, disentangling the impact of different factors on experience as a suspect is complex, especially since demographic characteristics such as ethnicity, age, education and class can be interrelated. We have carried out two ordinal regression analyses on the merged dataset of PFLS and BCS to identify the demographic

---

[9] The age profile of the black Caribbean group is much closer to that of the white population.

[10] The proportion can only be estimated roughly, as it includes a category 'too many to count', which we have arbitrarily taken to be 20. This assumption yields a figure of 48%. It is very unlikely that those who were frequently stopped could accurately remember numbers or dates.

characteristics most associated with being stopped on foot and being stopped in vehicles. Table 4.9 summarises the picture for car stops, and details are given in Appendix 3, Table A3.3.

Table 4.9. Variables affecting car stops 1999–2000

1. Owning a car
2. Being black
3. Being male
4. Being aged under 30
5. Being single
6. Being from a manual household
   (Being Asian, living in deprived inner boroughs and income were not significant)

Source: PFLS and BCS (2000)

Table 4.9 shows, unsurprisingly, that having access to a car is the best predictor of being stopped in a car; youth is also a predisposing factor, as is being male and being black. However, it must also be borne in mind that surveys do not provide information on other possible explanatory factors. In particular the PFLS did not include many 'lifestyle' or behavioural variables such as patterns of evening activity and consumption of alcohol. Nor is information available on the age and condition of the respondents' cars. And in any case, there is a point beyond which surveys cannot practically go in measuring the sorts of behaviour that may attract police attention, such as involvement in crime and disorderly behaviour, or erratic driving.

A similar logistic regression analysis was mounted for foot stops. Being young, being male, being black and coming from a manual background significantly increase the likelihood of being stopped (see Table 4.10 and, for details, Appendix 3, Table A3.4).

These findings suggest that the MPS draw 'foot' and 'car' suspects from similar – but not identical – pools of people. Similar analysis for England and Wales as a whole (Clancy *et al* 2001) confirms that being young and male are predisposing factors but that other factors (such as unemployment and often spending evenings out) may also contribute.

Table 4.10. Variables affecting foot stops 1999–2000

1. Being aged under 30
2. Being male
3. Being black
4. Being from a manual household
   (Income, being single, and car ownership were not significant)

Source: PFLS and BCS (2000)

In presenting these findings we have drawn attention to the limitations of regression analysis of survey data. In particular, the technique can identify fairly conclusively situations in which ethnic minorities are being stopped at a higher rate than white people *for reasons other than their ethnicity*. However, where factors *are* significantly associated with stops this cannot prove that ethnicity or age or being single are *in themselves* the factors that prompt the police to carry out stops.

Vicarious experience

Discussion of police practice in stopping or searching suspects has understandably focused on the experience of individuals during a limited, recent period. Yet, as the introduction to this chapter pointed out, experience can be vicarious and people's views can be strongly shaped by experience outside the standardised time frame set by a survey. The PFLS, therefore, included a battery of questions about experience of stops over the long term and about vicarious experience of foot stops – asking respondents whether their close friends, family members, neighbours and colleagues had ever been stopped on foot by the police. (It was decided not to ask about vicarious experience of car stops, as we reckoned the experience was sufficiently commonplace that life-time knowledge of suspects would be distributed evenly and fully across the population.)

The results show that vicarious experience of foot stops is fairly widespread amongst men, and young men in particular, but less widespread than we had expected amongst women. Forty-two per cent of men under 35 claimed direct or indirect knowledge of stops; the figure for older men was 32%; for women under 35 it was 18% and for older women 17%. Those people under 35 who reported vicarious experience usually mentioned that a close friend had been stopped. Older people were more likely to mention the experience of their children, neighbours and colleagues. (See Figure 4.7)

There were large differences between ethnic groups within younger age groups. Sixty-seven per cent of young black men reported direct or vicarious experience of being stopped. Pakistani or Bangladeshi males under 35 reported lower levels of knowledge (43%), but the proportion for white young men (38%) was still higher than that for Indians at 28%. Amongst older men and women, however, the differences between black and white respondents largely disappeared. Even though only a *minority* of any given group has direct experience of foot stops over a 12-month period, the proportion with at least vicarious knowledge will be much higher.

Figure 4.7 Percentage of population with direct or vicarious knowledge of foot stops

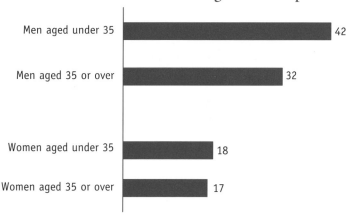

Note: Weighted data, unweighted *n* = 2,795
Source: PFLS

This is the case for the majority of young black men, two thirds of whom will have either been stopped themselves or will know close friends who have been stopped. It would be surprising if the cumulative weight of this collective experience had no influence on their perceptions of the police in general and, in particular, in the context of stops.

Key findings

- Half of Londoners have some form of contact with the police in each year, but many others may get to know of their experiences.

- Over half of those who themselves seek contact with the police mainly do so to report crime, though there are many other reasons for doing so.

- The police contact people mainly as suspects and the majority of these contacts are car stops.

- The same people often have contact with the police both as 'users' and as 'suspects'.

- The extent of police–public contact of either type has fallen since 1980, and in both cases the fall has been much steeper in London than elsewhere.

- Levels of contact are higher in inner London boroughs where the police presence is more intensive. But contact as users is greater in the more affluent inner boroughs while contact as suspects is highest in deprived inner boroughs.

- Although a smaller proportion of the population is now stopped by the police, the minority within this who are stopped more than once has increased.

- Once access to a vehicle is taken into account, the best predictors of being stopped by the police are being young, being male, being black and being single. But surveys are unable to take account of other factors which may determine patterns of police activity.

- Although foot stops are much rarer than car stops, 42% of men under 35 had either been stopped on foot at some time or had close friends who had this experience. For black young men the figure rose to two thirds.

- There is little difference between forces in the extent to which the police stop members of the public but officers in London are significantly more likely to search those they stop.

Chapter Five: Reactions to Police Contact

This chapter examines Londoners' reactions to the contacts they have with the police. The Policing for London Survey (PFLS) and the British Crime Survey (BCS) asked questions about the effectiveness of police action on the one hand, and about fairness and politeness on the other. Work in our case-study areas provided further important insights. It not only puts flesh on the statistical bones of the survey but also brings in the experience of younger people and illuminates differences in the dynamics of police–public encounters in different areas, as seen from both perspectives and from our own direct observation.

We begin by presenting our survey findings on people's reactions to the contact they sought with the police, largely as victims of crime, and then consider their experiences as suspects before examining contacts that led to people considering making complaints against the police. This is followed by a discussion of the possible reasons for the findings which includes insights into police attitudes in these situations.

Satisfaction amongst victims of crime

In the PFLS we replicated PSI questions asked of victims about satisfaction with the police, and can thus map changes since 1980–81. Victims who notified the police were asked about levels of satisfaction, and then asked reasons why they were satisfied or dissatisfied. Numbers in both surveys are low for individual types of crime; for example, the PFLS uncovered 117 (unweighted) reported cases of burglary.

Two thirds of victims of crime were satisfied with the police response. Of the 722 crimes reported to the police which were analysed by the PFLS,[1] victims had been fairly or very satisfied in 66% of cases (and nearly half of these had been 'very' satisfied). Table 5.1 provides a breakdown by offence.

Table 5.1: Levels of satisfaction with the police amongst victims who reported (%)

Crime	Very satisfied	Fairly satisfied	Bit dissatisfied	Very dissatisfied
Burglary (n = 117)	44	35	17	4
Vehicle theft (n = 164)	23	52	16	10
Theft person (n = 85)	19	36	17	28
Other theft (n = 76)	27	30	28	15
Criminal damage (n = 146)	30	33	20	17
Assault (n = 62)	50	19	3	28
Other crime (n = 72)	39	30	16	15
Total (n = 722)	32	34	18	16

---

[1] The number of cases is larger than the number of victims since individuals may have reported more than one type of offence in the previous year. However, where individuals had reported the same type of crime more than once, they were asked about their perception of the police response *only* on the most recent occasion.

Overall, there has been a decline in satisfaction between 1981 and 2000. Table 5.2 shows changes that are highly statistically significant.[2] The proportion of incidents where victims were very satisfied fell from 45% to 32%. Including the 'fairly satisfied', 87% were satisfied in 1981, a figure which fell to 66% in 2000.

There could be many reasons for the change. The most obvious is that the quality of service actually given to victims has fallen. However, this cannot simply be assumed. The same pattern of findings would be seen if *expectations* of the police had risen – a likely possibility given the development of more consumerist attitudes to public services discussed in Chapter 2. Similarly a fall in overall confidence in the police might be reflected in lower ratings of specific experience.

Another possible explanation for the fall in levels of satisfaction is that the Policy Studies Institute (PSI) survey uncovered a larger proportion of crimes in more serious offence categories – which are likely to have attracted more police time and effort. In other words, the fall could be a function of changes in the 'crime mix' experienced by victims. We tested this by reweighting the data so that the PFLS had the same 'crime mix' as the PSI survey: the decline in satisfaction remained.

**Table 5.2: Trends in satisfaction amongst victims:
PSI and PFLS surveys (%)**

Satisfaction level	PSI 1981	PFLS 2000
Very satisfied	45	32
Fairly satisfied	32	34
A bit dissatisfied	12	18
Very dissatisfied	11	16
Total	100	100
Unweighted *n*	444	722

The PFLS, the BCS and our focus groups all suggest that perceptions of lack of effort or lack of interest on the part of the police were key irritants, and these were often more important to victims than getting a 'result'. That is, in reporting to the police, victims seem to have realistic expectations about the chances that the police will actually solve the crime in the classic sense of detecting the people responsible and securing a conviction. However, they wanted the police to do *something*. Dissatisfied victims were asked the reasons for their dissatisfaction. Table 5.3 shows that failure to do anything, or to do enough, was the most frequent response. Other reasons for dissatisfaction included the length of time people had to wait before the police came and whether or not they felt they were kept well enough informed of progress in the case.

[2] *P*<.01. It should be recognised that this analysis is at the level of incident, rather than respondent – in other words, multiple victims are entered into the analysis more than once. We have not adjusted the weighting to take account of multiple victimisation within offence type.

Table 5.3: Reasons for dissatisfaction by crime types, PFLS (%)

Reason for dissatisfaction	Burglary	Vehicle theft	Theft person	Other theft	Damage	Assault
Slow to come	27	27	6	17	5	5
Failure to arrest/recover property	49	18	22	3	5	6
Did nothing/Didn't do enough	57	64	74	62	77	67
Incompetent	1	2	15	7	2	–
Failure to keep victim informed	9	36	13	10	18	5
Not interested	7	4	24	22	16	1
Rude manner	4	2	–	5	3	3
Other	1	2	–	7	4	28

Note: more than one response option allowed, so totals exceed 100%.

A similar picture emerges from the London subsample of the 2000 BCS, although a different set of questions was asked of *all* victims reporting crimes to the police. Thirty-six per cent of all victims in London thought the police had shown 'less effort' than they should and in 29% of cases they also complained that the police had shown 'less interest than they should'. The BCS suggests that victims in London were more satisfied with the police response than those elsewhere, especially those in other urban forces (see Table 5.4). In terms of both effort and interest shown, differences are statistically significant. However, the Metropolitan Police (MPS) fared a little worse than other forces in terms of speed of response.

Table 5.4: Victim dissatisfaction in London compared to other forces (%)

Reason	London	Other urban	Shire forces
Made less effort than they should	36	47	41
Showed less interest than they should	29	41	35
Unreasonable delays	19	15	15
Victim 'not at all well informed'	32	33	30

Notes: 1. Figures based on all victims reporting to the police, excepting for keeping victims informed: only those whose cases were investigated were asked about this.
2. Weighted data, unweighted *n* = 4,130.
Source: BCS (2000) (core only).

Members of our focus groups who had been dissatisfied with the police response also tended to emphasise slow response and failure to keep people informed, as in the following account from a focus group with schoolgirls in Borough C:

Girl 1:
My mum was waiting three and a half hours for them to come the other day, they told her to wait on the corner. My brother was hit .... my little brother was hit by an old man ... My brother came home and told my mum and my mum wanted to go down there and have a go at him but she didn't want to get in trouble so she rung the police and that and

they told her to wait on the corner where it happened. She had to ring
them at least six times in three and a half hours. She was waiting there
[All that time] – and then nothing … They haven't even got back to us
on it yet. That was about two months ago.

Girl 2:
They just tell you they'll get back to you and they never do.

They, too, were not unrealistic in expecting the police to 'solve' crimes where there
was little evidence to go on. However, a number of people who had reported
incidents in which they could identify the people concerned were aggrieved where
they believed the police had taken no action.

Victims in the PFLS who *were* satisfied were less likely to stress the speed of response
– except in the case of burglary, where it was mentioned by 48%. Large minorities,
though, appreciated the way the police took the matter seriously and showed interest
(see Table 5.5).

Table 5.5: Reasons for satisfaction, by crime types, PFLS (%)

Reason for satisfaction	Burglary	Vehicle theft	Theft person	Other theft	Damage	Assault
Came promptly	48	16	1	7	20	20
Dealt with matter efficiently	34	53	61	63	61	85
Showed interest	39	24	20	21	29	47
Took the matter seriously	39	26	39	29	28	45
Kept victim informed	21	3	18	7	–	13
Behaved with sensitivity	16	4	4	–	9	5
Other	20	16	11	13	14	1

Notes: 1. More than one response option allowed, so totals exceed 100.
2. Weighted data (see Table 5.1 for unweighted numbers).
Source: PFLS.

In our focus groups, a white woman in Borough A who said she had always had a
low opinion of the police had called them when her house was ransacked. Even
though they had failed to detect those responsible, her opinion of them had
improved 'a little bit' because 'They were like desperate to be helpful. They were
great towards me…' And a black woman in Borough B who had reported a flasher
found them 'sensible, practical and supportive'.

Variations in victim satisfaction
The PFLS additionally shows clear demographic patterns in satisfaction (see Table
5.6) and these are echoed also in the BCS.[3] Women were more likely to be satisfied
than men, older people than younger people and white people more than minorities.
There were also area differences, with victims in deprived areas being less likely to be
very satisfied.

[3] The 2000 BCS shows that only 13% of Londoners under 30 said they were 'very
satisfied' after reporting a crime compared to 22% of those between 30 and 59 and
29% of those over 60. Fewer victims from minority ethnic groups expressed satisfaction
than white victims.

Table 5.6: Demographic differences in victim satisfaction (%)

	Very satisfied	*Fairly satisfied*	*Bit dissatisfied*	*Very dissatisfied*
Men	25	36	20	18
Women	38	32	16	14
Under 30	39	34	4	23
30–59	25	36	25	14
60+	46	28	15	11
Non-manual household	34	31	21	14
Manual household	27	42	13	18
Affluent borough	34	34	18	14
Mixed boroughs	35	28	13	24
Deprived boroughs	24	41	23	11
White	36	34	17	14
Black	30	28	20	24
Indian	22	38	20	20
Pakistani/Bangladeshi	11	42	26	21

Notes: Weighted data, unweighted *n* = 722.
Source: PFLS.

As we have seen, though, there are important area differences in the distribution of the minority ethnic groups and they also tend, on average, to be younger than white people. To disentangle these factors, we mounted a logistic regression analysis to determine which of the demographic factors in Table 5.6 were most predictive of satisfaction. Gender was the strongest predictor, followed by living in better-off boroughs. No other demographic variables were included in the model. A similar model to predict who was most likely to be *dissatisfied* identified only one variable: victims from manual households were more likely to be dissatisfied.

We explored whether recent experience of the police as a suspect was also predictive of satisfaction and dissatisfaction. When variables measuring experience of foot stops and car stops were added into the model, these emerged as stronger predictors than any of the demographic variables – though gender was still retained in the model. Ordering variables according to their predictiveness, being stopped on foot was the strongest predictor of satisfaction (reducing the likelihood of being satisfied), followed by being stopped in a car, and then by gender. When the model predicting *dissatisfaction* included these variables, being stopped on foot was the strongest predictor of dissatisfaction, followed by social class (coming from a manual background) and, thirdly, being stopped in a car. These findings are complex to interpret. On the one hand, they could mean that even when they seek police help, those who are the object of police suspicion are treated in a characteristic way which leads to dissatisfaction. Alternatively this group may be more likely than others to be hostile to the police, which could shape the nature of the interaction. However, even if it did not, this hostility might tone ratings of contact with the police when their help is sought.

Ratings of contact as suspect

Most of those who were stopped by the police rated their professionalism highly. Overall, 37% of those who had been stopped in cars were very satisfied with the way the police handled the incident, and a further 34% said they were fairly satisfied. However, there were large differences in satisfaction between groups following a stop, as shown in Table 5.7. The differences between age groups and between white suspects and other ethnic groups are statistically significant, as are those between affluent and poorer boroughs. Reflecting the small number of women stopped in cars, the differences in gender did not reach statistical significance. A logistic regression model found only two predictors of dissatisfaction with the outcome of the stop – being young and being black.[4]

Table 5.7 Demographic differences in satisfaction amongst those stopped in cars (%)

	Very satisfied	*Fairly satisfied*	*Bit dissatisfied*	*Very dissatisfied*
Men	34	39	15	12
Women	42	28	17	13
Under 30	19	43	24	13
30–59	47	28	11	13
Non-manual household	39	34	15	11
Manual household	32	36	17	14
Poorer boroughs	30	36	17	17
Richer boroughs	43	33	15	9
White	40	36	13	11
Black	23	30	25	23
Indian	27	50	15	9
Pakistani/Bangladeshi	28	50	11	11

Notes: 1. Weighted data, unweighted n = 639 (max).
2. Respondents over 60 excluded, and area variable simplified owing to low numbers.
Source: PFLS, BCS.

Respondents who had been stopped in a car were also asked to rate the police on their fairness and politeness. Forty-five per cent rated the police as 'very polite' and a further 36% said they were fairly polite. Forty-one per cent felt the police were 'very fair' and a further 41% thought they were 'fairly fair'. As one would expect, these variables were closely intercorrelated with satisfaction; rating the police as fair and rating them as polite were both strong predictors of satisfaction – stronger than any demographic predictors.[5]

A similar pattern emerged for foot stops, but with somewhat lower overall ratings: overall 54% said they were satisfied with the way they were dealt with, as against 71% of those stopped in cars. Sixty-five per cent of those stopped on foot found the police polite, and 63% fair. The respective proportions saying 'very polite' and 'very fair' were 29% and 36%. The numbers stopped on foot are very small and do not support detailed analysis, though those in deprived boroughs were much more likely to be dissatisfied than those in affluent ones, and respondents under 30 much more likely to be dissatisfied than older ones.

---

[4] This was true whether the measure of satisfaction was being 'very/a bit dissatisfied', or being 'very satisfied'.
[5] When these variables were introduced into the model, age and ethnicity were no longer statistically significant predictors.

Visiting the police station

Respondents were asked if they had visited a police station in the last three years. Thirty per cent said they had done so – presumably for a variety of reasons, some relating to experience as victims or witnesses of crime, some relating to offences committed, and some relating to non-criminal matters. This figure excludes occasions when they had been taken by the police to the station – for example, when under arrest.[6] Those who had been to a station were asked about the quality of response they received.

Overall ratings of satisfaction were impressive. Eighty-five per cent said they found the staff helpful, and nearly half (43% of the total) said they were very helpful, 28% said they were dealt with very quickly and 40% fairly quickly. There were variations across area and between groups. Notably, respondents from deprived boroughs, and those from ethnic minorities, gave lower ratings than others. Table 5.8 provides a breakdown of ratings of helpfulness. Differences between the under-30s and older respondents are statistically significant, as are those between white and minority ethnic respondents.

Table 5.8: Demographic differences in perceived helpfulness of desk staff (%)

	Very helpful	Fairly helpful	Bit unhelpful	Very unhelpful	It depends
Men	38	49	7	4	2
Women	46	36	8	7	4
Under 30	27	46	13	11	4
30–59	44	44	6	4	1
60+	56	33	6	–	6
Non-manual household	43	41	8	4	4
Manual household	41	45	7	6	2
Poorer boroughs	36	44	11	7	2
Richer boroughs	46	43	5	4	3
White	46	41	6	5	3
Black	29	52	13	5	1
Indian	17	58	12	9	4
Pakistani/Bangladeshi	19	58	14	7	2

Note: Weighted data, unweighted *n* = 720 (max).
Source: PFLS.

Our fieldwork additionally provided ample opportunity for direct observation of police–public interaction at front counters. For the most part, we too were very impressed with how staff handled apparently endless queues and a very diverse range of callers and queries. However, they also suggested additional factors that may come into play in reducing satisfaction, of which two in particular are worth mentioning.

---

[6] Due to an error in programming some of those who had *sought* contact with the police in the last three years were not asked the question. The 30% is therefore a slight underestimate.

First, the physical surroundings vary considerably from one police station to another. In part this depends on age, but the extent of other wear and tear, including vandalism, can alter the physical environment in which people wait and may also have implications for security arrangements. In one station in Borough B the waiting area was extraordinarily cramped: people waiting often had to stand and it was impossible not to overhear the explanation each initially gave the officer on duty for being there.[7] Another, in one of the most deprived high-crime parts of Borough C had a floor-to-ceiling screen between the front counter and the waiting room: members of the public were given access one at a time to a narrow moat between the screen and the counter. Yet another had no internal phone in the waiting area, so callers on business could not phone their contact direct but swelled the queue, or jumped it to avoid being late for appointments, thus giving the impression of receiving favoured treatment. The station in Borough A was better equipped on all these counts and included a well-kept public toilet. However, it was the only station open in the whole borough, so inaccessibility was a frequent complaint and, despite being a low-crime borough, the queues tended to be at least as long as anywhere else.

Secondly, the atmosphere in the waiting area tended to vary considerably according to who else was waiting, and this could change with time of day as well. The presence of other people being aggressive – towards each other, the world in general or the police in particular – could be intimidating in a very small space. Sometimes such individuals might be drunk or on drugs or mentally disturbed and, in the nature of police business, they may be disproportionately present at police stations.[8] However, our strong impression was that they presented most often in the poorer areas, so a member of the public who visited one station might have a completely different experience visiting another station on the same business – even if they waited the same length of time and received comparable service once they spoke to the staff on duty.

Sources of serious annoyance

Respondents in both PFLS and BCS were asked whether they had ever been really annoyed about the way in which the police behaved towards them or people they knew. Thirty-two per cent said they had, and 21% said this had happened in the last five years. This figure was no different in other parts of the country (20% according to the 2000 BCS).

The trend does not show a great deal of change over time. Figure 5.1 shows that the figure was highest in 1982 at 25%, falling over the 1980s, rising into the 1990s and then falling again to its current 21%. There also seems to be some convergence over time across area: in 1982, 1992 and 1998 the differences between the MPS and shire counties were statistically significant in 1982; in 2000 the gap was only two percentage points, not a statistically significant difference.

In almost three quarters of these cases the respondent had been personally involved in the incident(s) which caused annoyance. (Neither the PFLS nor the BCS collected any information about the identity of the people who were involved in the third of cases where others had been involved, with or without the respondent.) Figure 5:2

---

[7] All stations, though, have facilities for private interview if the reason for the visit turns out to be particularly sensitive.

[8] Police officers may refer to them as their 'regular customers' and some may present several times a day.

Figure 5.1: Trends in annoyance with the police

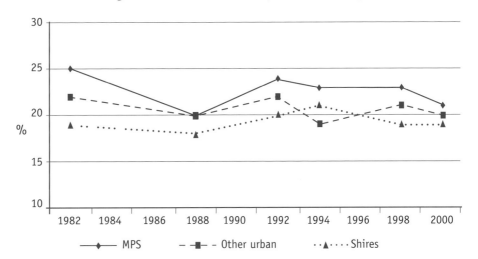

Note: Weighted data.
Source: BCS (1982–2000); PFLS.

Figure 5.2: Reasons for annoyance with police in the last 5 years

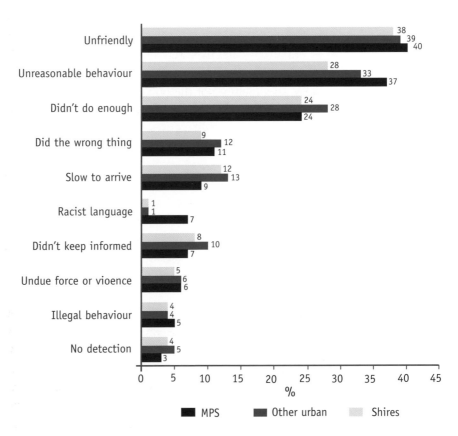

Notes: 1. Weighted data.
      2. London sample = 1,408; Other urban=855; Shires = 722.
      3. More than one response option allowed. Totals therefore exceed 100%.
Source: PFLS (2000); BCS.

presents the reasons for dissatisfaction, comparing the MPS with the rest of the country. Those Londoners who had been really annoyed were slightly more likely to complain about unfriendly, unreasonable or racist behaviour by the police, but less likely to feel annoyed about a slow response or unsolved crime.

Lack of friendliness topped the list of complaints, highlighting the importance of the *style* of police behaviour as well as *content*. Although there were no gender differences overall, younger people were more likely than others to have been really annoyed. And men under 30 were much more likely to have been annoyed than women of the same age (34% compared with 25%) – probably reflecting the fact that young men are more likely than any other group to have had unsought contact with the police. White respondents were far less likely to report being annoyed in last five years than black respondents, but annoyance was also greater among the Asian groups, and in particular the Pakistanis and Bangladeshis.

We mounted a logistic regression to identify the best predictors of being very annoyed with the police in the last five years. Predictors, in order of predictiveness, were:

1. Being young.
2. Being black.
3. Having an income over £15,000.
4. Coming from a non-manual household.
5. Having the use of a car.

Being Asian and being single did not emerge as predictors; nor did gender, although it approached statistical significance. The explanation for this is probably that the question asked about experiences encountered by the respondent or friends; thus women may have been annoyed at the treatment of partners. The fact that having a non-manual background predicted annoyance may reflect greater expectations of police deference. Having an income of over £15,000 a year could be interpreted in several different ways. First, as with social class, higher-income earners could have expectations which, if unmet, would lead to annoyance. Alternatively it could provide people with the means to pursue a lifestyle that exposes them to police contact. The variable measuring access to cars is probably a significant predictor because it increases the chances of adversarial contact with the police.

When measures of experience of the police are added into the model, the best predictor of annoyance is seeking police help; this is followed by being stopped in a car – and the variable measuring access to cars is dropped from the model. Being black is the third strongest predictor, followed by age and being stopped on foot. It is hardly surprising that contact with the police as suspect should be a predictor of annoyance, but more worrying that the experience of seeking police help should be.[9]

Complaints against the police

Forty-three per cent of people who had been really annoyed in the last five years (or 14% of the total sample) said they had felt like making an official complaint. Black, Pakistani and Bangladeshi respondents were more likely to say this than whites and Indians; in other words, the former groups were more likely than the latter to feel

[9] It was not the experience of being a crime victim that increased the risk of annoyance. This was included in the model and had a weaker predictive power than seeking contact.

annoyed and, in the cases that did arise, they were more likely to consider complaining.

Of those who felt like making a complaint, a quarter tried to do so, and a fifth succeeded. In total, 2% of the combined PFLS and BCS sample reported making a complaint. The (unweighted) total of complainants was 131. Forty-six per cent of these were very dissatisfied with the outcome, and a further 17% a bit dissatisfied; 25% were fairly satisfied and the remaining 12% very satisfied. Of those who felt like complaining but failed to do so, half said they couldn't see any point in doing so. A tenth said this was because they didn't know how to; a further tenth were worried about the police response.

Direct experience of the complaints process was obviously limited but, regardless of their experiences, people were asked what they thought about the complaints system. The vast majority of respondents (85%) said they would make a complaint if they were seriously dissatisfied with something the police had (or hadn't) done. There were no marked differences between groups, though Pakistanis and Bangladeshis were least likely to envisage complaining (77%). Of these prospective complainers almost all (four out of five) envisaged complaining to a supervisor and/or to the local station; 12% mentioned New Scotland Yard or, more specifically, the MPS's complaints bureau; 4% mentioned their MP, 3% solicitors and 15% others. (Respondents were allowed to nominate more than one point of complaint, which is why the total exceed 100.)

Respondents were fairly uninformed about the system, though. Seventy-seven per cent said they knew too little to say whether it worked well, 9% thought it worked well, and 14% thought it did not. Black respondents were a little less likely than others to say they couldn't assess the system (71%) and rather more likely to say it didn't work well (22%) – statistically significant differences. Those who didn't think the system worked well were asked why. The most common reasons were lack of independence (41%), no value in making a complaint (23%) and no confidence in the police (18%).

Key findings

- Public satisfaction with police service has fallen since 1980–81; 45% of crime victims who called the police were very satisfied in 1981, compared with 32% in 1999–2000.

- However, victims in London tend to rate the police response a little higher than elsewhere.

- Satisfied victims stressed efficiency, fast response (in relation to burglary), taking the matter seriously and showing interest, and keeping the victim informed.

- Sources of dissatisfaction include: failure to do enough (or anything), slow response (especially for burglary) and failure to keep victims informed.

- Overall, those approached by the police rated their professionalism highly: 81% of those stopped in cars said the police were polite (45% saying 'very polite'); 82% found them fair; and 71% were satisfied overall with the way they were treated.

- Of those on stopped on foot, 54% were satisfied with the way they had been dealt with, 65% thought the police were polite, 63% fair.

- Young people and black people were significantly less likely than others to rate police behaviour in stopping them as satisfactory.

- Satisfaction amongst those who had visited police stations was high: 85% said the desk staff were helpful (43% of visitors saying 'very helpful'); 68% were dealt with quickly.

- Younger people and those from minority ethnic groups were less satisfied than others.

- A third of Londoners had ever been 'really annoyed' at the way the police had treated them or people they knew. One in five (21%) had experienced something really annoying in the last five years.

- There has been a small fall over time in this proportion, and there are some signs that the MPS rate is converging with the lower rates of other forces.

- The main reasons for annoyance in the last five years were unfriendly manner, unreasonable behaviour and failure to do enough. Failure to detect crimes rarely caused annoyance.

- Londoners who had been really been annoyed were more likely to cite unreasonable behaviour and racist language than people living elsewhere.

- There were big differences between groups. Young people were more likely to report annoyance than older people, and ethnic minority respondents more than white ones. A third (34%) of black respondents reported annoyance, compared with 19% of whites.

- The best demographic predictors of reporting annoyance in the last five years were: being young, being black, having an income over £15,000, coming from a non-manual household, and having the use of a car.

- Four out of ten of those who had felt really annoyed – or 9% of the total sample – felt like complaining; 2% of the sample actually did so, and the majority of these (around two thirds) were dissatisfied with the outcome.

Chapter Six: Confidence in the Police

This chapter examines Londoners' views about the competence and fairness of their police and aims to identify some of the links between experience and attitudes. It begins by considering where people get their views of the police. We then draw on several measures of confidence, relating to perceptions of competence and integrity. We end with some findings on people's willingness to help the police.

Measuring confidence in the police

It is increasingly common to measure the satisfaction of *users* of public services so that areas of weak performance can be identified and remedied. The previous chapter has focused on police users' experiences. For many public services there is little point in developing measures that include the attitudes of *non-users*. Certainly the latter will answer survey questions about service performance. However, in general their ratings tend to be below those of users.[1] It is also difficult to interpret the responses of those with little or no experience of the service under investigation; responses such as 'fairly satisfied' are often interpreted by researchers as the equivalent of 'no opinion' or 'don't know' (Cabinet Office 2001). For most public services, an argument can be made for restricting surveys of satisfaction and confidence to those with direct experience of the service in question.

An exception needs to be made, however, for the criminal justice system in general, and for the police in particular. Public confidence in the institutions of justice is likely to be related to people's commitment to civil and law-abiding behaviour. By contrast, public confidence in the health service is unlikely to affect levels of public health directly.[2]

In measuring confidence in the police, we have aimed to assess people's views on the *effectiveness* of the police, and on their *integrity*.

Sources of information about the police

A starting point in exploring people's confidence in the police is to find out how their views are formed. Any attempt to improve public confidence needs to take into account the sources of information they draw on since it is apparent that the majority do not have recent, direct experience of the service. Also, those who *do* have contact with the police do not do so in a vacuum. Their attitudes and expectations may be important in influencing the encounters themselves as well as their assessment of them afterwards. So it is important to understand what shapes those attitudes and expectations.

We asked our sample to say where they got their information about the police. Most referred to a number of different sources, as Figure 6.1 shows. The most frequently mentioned sources were newspapers and television and radio news. Just under a third referred to fictional media programmes; 8% specifically mentioned TV soap-operas. Even though half the sample had had some sort of contact with the police over the previous year, only a fifth referred to direct personal experience. Rather

---

[1] For example, 80% of users of secondary schools are very or fairly satisfied with their performance, compared with 30% of the general population (Cabinet Office 2001).
[2] With some important exceptions, however: lack of confidence in immunisation regimes, as with MMR vaccinations, may lead to reductions in public health.

more (43%) referred to word of mouth – from friends, relatives and others they knew. That is, direct and vicarious experiences of the police are important in shaping people's views but they are by no means the main influence on them.

Figure 6.1: Londoners' sources of information about the police (%)

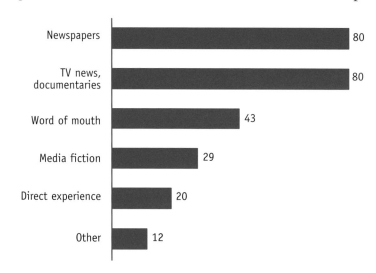

Note: Weighted data, unweighted *n* = 2,759.
Source: PFLS.

Asked which of the various sources of information was their main one, 28% said the TV and radio news, 16% broadsheet papers, 15% tabloids and 11% TV documentaries. The vast majority (92%) saw their main source as accurate. People under 45 were more likely than older people to rely on personal experience or that of their friends and acquaintances. There were only small differences between ethnic groups.

Older people were a little more likely to rely on newspapers, and some in our focus groups referred to this as a matter of concern. Especially in areas where they were increasingly less likely to see the police at all and rarely had to call on them, they were aware that their impressions were formed on the basis of stories that were newsworthy and, not least for that reason, tended to cast the police in a negative light. One woman in Borough A drew an important contrast: 'Obviously out there, there are police who are racist, who are sexist and those kind of things that we read about in general terms – and then there's our own personal experience...' While she did not disbelieve what she read, it did not square with her personal experience. However, her own experience was not only limited; respondents like her were often aware that, given their class, age and gender they were less likely to see the negative aspects of police behaviour (see also below). It was, therefore, difficult for them to know the extent to which problems such as racism and sexism were endemic or confined to a minority of officers.

A man in Borough B claimed to be 'an avid reader of the local newspaper' and said it made his 'blood curdle every week to read of the rapes, the murders, the muggings and assaults which go on'. A woman in the same group, though, highlighted the implications this had for their perceptions of police performance, as follows: 'Well, it talks of all the terrible things that have happened and so on, but it never seems to talk of crimes that are solved.' Similarly an older black woman in Borough C said the media were not interested in good news 'So they always pick up on the failures'.

It is often suggested that fictional TV programmes are important shapers of public views (Reiner *et al.*, 2000). However, the Policing for London Survey (PFLS) found only a minority citing this source, and our focus groups also suggested that people were well aware of differences between these representations and reality. A cynical example came from a group of white 18–24-year-olds in Borough C:

> *Young woman*:
> If the police was like The Bill I'd love 'em – but they ain't. Know what I mean?
> [Laughter]

> *Moderator*:
> So, do you think that's different?
> [Chorus of 'Yeah']

> *Young woman*:
> Completely different. The Bill is the best police going. But *our* police don't give fuck all.

The police and other occupational groups

PFLS respondents were asked to rate the quality of work done by several public sector services. Table 6.1 shows that the Metropolitan Police (MPS) are rated higher than judges but lower than most other comparators.

Table 6.1: The police and other occupational groups – percentage of Londoners saying they do a 'very good job' or a 'good job'

	'Very good job'	*'Good job'*
Firemen	73	99.7
Nurses	64	97.0
Teachers	39	90.0
Doctors	37	87.0
Social workers	20	73.0
Police nationally	18	83.0
Police locally	18	79.0
Judges	11	68.0

Notes: 1. Don't knows/NAs excluded.
2. Weighted data, unweighted n = 2,059 to 2,711.
Source: PFLS.

Satisfaction measures such as these need to be interpreted with caution. Whilst the majority of Londoners have some direct or indirect contact with doctors, teachers and nurses, very few will know much about the work of judges, who fall at the bottom of the list. And although almost all Londoners think that firemen do a good job, only about 1% of households call out the fire brigade to deal with a fire in any one year.[3] Similar questions have been asked nationally, for example in MORI polls (e.g. MORI 2000) and these show similar rankings. However, when the questions are asked about trustworthiness rather than effectiveness, judges score rather better than the police.[4]

Figure 6.2: Londoners' ratings of performance of criminal justice agencies (%)

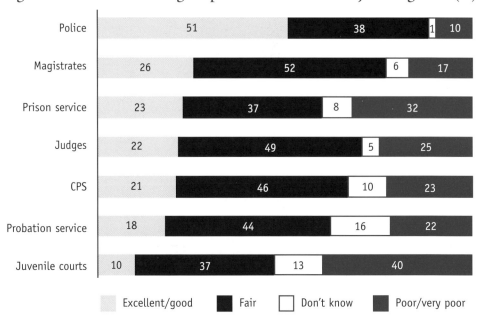

Note: Weighted data, unweighted $n = 1,082$
Source: BCS (2000)

However the police rank against other professions, the MPS is thought by Londoners to do a better job than other parts of the criminal justice system in London. Figure 6.2, from the 2000 British Crime Survey (BCS), shows strikingly higher ratings of police performance relative to other parts of the system. The youth courts fare worst of all, followed by judges and the probation services. As one might expect, the proportion of respondents who 'didn't know' or otherwise were unprepared to respond was highest for the less well-known services, in particular the Crown Prosecution Service (CPS), the probation service and the juvenile courts.

Trends in ratings of effectiveness over time

The PFLS and the BCS can provide long-run trends in Londoners' views of police performance. The surveys have asked 'Would you say the police in this area do a good job or a poor job?' Figure 6.3 shows the results. There are some fluctuations from year to year, and it should be remembered that sample sizes for some BCS subsamples are small. There are also clear differences in the way that different survey contractors have handled 'don't know' responses.[5] Nevertheless, there are clear and statistically signficant changes over time. The proportion of Londoners thinking the police do a poor job doubled from 9% to 18% over the two decades, and the proportion saying 'very good job' fell from 25% to 17%. Ratings appear to have been fairly steady – albeit with fluctuations – between 1982 and 1994, with a more marked decline since then.

---

[3] Source: 2000 BCS.
[4] MORI respondents were asked: 'For each [professional group] would you tell me whether you generally trust them to tell the truth or not?' Doctors topped the list with 87% expressing trust; 77% trusted judges and 60% trusted the police.
[5] For example, 'don't know' responses fell from 21% to 9% between 1982 and 1984. There appears to have been a compensating growth in the 'fairly satisfied' group.

Figure 6:3: Trends in ratings of local police performance in London (%)

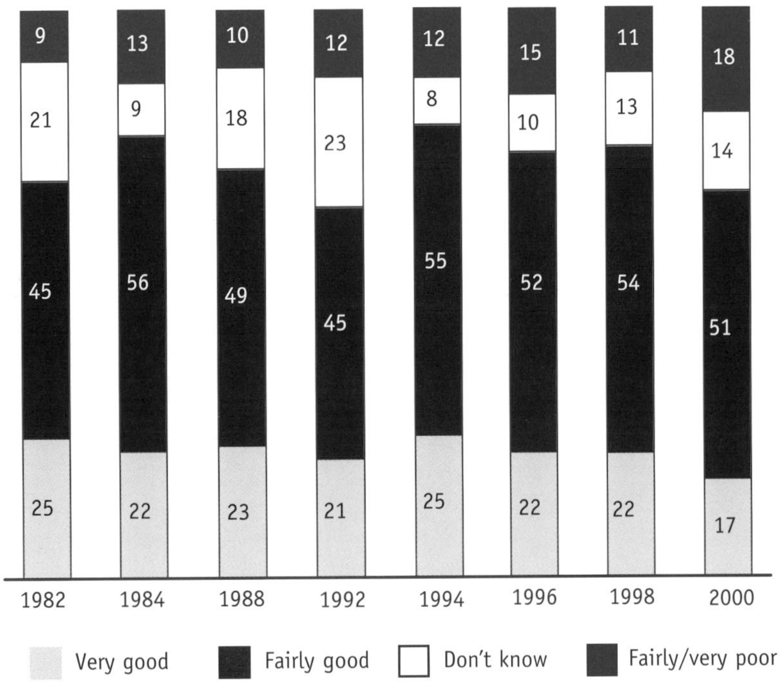

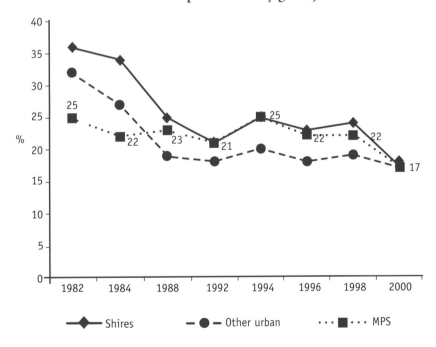

	1982	1984	1988	1992	1994	1996	1998	2000
Fairly/very poor	9	13	10	12	12	15	11	18
Don't know	21	9	18	23	8	10	13	14
Fairly good	45	56	49	45	55	52	54	51
Very good	25	22	23	21	25	22	22	17

Very good ▪ Fairly good □ Don't know ■ Fairly/very poor

Note: Weighted data, unweighted *n* (82–00), 1,331; 932; 641; 726; 983; 1,187; 1,149; 5,473.
Source: PFLS (2000); BCS (1982–2000).

Figure 6.4: Area differences in confidence – per cent saying local police do 'very good job'

◆ Shires ● Other urban ■ MPS

Note: Weighted data, unweighted *n* (82–00): 6,329; 6,582; 4,907; 5,114; 7,237; 7,923; 7,408; 14,290.
Source: PFLS (2000); BCS (1982–2000).

We cannot say, of course, whether this picture is just one frame in a series showing longer-term decline. It is possible that the 2000 figures may reflect the impact on public opinion of the extended period of high-profile criticism of the police during the Macpherson Inquiry. Certainly, whatever processes underlie the change, they appear to have affected forces outside London rather more sharply than the MPS. Figure 6.4 compares the trend in the proportion of respondents who thought their local police did 'a very good job' with that for shire forces and for other urban ones. It shows that the MPS has actually fared rather better than other forces over the last two decades: whilst ratings in all areas show a fall, this is steepest in the shire counties, and shallowest in the MPS. The gap between the MPS and other forces was greatest in the early 1980s. By 2000, 17% of respondents in London and other urban forces, and 18% of those in shire forces said their police did a very good job.

Who thinks the police do a good job?

Table 6.2 summarises differences between social groups in their assessment of police performance, showing those at opposite poles as well as those who assumed a neutral position. Perhaps the most striking thing about the table is that the differences between ethnic groups are much less marked than the ratings presented in Chapter 5 based on respondents' actual experience of the police. Yet the patterns within this are similar to those in Chapter 5, with ethnicity and age important factors, and ratings in deprived areas lower than elsewhere.

Table 6.2: Demographic breakdown of rating of local police performance (%)

	Do a very good job	Do a fairly good job	Don't know	Do a bad job
Male	17	53	11	19
Female	17	50	16	17
Aged 16–29	12	52	14	23
Aged 30–59	17	52	13	17
Aged 60+	23	48	15	14
Income under £10,000	19	48	14	19
Income under £20,000	17	49	14	21
Higher income	17	54	13	16
Social class: non-manual	16	55	14	16
Social class: manual	19	48	12	21
Deprived inner boroughs	13	47	16	24
Poor outer boroughs	16	50	15	20
Affluent outer boroughs	17	54	13	16
Central London	24	53	9	14
White	18	52	13	17
Black	14	50	18	18
Indian	12	56	12	21
Pakistani/Bangladeshi	14	49	11	26

Note: Weighted data, unweighted *n* = 5,743 (max).
Source: PFLS; and BCS (2000).

We mounted a series of logistic regression analyses to identify what personal characteristics and what experiences predicted views. A demographic model predicting who thought the police did a bad job identified three predictors (details in Appendix 3, Table A3.6):

1. Living in a poor borough.
2. Being young.
3. Having a low income.

After taking these factors into account, gender, class, ethnicity and marital status were not predictive. We ran a similar logistic regression model to identify which groups were most likely to say the police did a 'very good' job. As one would expect, the converse broadly applied: the strongest predictors were living as a couple; age (older people being more positive); living in affluent boroughs; and having an above-average income. After taking these factors into account, those from manual backgrounds held more positive attitudes.

We then carried out a second set of logistic regression analyses which included variables measuring police contact and experience of crime as well as respondents' socioeconomic characteristics. The predictor factors associated with negative views are listed below in order of predictiveness:

1. Being stopped on foot.
2. Seeking police help.
3. Living in a poor borough.
4. Being young.
5. Having below average income.

As one might expect, the model suggests that experience as suspect is associated with poor ratings. However, seeking help from the police is also associated with low ratings of police performance, independently of the experience of being a victim of crime.[6] People in poor city areas, young people and the less well-off tended to hold a poorer opinion of the police than others, after taking account of their experience of the police and crime.

Given the large difference between black and white respondents described in the previous chapter in ratings of police contacts, it is surprising that being black did not emerge as a predictor. In the past there were large differences, but these seem to have narrowed over time. Figure 6.5 shows there has been quite a marked convergence over time between white and ethnic minority respondents in their views of police performance. Between 1982 and 1994 there was, on average, a gap of 11 percentage points between white and minority respondents' scores; since then this gap has narrowed to an average of 7 percentage points.

---

[6] A variable measuring victimisation was initially included in the model, but it was not selected as a predictor. This suggests it was not the simple fact of victimisation that reduced the ratings of those who asked for police help.

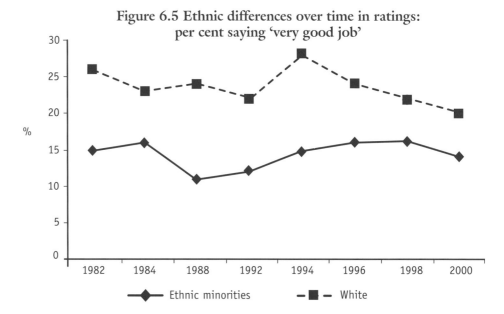

Figure 6.5 Ethnic differences over time in ratings: per cent saying 'very good job'

Notes: 1. Weighted data.
            2. Ethnic minority booster samples used for BCS where possible.
Source: PFLS (2000); BCS (1982–2000)

Views on fairness and integrity

By far the most common perception of discrimination to emerge from our focus groups was the perception that young people generally were picked on by the police. In addition to the examples already cited, the view that they were negatively stereotyped was summed up by one girl in Borough A thus:

> They're very suspicious of teenagers…They forget they're just normal, average people. If they see a group of teenagers, they think 'What are they doing?' [They] just go up … because they're wearing a uniform, go up and ask them questions.

Many respondents of all ages thought the police picked on ethnic minorities although some, including this group of schoolgirls in Borough A, believed they had recently become inhibited about engaging with minorities at all and that this was now exploited on occasion:[7]

> *White girl 1*:
> If there's a fight between a black boy and a white boy … Whereas, I mean, a long time ago they'd probably blame it on the black bloke … but now they won't even get involved. They'll just let the fight carry on and they'll say 'No. We're not getting involved because we don't want to be done for being racist'.

> *Black girl 1*:
> Black people use that a lot now … 'Racist' …

> *White girl 3*:
> And white people say, you know, ''cos he's black, you know, he can do

---

[7] Another girl of Indian origin volunteered: 'Even my Mum … say something bad happened to her [a crime] and she reports it and they don't do anything about it, she says: "You're not going to do anything about it because of the colour of my skin". And she brings it out herself. She even admits it. She just uses it, just to get … notice because [otherwise] they don't do anything.'

anything to me – 'cause they [the police] think *I'm* being racist towards *him*'...

Asian girl: I think it's been blown out of proportion... And so now instead of anything getting better it's just going to get worse.

A number of older people, though, also raised the question of discrimination against minorities. For the most part (as with the woman from Borough A cited previously) this tended to be based largely on newspaper accounts, and coverage of the Macpherson Inquiry had almost certainly heightened consciousness of police racism in the period immediately preceding the study. An older black woman in a focus group in Borough C said her views had recently changed as a result of what she had seen on television:

> They do have a lot of discussions on cases of black people and they ... are saying that we couldn't get justice or nothing like that because justice is only for certain people.

Importantly, though, the focus groups bring out the extent to which similar individuals of the same ethnic origin may hold different views. Another woman in the same group insisted, nonetheless, on comparing the police treatment of minorities with police services elsewhere in the world:[8]

> ... if you compare them, I really admire the English police because I believe in anything there is some good and some bad and the English police, most of the time, they are very dedicated. I also believe that maybe it's time, as a black people, to stop taking this view that they're racist as a first thing against them.

Some white respondents, though, drew their perception of police racism from their own experience and observation. Thus one white professional noted that he had only ever been stopped in his car when he had been with colleagues of minority ethnic origin.

At the same time our focus groups highlighted an important corollary of this negative discrimination against some groups. Several respondents raised the possibility that the police might also discriminate *in favour of* other sections of the population. Girls in particular were aware that they got away with far more than boys – not only because the police were less likely to suspect them but also because male officers were not allowed to search them.[9] A middle-aged white woman reported a very positive experience of being stopped in her car which contrasted starkly with the account given by an Asian man in the same group. She had crossed a red light but the police were 'very, very nice about it', she reflected, '...maybe because I was a woman'.

Almost none of our respondents, however, raised concerns about police corruption. On the only occasion when the question of bribery was raised, it was assumed that if this occurred it was likely to be confined to specialist units (in particular CID) rather than the sort of officers the public were most likely to meet.

---

[8] One respondent of North African origin in Borough B said: 'I've been studying in Paris for 10 years and then I moved to Germany. I'm going to tell you the difference between the police there and here. They [the English police] are the best in the world'

[9] One who hung out with a group of boys on one of the poorest estates in Borough A would routinely secrete their 'joints' on her person when the police came into view.

Survey measures of police malpractice

The survey asked explicitly about corruption, replicating a series of questions in the Police Studies Institute (PSI) survey. These covered unnecessary use of force, use of violence in police stations, planting of evidence, taking bribes and extracting favours. Findings are presented in Table 6.3. There appear to be two conflicting trends. On the one hand, the proportions believing that the police *never* act illegally has fallen quite significantly for most items. On the other, the proportion believing that illegal behaviour is common has either remained the same or declined only slightly. There was, however, a statistically significant fall in the proportion thinking that unreasonable force was used in police stations.

Table 6.3: Beliefs about police malpractice:
per cent saying it 'often happens' and 'never happens'

	PSI 1981		PFLS 2000	
	Never	*Often*	*Never*	*Often*
Threats, etc. during questioning	30	25	24	23
False recording of interviews	56	11	53	10
Excessive force at arrest	63	13	45	11
Excessive violence in station	53	12	40	7
Fabricating evidence	40	9	29	9

Notes: 1. Don't know and n.a. included.
2. Weighted data, unweighted n = 2,420 (PSI); 2,800 (PFLS).

Two further questions about the prevalence of bribes and other forms of graft showed significant improvements in people's perceptions of police integrity. In 1981, 8% of the sample thought that most or quite a lot of officers took bribes; but by 2000 this had fallen to 4%. In 1981, 14% thought that most or a lot of officers accepted goods or favours from people who wanted to keep on the right side of the police. In 2000 the figure was 7%. (Both differences are statistically significant, the former at the 5% level, the latter at the 1% level.) There was no change in the proportion who thought these things never happened.

There were some demographic differences in views about police integrity, though these were less marked than those relating to police effectiveness and were not always consistent across items. We therefore constructed a scale to summarise beliefs about malpractice, summing the responses to the variables in Table 6.3 and the two items about bribes and accepting favours. We then carried out a multiple linear regression analysis. Only four demographic variables were significant predictors. These were, in order of predictiveness:

1. Being black (predictive of negative views).
2. Being young (predictive of positive views).
3. Being male (predictive of positive views).
4. Having a low income (predictive of positive views).

Our black sample were very much more likely to think the police used threats, force, false recording and fabrication of evidence than white or Asian respondents. For example, 22% of white respondents thought that threats were often used, as against

33% of black respondents. This is consistent with the PSI survey, and consistent with PFLS findings about greater levels of dissatisfaction with the police amongst black respondents. The findings about age and sex are surprising, however. People under 30 were generally *less* likely than their elders to think the police often acted illegally, and men were *less* likely to think this than women. Well off respondents held more negative views than poorer ones.

We then developed the model, adding in experience of the police either as police 'users' – such as reporting crimes – or as police suspects. Those who had experience of the police as suspects were more likely than others to question police integrity. Being stopped on foot and being stopped in a car were both included in addition to the demographic variables already in the model, predicting negative views.

These are a complex set of findings, with various possible explanations. The fact that young people, and young men in particular, are more positive about police integrity than others might suggest that it is because they speak from direct experience. On the other hand, the fact that those with direct experience as suspects were *negative* about police integrity calls this explanation into doubt. Another possibility is that the views of people under 30 have not been shaped by the corruption scandals of the 1960s and 1970s, and the series of wrongful convictions that occurred in the 1970s and 1980s.[10]

Survey measures of fairness
As with illegality, the survey asked a series of questions on fairness and integrity that replicated those in the PSI survey. Table 6.4 shows trends in the proportion of people who think the police treat different groups unfairly. It is clear there has been a large rise in the proportion of Londoners who think that minority ethnic groups receive unfair treatment; otherwise, however, the picture has changed little over time.

Table 6.4: Per cent saying the police treat different groups unfairly

Group	1981 (PSI)	2000 (PFLS)
Ethnic minorities	22	36
Young people	10	12
Poor people	1	1
Criminals	1	1
Gay people	<1	1

Note: Weighted data, unweighted n = 2,420 (PSI); 2,800 (PFLS).
Source: PSI; PFLS.

There were differences between demographic groups in responses to treatment of minorities. Table 6.5 shows differences between black, Asian and white respondents. It is clear there has been a convergence of views, with the ratings of white respondents now much closer to those of ethnic minorities. Nevertheless, the differences between the views of black and white respondents in 2000 are highly statistically significant, and those between white and Asian respondents approach statistical significance.

---

[10] Whilst some of these involved police forces other than the MPS, it seems unlikely that many respondents would be aware of this distinction.

There were other demographic differences. Middle-aged respondents were more likely to think minorities received unfair treatment than others; so were middle-class respondents, and those who were affluent. This demographic profile – affluent, middle class, middle aged – suggests that those white respondents who were most likely to keep abreast of current affairs may have been sensitised by the Macpherson report to unfair treatment by the police of minorities.

Table 6.5: Per cent saying the police treat ethnic minorities unfairly

Ethnic group	1981 (PSI)	2000 (PFLS)
Black	48	53
Asian	36	39
White	20	34

Note: Weighted data, unweighted *n* = 2,420 (PSI); 2,608 (PFLS).
Source: PSI; PFLS.

Willingness to help the police

As with questions on integrity, we replicated questions in the PSI survey about people's willingness to help the police. People were asked about several scenarios in which they might help the police. Table 6.6 compares responses in 1981 and 2000, broken down by ethnic group, for two of the scenarios. In the first they were asked if they would be prepared to call the police if they saw someone beaten up outside a pub; in the second they were asked if they would be prepared to identify people whom they had seen vandalise a bus shelter.

Table 6.6: Preparedness to help the police, by ethnic group (per cent prepared to help)

	PSI 1981		PFLS 2000	
Would you be prepared to	*Report pub fight*	*Identify vandals*	*Report pub fight*	*Identify vandals*
Black	54	37	72	50
Asian	64	70	83	76
White	65	70	81	75

Notes: 1. Don't know and n.a. included.
     2. Weighted data, unweighted *n* = 2,420 (PSI); 2,608 (PFLS).

The findings are surprising in the light of the decline in ratings on some measures of police performance reported in this and the previous chapter. The increase in reporting is fairly consistent with findings of the BCS, which shows that Londoners actually are reporting a greater proportion of less serious crimes than they did 20 years ago (Aye Maung 2001). The difference between black respondents and others is striking. The fact that the gap in preparedness to report has narrowed is reassuring but, especially in relation to identifying an offender, it remains large.

Other demographic differences in preparedness to help the police were generally small. There were no statistically significant differences across class, gender or area. However, people under 30 were less likely to report the pub fight (72% compared with 82% for older people) and less likely to identify the vandals (82% compared with 91%).

Whether people would actually behave as they claim they would when answering hypothetical questions is, of course, always open to doubt. Just as people may wish to give interviewers the impression their opinions of the police are informed by fact rather than by hearsay, so too their answers may in part be influenced by what they feel they *ought* to do in the situations described to them. This may in part explain the less reassuring picture that emerged from our focus groups. Even those who were most supportive of the police often qualified their willingness in principle to report crime and act as witnesses. Many of our respondents said they would only be happy to do so if their anonymity could be guaranteed, but often they were very reluctant to get involved at all. This was either because of fear of reprisals or a communal taboo on 'grassing' which seemed especially marked among white working-class people in Borough C and young Bangladeshi men in Borough B (although some of the latter claimed they would readily 'grass up' a member of another ethnic group).

Police officers themselves found many victims in high-crime areas unwilling to report and this was even more true of potential witnesses. For example:

> *PC Borough A:*
> Most people will look after themselves and if somebody's witnessed an offence and you approach them to help you with it, then yes they've seen it but no they're not going to help you with it. 'Because it doesn't affect me' and 'Why should I go out of my way and have some comeback on me?' We've become a walk-on-by society. I had an incident recently where a woman was attacked in the street by her boyfriend who was armed with a police style friction lock baton, and we had about 18 calls on it. One person would give me his statement. And that was because he wanted to be a police officer. It just says a lot about the walk-on-by society that we've become.

This could create particular problems in securing convictions where – as might often happen in public order situations – cases increasingly rested on police evidence alone.[11]

Considering joining the police

In the survey we repeated a set of PSI questions about joining the police. Table 6.7 shows the proportion of respondents under 45 who said that they had 'ever considered joining the police'. In both PSI and PFLS, only a small proportion had done so – but this proportion had doubled for both black and Asian groups.

Table 6.7: Per cent of under 45s who had ever considered joining the police, by ethnic group

Ethnic group	1981 (PSI)	2000 (PFLS)
Black	13	27
Asian	10	22
White	20	20

Note: Weighted data, unweighted *n* = 2,420 (PSI); 2,608 (PFLS).
Source: PSI; PFLS.

---

[11] Officers in more than one group also believed that the judiciary in London were far more sceptical of police evidence than in provincial forces.

As with other questions about supportiveness towards the police, our focus groups with members of the public presented a complex and more ambiguous reality behind the answers people give to survey questions. Respondents were asked: 'If a friend of yours or someone in your family was thinking about joining the police and asked your opinion, what would you say to them?' People recognised the importance of the police role and they tended to want to see significant increases in the numbers of officers accessible to the public. The extent to which this was true of respondents *irrespective* of age, area or ethnicity was one of the most striking findings from our focus groups – albeit, as previous chapters have indicated, they wanted to encounter the police in non-adversarial roles and to see them targeting groups 'other' than themselves. Few would themselves consider joining the service, though; and, while they would not dissuade others, most had concerns about the dangers of the job and the hostility they would encounter. As one girl in Borough A put it:

> They'd probably end up getting hated, wouldn't they? . . . And they'll probably end up getting hurt as well.

Many did not rate it highly as a career, and minority ethnic respondents assumed they would inevitably face barriers of racism – and not only *within* the service. Thus an older black woman in Borough C:

> The prejudice there is too much – first prejudice with your colleagues and [then] prejudice outside with the people you're protecting.

Meanwhile, teenagers in a school in Borough C also referred to a traditional antipathy towards joining the police among the white working class in the area which almost amounted to a social taboo:

> *Moderator:* What would your advice be?
>
> *Boy:* No, no ... I'd disown them.
>
> *Moderator:* Why would you do that?
>
> *Boy:* No, you just don't, you don't join the police.
>
> *Moderator:* Why?
>
> *Boy:* My family just don't join the police. It'd be ... it wouldn't be right.

Some young people, nonetheless, would actively encourage others to join – despite their generally negative views of the police and their more personal concerns about the individuals' safety. They tended to express this in terms of their potential role as catalysts for improvement generally and – especially in the case of minorities – in order to tackle institutional racism. This attitude was more likely to be expressed by young women rather than by young men. For example, a young Bangladeshi woman in Borough B argued:

> *Woman:* Yes [I'd encourage someone I knew to join] because they're not going to be as racist against, like, Asians ... Yes, I mean – one person could make a difference. You never know, one person could help.

Moderator: You think it might help in terms of overcoming problems with racism?

Woman: Yes, like you could become a leader, or you might turn into a Superintendent.

Key findings

- Londoners say the news media are their main source of information about the police, though people under 45 were more likely than their elders to rely on personal experience.

- Asked to rate the quality of MPS work, Londoners rank the police below firemen, nurses, teachers and doctors, and on a par with social workers.

- However, the police are ranked higher than all other criminal justice agencies.

- The proportion of Londoners saying the police do a 'very good job' has fallen from 32% in 1982 to 20% in 2000. The proportion thinking the police do a bad job has doubled, from 9% to 18%.

- Other police forces have fallen from a higher starting point to the same level.

- Young people, poor people, those in deprived areas and ethnic minorities rate the quality of police work lower than others.

- The best predictors of dissatisfaction include being stopped on foot, being stopped in a car and seeking police help.

- In 2000 Londoners were more likely to say the police treat ethnic minorities unfairly than in 1981. The greatest increase was amongst white respondents.

- Some measures of confidence in police integrity show improvements, others no change.

- In 2000 Londoners were more likely to say they would report a pub fight and identify an offender who had vandalised a bus shelter than in 1981.

- In 2000 more black and Asian respondents under 45 said they had considered joining the police than in 1981 – though figures for white respondents showed no change.

- The results of focus groups reveal considerable ambivalence about the police as a career.

Chapter Seven: Group Perceptions and Area Differences

The reasons for the differences between groups in their experience and perceptions of the police are complex. In particular, group perceptions are not shaped solely by the direct experience of individual members of the group, but those individuals' experiences themselves will also vary. The same individual may have a number of different experiences of the police – whether as a victim of crime, a suspect, or both; and he or she may feel more positive about some of these experiences than others. But the experience of members of the same group may also differ, depending on which other groups they also belong to. Thus members of the same minority ethnic group may have different experiences of the police depending on their age, gender, socioeconomic status, lifestyle and – as became increasingly apparent in the course of our study – what type of area they live in.

Importantly, the history of the group and its sense of collective experience may come into play in individuals' encounters with the police. It can shape the way in which the encounter is interpreted and can even influence the dynamics of the encounter. Some of our police respondents understood this and the ways in which they explained the reasons for the way the public saw them was particularly illuminating. The explanations in part reflected their views of what was currently wrong with the service, but they were also influenced by the officers' own group perceptions. As Chapter 9 illustrates, some of these perceptions relate to their sense of themselves as a group *within* the service, but some were also strongly influenced by their views of the public. Again, direct and indirect experience were important factors but long-established group norms also came into play and here, too, there were stark distinctions by area.

In trying to identify and address the causes of public dissatisfaction with the service, some recognition needs to be given to these group perceptions and to the ways in which these may interact in police–public encounters – not least because these perceptions are the realities of the parties concerned.

Focus groups with the public

One of the most striking findings from our qualitative work was the extent of the sense of a group experience of the police among young people. Negative views of how the police approached young people tended to transcend both ethnicity and area. Possibly because a higher proportion of young people have direct experience of being targets of police attention, negative accounts of these experiences also tended to over-ride positive experiences. At the same time, the numbers who had had this type of contact and the strength of peer networks among people at this age tended further to reinforce a collective, negative view. Thus a black schoolgirl in Borough C 'used to think they [the police] was great' because of the concern they had shown when she was the victim of an accident several years previously. Now, though, echoing many others (like the white schoolgirl in Borough A, quoted in Chapter 3):

> ... friends of mine, like kids our age ... if they're in a tracksuit or something and a cap and they look like they are up to something but they're not, just by their appearance the police look at them and think

'OK, let's go and search them'. The police will go up to you and say 'What are you doing?' and 'Where are you going?' and they will question them for no reason.

Among young people, those with more positive perceptions were apt to remain silent in a group situation, so the vicarious impressions formed by those with little or no direct experience tended to be negative.[1] And our schoolboy respondents in particular seemed more likely to gravitate towards a negative group norm.

Irrespective of age, though, it was apparent that the groups in higher-crime areas tended not only to have more experience of the police (both directly and vicariously) but this experience more often combined experience as suspects *and* as victims. These mixed experiences of the police and a shared, negative view of the service were most apparent in Borough C;[2] and here, too, a sense of collective history came into play. Thus an older woman talked about her brothers being targeted by the police as young men when they were growing up in the area. A middle-aged man had hesitated to report a theft to the police because he was 'known' to them and, therefore, did not expect his victimisation to be taken seriously. And, as the previous chapter illustrates, school pupils implied that not trusting the police (or co-operating with them) was effectively a communal norm handed down to them from previous generations.

An important factor in group perceptions of the police, however, appeared to be the perception of how *other* groups were treated. In particular, our focus groups highlighted the ways in which people might explain their negative views of the police in terms of their belief that other groups received better treatment. White respondents in our 18–24-year-old group in Borough C believed people in the 'black' areas of the borough were being allowed to get away with crime. But the equivalent group of Bangladeshis in Borough B, while admitting that a lot of violence went on between groups, asserted that the police targeted them instead of or more than the white young people involved.

Police bias, though, was not only seen in terms of race. As we have seen, age was commonly seen as important, but so too were class and area, as well as gender. A black schoolboy in Borough C claimed that 'If someone's in trouble … You make a phone call and there's two people on the phone and someone says 'X' [a poor area of the borough] and next person says 'Y' [the most affluent area], they're going to go there first and X second'.

Two schoolgirls of different ethnic origins in Borough A thought this affected police attitudes as well as the level of service:

> *Girl 1*: Working class areas and in middle class areas they're different. They're like the police are more friendly in like middle class areas, and they're more like … yeah? And in working class areas they're just like …
> *Girl 2*: … they think they're above you.

---

[1] Thus two young women spoke to us privately after our focus group with Bangladeshis in Borough B: they knew several of the young men in the group as trouble-makers in the area and their accounts were at odds with the experience of the girls' own brothers. But they were not prepared to say this in discussion.
[2] This was less the case for the one focus group we conducted in an affluent neighbourhood.

That is, where people are dissatisfied with the treatment they receive from the police, this may be compounded by an automatic *assumption* that they have been treated worse than someone with different characteristics in the same situation. A Bangladeshi schoolgirl, for example, reported that her cousin had been searched by the police but, solely because they had found nothing, believed that the search must have been racially motivated.

Focus groups and interviews with the police

Our police focus groups were expressly asked how they thought local people perceived them. They were very conscious of being seen in a negative light and this was clearly a source of profound personal frustration for many. In the case of victims of crime, officers frequently shared the view they were receiving a poor service and this intensified their own dissatisfaction with the organisational environment.

One PC in Borough B commented:

> ... we don't get enough time to deal properly with incidents because we go somewhere and we deal with it and we don't have the time to stick around and talk to and reassure the people. It's always: 'Yabber, yabber, yabber' on the radio. And you give the impression to the victim, or people on the street or whoever – they'll think I'm not interested ... will think I just want to get off and do something else ... The most rewarding thing is when I turn my radio off and I can actually sit down ... and help them with their individual problems – [when] I can find the time to help them or whatever without being interrupted ... rather than just get going and rushing out.

A colleague in another area complained specifically about the problem being compounded by the knock-on effect of having to clear paperwork from a previous shift before he could get out on duty:

> So of course you could go to a burglary or ... anything: it's an hour and a half old – maybe even longer. And of course, that may be the most ... a smashed window, for instance, for that person ... that is the most important thing in his life or her life that has ever happened. And all of a sudden you turn up in a car, jump out the car, up to the door and they go: [in a sarcastic tone] 'It was nice of you to get here wasn't it?' Of course that's their first impression.

The problem was also recognised by their managers. A focus group with sergeants and inspectors characterised public perceptions of the police as follows:

> *Manager 1:*
> We are seen as rude, uncaring and abrupt by a lot of people; and it's ... not the officers' fault. That's important. They just don't have the time these days to sit down and spend an hour to two hours dealing with a burglary or whatever, they're just wanting to go to the next one – or being called up for something else. That is something that will be very difficult to address.

> *Manager 2:*
> Years ago you would go to the scene of a burglary and sit down and
> have a cup of tea with the victim and chat with them and take time with
> them … The common concern I've heard bandied about more than once
> now is 'chasing the CAD'.[3] Out there, it's like a ping pong machine.

However, as our survey findings have shown, the people the police encounter do not
divide neatly into victims and suspects. If only unconsciously, the process of
categorisation starts with the subdivision of those who call on the police for help –
some of whom are victims but many of whom may also be past, present or potential
suspects, and the balance of these groups tends to vary by area.

Many officers – like those cited above – felt passionately that the reason they had
joined the job was to protect 'genuine' victims and secure justice for them. By
contrast, some types of victim were particularly frustrating to deal with because they
were difficult to help, and those who were also 'known' to the police as offenders
evoked a mixed response at best.

Officers often seemed to frame their perceptions of police–public contact in the
context of differences between areas. Differences in the ethnic make-up of different
areas tended to be taken as a given within this, but reference was made to what some
saw as the racialisation of people's perceptions of the service – both as victims and as
suspects.

Cases where victims were seen to be unco-operative appeared to fall broadly into
three categories. In some instances people would call the police to intervene in a
personal dispute but with no intention of taking the matter any further. Effectively
they were using the call to the police simply to strengthen their hand against the
other party or – as in the most trivial instance we were given – to bolster their
authority. The dispute could be very minor. (Separate references were made in
different groups to squabbles over who had the remote control for the television,
and one officer in Borough A had been called by a mother to an argument between
her children over their Christmas presents.) Equally, they could involve the threat of
serious violence – even if the trigger for the dispute was trivial.[4] But the common
factor was that the caller did not want any further action taken and would usually not
provide enough information for the police to take any action independently.[5]

These cases tended to overlap with the second category. In these instances, someone
who was not directly involved in the incident would call the police. Sometimes the
call would be anonymous but, especially in cases where the caller was known to the
parties involved, this placed a particular onus on the police to protect their identity.
Yet the parties themselves would deny that there was any problem – even if there was
apparent evidence of violence. Not only would they refuse to provide the police with
any information, they might also demand to know who had called them. Even

---

[3] Command and Despatch – the control centre which relays calls to officers on patrol.
[4] Officers in Borough C in particular tended to comment on the speed with which the
most trivial incidents could escalate in this way: one cited the case of someone being
killed in an argument over a football score.
[5] This problem is also common in classic domestic violence cases, and the current policy
of automatic arrest represents an attempt to overcome this. However, our focus groups
threw up cases of men who claimed that female partners had picked a fight and then
used the system against them in this way. They felt aggrieved that the police
automatically presumed them guilty without hearing their side of the story.

though the police did not divulge this, they might work it out for themselves (rightly or wrongly).

In turn, this second category tended to overlap with the third, where the police directly came across victims of violence who simply refused to admit where they got their injuries. These cases might come to light in other ways also, sometimes resulting from street fights but also violence in pubs or clubs. Victims in these instances had mixed reasons for not giving the police information. They ranged from fear of reprisal, through norms of 'not grassing' (possibly combined with a resolution to 'sort it out' for themselves) to being too drunk or high to remember what had happened – even if they wanted to and were capable of providing a coherent account. Officers' feelings about these cases were illustrated by the following exchange from a focus group with PCs in Borough C:

> *PC 1:*
> A lot of the time, I mean, we get called to a domestic situation or fight or whatever; but nine times out of ten, you'll get there all they want us to do is break up the fight or whatever was going on. But they don't want [us] to take any action: they want the best of both worlds. You won't get them … to make a statement.

> *WPC:*
> We've had horrific fights – I mean where a bloke's bleeding from every place you can see on his head and he's like: 'No I fell off a kerb.' Well hang on, we know he was in a fight because we had several calls, independent of the people in the pub; and we know there's something going on. But he's like: 'No, no, no – I fell off the kerb and bumped my head on the kerb.' And it's actually quite frustrating, to think: 'Well, I wanted to do something … We're *here* to do something . . .We're here to stop this sort of thing – to find the sort of people that are responsible for this.'

> *PC2:*
> It's a macho thing as well isn't it? … kind of: 'I don't need you …'

> *WPC:*
> Yeah: 'I'm not going to tell you anything: I'm going to deal with it myself …'

All these different categories of victimisation could occur in all areas. Indeed, the particular problem with night-clubs was raised by officers in Borough A, but references to the failure of victims to co-operate seemed to occur most frequently in Borough C. It was here that the incidence of violence between local residents appears to have been highest. And officers explicitly drew attention to the extent to which people they dealt with as victims were also likely to be known to them as suspects and offenders:

> *PC 1:*
> There are more criminals in this area than in other areas. You go to something that comes to our attention, you do a name check on

someone [i.e. on the Police National Computer]. It's rare that they're not known …

PC 2:
Go to a domestic and do a name check on the partners or whatever. Nine out of ten times, they're known to the police for one reason or another.

Respondents in our police focus groups usually had experience of working in different areas and tended spontaneously to divide boroughs (and sub-areas within these) into three. The first two contrasting categories were those with substantial residential populations, even though they might also include large shopping centres and leisure venues.

On the one hand, there were the more middle-class residential areas where people tended to be well disposed towards the police generally and were more likely to co-operate with them, whether as victims or suspects. A female police manager said that Borough A was much busier than people supposed but, compared with two inner-city boroughs where she had worked previously:

I haven't found it has so much in-your-face aggression. Particularly, I can think of being a custody officer. When I was custody officer at [the boroughs referred to] someone would walk in and would instantly insult you, just because of who you were and what you represented. People tend to be a bit more polite here. I don't think you get so many public order offences here – or arrests for it …

On the other hand, there were areas that were highly deprived, creating high stress levels among the local population and where verbal aggression was common. Crime was generally high and interpersonal violence was triggered easily, with an increasing use of knives and guns. In these areas people were seen as generally hostile to the police and much more likely to be unco-operative. As a group of constables in Borough C put it:

PC:
The police are *not* liked; [so] you have an uphill struggle from the start. Whatever you do, people are very wary of you.

WPC:
I was a Special for several years before I joined; and the last year of that I worked full time. And that was in [a middle-class area of an outer borough]; and you see the difference in how people react to you. You could be going down the street and you'd get kids saying to you: 'Hello policeman. How are you?' And they actually talk to you … But *here*, you even *dare* to say hello to anyone and you get the death stare; or you just get: 'Don't talk to me: I don't want anything to do with you.'

The third category was areas of central London that were intensively policed because they were high-crime areas but where most of the crime the police dealt with did not involve local residents. There were parts of the West End where most people (and many tourists in particular) held very positive attitudes towards the police.[6] In other parts of central London, though, non-residents might be attracted by drugs markets or for prostitution; even those who were simply passing through might prefer not to get involved in helping the police. Thus an officer in Borough B contrasted this type of area (Z) with (Y) – another part of the same borough that was middle class and residential:

> The sorts of people that deal there ... they've all got very long criminal records ... There's a high profit margin to be made there. They're not going to be reported by members of the public most of the time, if they do commit a crime. They'll very rarely phone us about it. Because even people passing through Z, law abiding citizens, they see a fight in the street – it's just standard in that area. They don't consider it a major issue, whereas if they saw it in Y, we'd get 25, 30 phone calls about it. We'd be round there like a shot and everybody would want us to do something about it and a lot of people would be willing to provide evidence. If you go to a fight on the street at Z, nobody wants to know. Even if people do get arrested subsequently it's difficult to do anything about it because nobody will give you any evidence.

Most of Borough A was perceived as falling into the first category while Borough C tended to fall squarely into the third and Borough B combined elements of both, along with the characteristics of the central area also (albeit with more of the problem elements and fewer of the compensations).

This tended again to confirm the findings of the policing literature almost from its inception, that there is a degree of collective police response to these different environments. The different patterns of interaction with the public and the local history of these interactions could combine with at least two other particular factors to produce overall differences in policing *styles* from one area to another. That is, the police reacted in some measure to public attitudes towards them – but their own attitudes might, in turn, anticipate what they expected to be the attitude of the public. In areas where public attitudes tended overall to be more hostile, the problem was compounded by the need for more intensive and intrusive policing methods because crime was high. But this higher police presence and the greater density of population, in turn, also meant officers were more likely to reach incidents while they were still in progress. This placed them in situations where feelings (and actual levels of violence) might be running high, and they would call for backup in the knowledge it would arrive in reasonable time. In all, this increased the likelihood of their being directly involved in (others') confrontation but minimised the need for them be able to defuse the confrontation. One manager in Borough A reflected on the difference it made when 'the Cavalry isn't around the corner', and another drew out more robustly the difference this could make to officers' attitudes and behaviour:

> The thing that really impressed me from where I'd been before was the attitude of the police officers when I came [to Area A]. I found the police officers on the whole on an outer borough (it was the first time I've been to an outer borough) were a lot more professional than I was

[6] An officer now in Borough A had previously worked in a deprived inner borough but transferred to the central area where he was amazed at first to find not only that people *wanted* to speak to him but to be photographed with him as well.

used to. I found the police officers that I was used to dealing with and supervising at [two central London stations] … the young ones in particular were very immature … aggressive [would] go over the top very, very quickly. They would get to something very quickly, because the ground is so small and they'd be right in the midst of it. Whereas places like [areas on the fringe of Borough A] the police officers would be small in numbers, so they wouldn't get to the confrontation so quickly. They would try to deal with it and send people home. By the time their colleagues turned up most of the problems had dissipated, had gone. So we didn't have that immediate confrontation: the atmosphere still wasn't as tense at the time they got there, and it's a completely different way of dealing with it. It seemed their attitude was a lot more professional, they didn't have that youthful aggression a lot of police officers up town have. I was quite impressed with them actually as a sergeant coming here.

Some officers in Borough C were conscious that their work gave them a distorted view of the local population. Running from one incident to the next in cars, they had increasingly less contact with the broad range of ordinary people in the area. They almost never met local people in normal circumstances but encountered them only as victims or suspects:

PC 1:
As a response team, the only people we tend to meet are either a victim or a criminal. You don't get [to meet] the broad range of people; and as we get shorter and shorter on the teams…

PC 2:
Go back a few years ago and I mean there are a few of us here from the [neighbouring] area or [X] area and you used to have times when you used to be able to go out and walk around the area, patrol the area. And you used to meet people and you would just meet somebody in the street and you would have a conversation. You'd would say 'Hello' or whatever and you would pass the time [of day]. Now you're in a car going literally from one call to another because there isn't the time to do anything else…

Some officers in Borough C were very articulate about the economic and social circumstances that generated the problems they were called on to deal with. As one manager put it:

You've got to step back. I mean, yes, as the police we've got to say that we're awfully busy – but think about how those people are feeling. They have no options: they have to live in these places that aren't very nice. Even if they try to maintain their own dignity in that area, it's nigh on impossible. Only I think that you have to accept *that* as well as … Yes – it's busy for us; and, yes – there is a lot of crime and all that sort of thing. But I think you have to look beyond it and look at that as well. I think that it's unfortunate that they think that we don't feel that way. And that's where the confrontation comes in.

Others, though, appeared to have taken on a collectively negative view of local people that mirrored the view they assumed people held of them. The tone on a different team was very different. Most agreed with a view that wrote off the area as dirty and run down, seeing the police called to 'childish' problems by inhabitants who were 'most unhelpful'. The only dissenting voice was that of a late recruit to the service who had grown up in the area and still had relatives there:

> ... so I *know* people that live in this area. And it *is* a dump; it *is* run down; and obviously when you do this job you only come into contact with people with troubles. But there are quite a few good people around as well – who *I* know, but, obviously, that's only because I've lived here and I know the area.

Although these negative stereotypes of the public were most likely to be expressed in area-specific terms in Borough C, they were not universally held but nor were they confined to that area. Unless they had a wider community brief, many of the officers coming into regular contact with the public were not dealing with a representative cross-section of the population. Developing a fairly jaundiced view of humanity was an occupational hazard which, at worst, created a beleaguered 'them and us' view of their role, especially in areas where the public tended to be least co-operative. As some officers recognised:

> *WPC 1*:
> We run the risk of starting thinking that everyone hates us...
>
> *WPC 2*: You get so used to being treated that way, you forget there are others that are quite happily welcoming and would give you a cup of tea.
>
> *Manager*:
> Yet there are people [here] that would welcome you. There are decent people who do respect the police; and that's a shame because we start losing that. We start forgetting that does exist...

One experienced officer who had moved into the area from outer London implied he had been struck by his colleagues' negative attitudes. Their expectation of hostility had almost become a self-fulfilling prophecy and, having tried at first to fit in, he had ended up rejecting their inhibitions and had gone back to what he always did ,which was just 'chat' to anyone he came across in passing.

The distribution of the minority ethnic population and the heightened likelihood of police contact with residents in the areas where they are most likely to live strongly suggest that some minorities (in particular the black, Pakistani and Bangladeshi groups) disproportionately experience these more confrontational policing styles. Certainly this is consistent with our survey findings in Chapter 5 about reaction to contact with the police.

The officers we spoke to rarely raised issues of race or ethnicity and it seems possible they were more than usually inhibited about doing so in the immediate aftermath of the Macpherson Inquiry. However, a recurrent complaint was the extent to which people of different ethnic origins saw the police as favouring other groups:

PC 1:

Certainly going to an incident [in a named area] where you have say a
black person and a white person with a dispute; and the black person
would be correct in the incident. And you turn around and say that; and
the white person turns around and says: 'Well you're only doing that
because he's black.' You know, you then get the other situation; and I've
had that several times as well. Again, you know – it's mad ... You can't
win, do you know what I mean?

PC 2:

No matter how we try to deal with some things we're not going to win.

Less explicitly, a number also hinted at resentment towards what they saw as
preferential treatment for victims who alleged racist motivation. The possibility
cannot be ignored that this may affect the response victims receive when they first
report such cases. And this, in turn, may be reflected in survey findings of lower
levels of satisfaction among victims of racist incidents relative to comparable
individuals' views of the police response to other crime reports. More commonly,
though, officers talked openly about thinking twice now about approaching
members of certain groups when they felt they had grounds for suspicion. The
concerns they cited did not include self-doubt about their own motives but rather the
threat to their mortgages and pensions if a complaint were made against them.

Other observation

Our observation of the police at work tended to corroborate officers' views of area
differences in attitudes to the police. It was apparent in custody suites in particular
that some individuals in any area would set out to wind the police up, but this
seemed to be most prevalent in Borough C. On a patrol observation, we were also
called more than once to the same address without being able to find out why the
police had been called. The householder seemed simply to be using the fact that he
could summon them to give him some leverage in a dispute with other people in the
house which none of the parties was prepared to explain.[7]

The higher incidences of adversarial or non-co-operative encounters in Borough C,
however, were by no means race specific; nor did officers appear to see them as such.
Despite the context, the dynamics between the police and those present in the drugs
raids we observed were surprisingly non-adversarial. Rather, the black suspect who
was arrested responded in the best tradition of 'It's a fair cop'.

Conclusions

The case study boroughs were selected in order to refine our understanding of
whether the dynamics of police–community relations varied according to the type of
area people lived in, *in addition to* their socioeconomic characteristics and the social
categories to which they were allocated.

Clearly, given the relatively limited scope of our work, it is not possible to provide
definitive answers. Taken together with the findings of earlier chapters, the material
here suggests the questions of group perceptions of each other among sections of the

---

[7] The same officers were also called later to an alleged stabbing where the victim at first
claimed to have been attacked in the street by other young men unknown to him.
Eventually it transpired that he and his girl friend had had a row and she had assaulted
him with a pair of scissors. They did not want any action taken.

public and of the police would be worth exploring further. The police literature is redolent with findings of the ways in which the police tend to categorise the public and the attitudes associated with this, but the ways in which these perceptions *interact* with public perceptions of and attitudes towards the police are relatively neglected. A question of particular interest is the extent to which this may systematically influence the style of police–public encounters by area. This may have important implications for groups who are not evenly distributed by area but who tend to be concentrated in areas where policing styles tend to be more adversarial.

Key findings

- This chapter and some of the earlier findings suggest that group perceptions of each other may be an important factor in shaping individual and group encounters between the police and the public. And these, in turn, may be reflected in police–community relations more widely.

- These mutual perceptions have a basis in direct experience, but the experience of other members of the group is also important and the *history* of the group experience may have a significant influence as well.

- The police and members of the public alike may make assumptions about how the other sees them. And the negative effects of this may further be compounded on the part of the public by assumptions that the police treat other groups differently.

- Young people in particular appear to see themselves as labelled negatively by the police, but people also perceive that this applies to some ethnic groups, poorer people and men.

- The police's views of the public are strongly conditioned by their perception of who is most willing to co-operate with them.

- To a degree, the police's 'usual suspects' tend to come from the groups who are also perceived to hold more negative views of the police. A higher proportion of these live in highly deprived, high-crime areas, and this lends itself to labelling by area.

- The problem is compounded by police deployment. In particular, officers on response teams encounter the public almost exclusively in adverse circumstances, and these encounters have greater potential for confrontation in higher-crime areas that are also more ethnically diverse.

Part III

Discussion and Conclusions

Chapter Eight: External Constraints on Responsive Policing

To summarise the findings reported thus far, our sources point to a degree of dissatisfaction amongst Londoners with the day-to-day policing they receive. At the risk of oversimplification, they find the police less responsive, less visible, less accessible, more intrusive in their policing tactics and less engaged with the community than they would like. The evidence also points to an apparent paradox of *declining* public confidence in the police at a time when crime – and anxiety about crime – appears to be falling and surveys suggest that the public are making fewer demands on the police than they were. This and the next chapter set out to examine the reasons for this.

Whilst specific to the Metropolitan Police (MPS), much of our analysis will also apply to other forces since the processes involved will not be unique to the MPS. In fact its position has improved relative to other forces. Twenty years ago Londoners were more sceptical about their police than others; now this is no longer true.

This chapter examines factors that lie largely outside police control and beyond the reach of immediate solutions by police management. Some of the argument is speculative and not readily amenable to empirical test; where possible, however, we have drawn on statistical evidence – including data provided by the MPS itself – and our own qualitative data.

Several factors external to the MPS could explain Londoners' perception that their police are unresponsive, and have become less responsive:

- The MPS has more work to do than previously.

- The MPS has fewer resources.

- Priorities imposed on the MPS impede responsive policing.

- Londoners expect more of public services such as the police than previously.

- Efforts to increase satisfaction amongst some groups may increase a sense of non-responsiveness among others.

Does the MPS have more work to do than previously?

At the time our study was undertaken the number of calls for police assistance as recorded through the computerised Command and Despatch (CAD) system had been fairly static. It will be remembered from Chapter 4 that the total number of calls fell marginally by 1% between 1996 and 2000. Crime calls showed an increase of 17% (see Chapter 4) but in view of both BCS and recorded crime trends it seems possible there have been changes in the way that CAD crime calls are recorded. Other types of call all fell between 1996 and 2000: traffic incidents fell by 4%; disturbance were down by 7%; and other accidents, injuries and incidents were 9% down. On the basis of CAD statistics there is no obvious basis for thinking the actual volume of work increased over this period.

Overall, crime statistics recorded by the police show a small decrease. The most recent crime figures recorded by the MPS, covering 2000–01, total just under a million. Adjusting to take account of changes in counting procedures,[1] the figure in 1995–96 was just over a million, with very little change in the intervening period. The main reasons why these figures have not fallen as much as survey trends would predict will include the following:

- A determined attempt by the MPS to increase victims' preparedness to call the police, especially in relation to hate crimes and domestic violence.

- Progressive familiarity amongst officers about the new Home Office requirements for crime recording, which from 1998 extended the range of crime categories to be counted and required fuller recording of various existing offence types (Home Office 1999).

- Increasing impetus from the Association of Chief Police Officers (ACPO) to ensure that crimes are recorded as fully as possible.

While demands on the police made by the *general public* have been in decline, however, there has almost certainly been growth in demands from commercial organisations and other public bodies. The private security sector has increased very substantially over the last 20 years, and especially over the last five, and this growth may itself have brought new demands – for example, as security guards in shopping malls or stores report suspicious conduct, anti-social behaviour and minor theft to the police.[2]

Respondents in our police focus groups also referred to local authorities and other public services as an important source of demand. Many of these new demands were related to 'risk management' functions for which public services have been held increasingly accountable over the last two decades. Officers talked most often about demand from these sources relating to 'vulnerable people' – in particular the mentally ill, the homeless, the elderly and people in children's homes. The CAD statistics appear to reflect this, for the largest increase in any category was for 'missing person' cases, which grew by 33% between 1996 and 2000.

The reasons for this growth are twofold. On the one hand public services are now expected to work in partnership to a greater degree than five years ago; thus other public services may feel more entitled to mobilise the police, and the police may feel more obligated to respond. On the other, most public services are – or feel – more accountable for their actions, and they are probably more inclined to head off the risk that if any harm befalls a vulnerable person, they might be held responsible. In the eyes of our police respondents, the extra scrutiny had led other public agencies to be risk-averse (or to 'cover their backs') in involving the police in potentially problematic cases.

Leaving aside the growth in calls for help in relation to specific incidents, the servicing of the Crime and Disorder Reduction Partnerships established in 1998 has

---

[1] The adjustment was made by uplifting the 1995–96 total by the percentage difference in the 1998–99 figures when counted according to the old and the new rules.
[2] According to one recent estimate, the number of people employed nationally in private security is now nearly double those employed in the public police service (Johnston 2000).

made significant demands on the time of both senior managers at borough level and of more junior staff. For example, in the mid-1990s boroughs were allocated relatively few staff to partnership work. In Borough C, for example, there was a Borough Liaison Officer at inspector level, supported by a sergeant. Both had additional responsibilities. At the time of writing, the partnership team comprised a team of eight, including an inspector and two sergeants with the remainder a mix of constables and civilian analysts. Although the direct call on resources represents only a very small proportion of the borough's uniformed strength, the team also stimulates a great deal of new project work that is undertaken by staff across the borough, largely funded by bidding to the Home Office for crime-reduction funds. The long-term benefits of this investment may well be substantial but, in the short term, the partnership initiatives associated with the Crime and Disorder Act 1998 have drawn resources away from boroughs' capacity to respond to demands from the public. According to the Commissioner's annual reports, expenditure on 'community safety and partnership' rose from just under 3% in 1998–99 to 24% of the total in 1999–2000. By contrast, the percentage of costs allocated to '24-hour response and traffic' fell from nearly 16% to half that. While partnership work alone does not account for this fall, it is illustrative of the other pressures on the service which militate against increasing the response capacity and may even detract from it.

With regard to the policing of public order, though, Chapter 2 has noted that London inevitably generates much higher demand than elsewhere. But, while trends in overall demands related to public order are hard to assess, there is no evidence these had been increasing in London at the time of the study;[3] and it seems likely they were actually lower throughout the 1990s than the 1980s.

In terms of increase in workload, one of the findings that emerged consistently in our case-study interviews with police officers was the demands on their time made by recording information. Much of this is not directly related to investigation or prosecution but feeds in to systems intended to increase legal and managerial accountability. Some of the information is required as a direct result of legislation or other government initiatives or to provide a range of national bodies (including central government, Her Majesty's Inspectorate of Constabulary – HMIC, and the Audit Commission) with standardised information on police performance. But some is for internal management purposes, although this is often driven by the need to monitor whether externally imposed targets and standards are being met. Additionally, the Macpherson Inquiry in particular heightened the perceived need for a more robust audit trail for decision-making than hitherto.[4] As one manager put it:

> This is one of the big lessons that I've learnt out of that Macpherson report ... If someone hasn't recorded it ... [if you say] 'Well my decision was to let him investigate it' [you will be challenged]. 'But what options did you weigh up before you came to that decision?' You've got to record all these options now.

---

[3] The Commissioner's annual report for 1998–99 refers to policing: 2,885 demonstrations, pickets and other public order events, 32 ceremonial events, 354 league football matches and 334 other sporting events. In 1999 the rules for counting such events changed, and there was a sharp – artificial – fall. Nevertheless the fall continued into 2000–01.

[4] Other cases have had a similar impact recently, albeit they have not had the same high profile until the recent inquiry into the murder of the child Victoria Climbié.

The impact of these developments combined with systems of accountability *internal* to the MPS are considered together in Chapter 9. But the consensus in the three case-study areas was consistent with the Home Office report *Diary of a Police Officer* (PA Consulting 2001): whatever benefits may have accrued in terms of accountability, the demands of record-keeping had inexorably eroded the time available for response work.

Have MPS resources shrunk?

The MPS, like other police forces in England and Wales, effectively has its budget set by central government.[5] Figure 8.1 shows that, adjusting for inflation, MPS expenditure grew by 62% from 1980–81 until 1994–95 and then fell back by 5% over the 3 years to 1997–98. It has since recovered a little and stood at just under £2.2 billion for 2000–01, 2% less than in 1994–95 in real terms. The MPS has fared less well than other forces in recent years. Since the mid-1990s the Home Office has allocated resources by means of a national funding formula. The MPS initially lost out significantly under the formula, but a case was made to give it special status in recognition of the unique problems in policing a capital city. The MPS's protected status for the purposes of national funding has continued to a degree under the new government and this was justified as follows:

> The Home Secretary has decided that the Receiver for the Metropolitan Police District should receive additional funding in recognition of the Metropolitan Police's distinct national and capital city functions. He also considers that it is particularly important to maintain public confidence in policing in the capital city. It would be difficult for the principal formula to take account of these special circumstances. He has decided, therefore, that a portion of the aggregate amount of grants will be assigned to the Receiver for the Metropolitan Police District over and above that available through the principal formula … The Home Secretary has set the amount of this special payment at £176 million (Home Office 1999).

**Figure 8.1: Expenditure (£ millions) in the MPS,
1980–81 onward, at 1980 prices.**

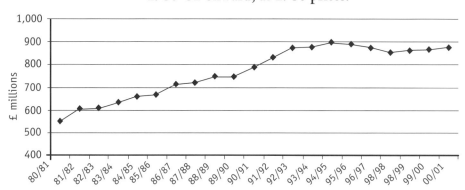

Notes: 1. GDP annual deflator applied, using 1980 as base.
2. Expenditure figures are for financial years.
Source: Commissioner's Annual Reports (1980–2000/01)

---

[5] The total budget is determined by the level of the 50% 'specific grant' allocated by the Home Office, although the total budget includes a block grant element and a proportion raised through the community charge. The local authority (in this case the Mayor) sets the budget, but the 'gearing' of the grant system tightly constrains their freedom.

The formula, that is, curtailed the previous highly favoured status of the MPS and brought relative financial pain. Although the service now receives a smaller slice of the cake than previously, it did not erode its position completely. The MPS still receives around a quarter of the main budget allocated by the Home Office to *all* police forces in England and Wales each year, compared to the seventh it would receive if resources were allocated simply in proportion to the population.

Of this total budget, by far the greatest part is consumed by staffing costs. The number and quality of people available for policing London are determined not simply by the budget allocation but by the capacity of the MPS to recruit and retain staff within pay scales that are still nationally controlled. By the end of March 2001 there were 11% fewer officers than in 1991 – 25,400, compared to 28,500 ten years earlier. Some of these officers were shed when the MPS lost responsibility in 2000 for some peripheral areas in adjoining shire forces – estimated to involve a transfer of the equivalent of 900 officers – or 3.5% of total strength. However, the figure had already begun to rise by August 2001 when it was up to 26,000.

Losses of civil staff have been steeper: there were 13,900 in post in March 1991, falling to 10,200 in March 2001 – a reduction of 26%. From the mid-1990s – and throughout the period of our fieldwork – the numbers of both officers and civil staff were consistently below their targeted strength.

There was a widespread perception of a crisis in the recruitment and retention of staff in London during the period of our research, and this impression was strongly borne out by material from our interviews and focus groups with officers. The reasons they offered included the declining status of the job, the cost of London housing and the poor quality of life in a large city (including concerns about education for their children). It was argued that skilled officers were leaving early or transferring out and were having to be replaced by recruits from outside London. Some were joining only after they had failed in applying to their home forces, but it was expected that – even where London was their first choice – many would eventually return and other forces would reap the value of the MPS's investment in them.

The point was also made to us by some respondents that, while overall staffing levels have fallen over the last decade, effective strength has been depleted further by alterations in working practices, some of which reflected changes in employment law. At the same time, though, reference has already been made to the fact that some boroughs had supplemented their core budgets with government grants won through competitive bidding processes. This additional funding represented quite a significant proportion of the total for Boroughs B and C, adding between 5% and 10% to the total police budget. This source of money was seen as something of a mixed blessing, however. The time and effort absorbed by the police and their partners in bidding were considerable, and often this effort was not repaid. More to the point, funding was contingent on pursuing government priorities, which did not necessarily match with local need. Thus successful bids could effectively skew service delivery away from local priorities. This is further discussed below.

Do priorities imposed on the MPS impede responsive policing?

The role of the MPS was originally described as preventing crime, protecting life and property, and keeping the peace (Mayne 1829).[6] A wide variety of functions falls under these three heads; and central government has recently also given primacy to the goal of crime *reduction*. Yet, as has often been recognised (not least by Lord Scarman), these functions are necessarily in tension, and the relative priority attached to each has changed from time to time, although the change is rarely made explicit. Precisely what balance should be struck is a highly contestable issue, and one that should be open to political debate at central and local government level.

Following the riots in 1981 and debate triggered by the Scarman report (1981), priorities within the MPS shifted markedly towards an order maintenance model of policing, supported by community policing strategies. This tendency was evident throughout the 1980s. At the turn of the decade, however, there were two significant political developments, which have already been described in Chapter 2. Public sector managerialism finally caught up with the police and, a little later, crime control emerged as highly visible party-political issue, when the Labour Party promised to be 'tough on crime, tough on the causes of crime'. Both party-political debate and performance-management regimes that depend on statistical targets certainly involve simplification and, arguably, oversimplification. Those targets that commanded political consensus through their common-sense plausibility related to crime control and involved the prioritisation of specific crime categories. The net effect on the police was to limit consideration about the balance to be struck between competing priorities, and this also had a significant influence on the unstated assumptions about the *purpose* of policing which rapidly began to be reflected in the way the service was managed. The implications of this are taken up in our final chapter but the way in which this occurred needs describing here.

The key *external* elements of the current MPS performance management regime are the Home Secretary's annually set Key Objectives, the Audit Commission's Best Value Performance Indicators and the performance indicators (PIs) used by HMIC. The Home Secretary's powers to set objectives were established by the Police and Magistrates Courts Act 1994. Initially these were specific and focused on crime categories. Towards the end of the 1990s they began to broaden out. In 1998–99, for example, they covered young offenders, drug-related crime, violence, burglary, response to emergency calls and crime reduction by the CDA partnerships. The priorities were then reduced in number, simplified, and generalised further. In 2000–01 they were to:

- reduce problems of crime and disorder in partnership with local authorities, other local agencies and the public; and

- increase trust and confidence in the police, especially among minority ethnic communities.

This retreat from specificity was triggered in part by a recognition that 'micro-management' by *central* government was incompatible with robust priority-setting

---

[6] Sir Richard Mayne is credited with this, as the first Commissioner of the MPS, but it is equally likely that the formulation was that of his co-Commissioner, Sir Charles Rowan, who jointly authored the *General Instruction Book* for the service when it was set up in 1829.

by *local* crime-reduction partnerships. However, this development was offset by the development by the Audit Commission of suites of increasingly elaborate PIs, including the 38 Best Value Performance Indicators (BVPIs), which were put into place in April 2000.

By the time of our study, the Home Secretary's objective-setting in the 1990s and the Audit Commission's PIs had set the basic framework of the performance management regimes of all police forces in England and Wales. Local policing plans were agreed by police authorities (as required by the Police and Magistrates' Courts Act 1994) and the performance targets set within individual forces followed their lead. The decision in 2001 effectively to bypass senior managers at force level by shifting the focus of HMIC inspections to the level of individual BCUs (Basic Command Units) also suggests a continuing tendency towards centralisation. And, while there are advantages in the fact that London boroughs will be inspected individually in future, there is a danger the comparisons made between them will not compare like with like.[7]

The intentions behind these initiatives were to drive up police performance, to improve value for money and to reduce crime. However, they had also begun to have some unintended consequences. First, the technical and unexciting nature of these performance management systems masked the fact they pre-empted political debate about the functions of policing, and the relative priorities that should be accorded to these. At national level political debate about 'law and order' was so intense and so populist in the mid-1990s that only the most self-destructive politician would challenge the crime focus of the Home Office objectives (see Roberts *et al* in press for a discussion). At local level, other members of crime-reduction partnerships were similarly feeling the pinch of managerialist regimes on the delivery of their own services, so both the police and their partners were pulled in two directions. There was an inherent tension between the imperatives of meeting the targets set for their own service and the expectation they would give priority to pooling their resources around mutual aims required by partnership working. Furthermore, these agency-specific performance measures could imperceptibly produce a shift in emphasis of the functions of individual agencies, which was likely to have implications, in turn, for their role within the partnership. In the case of the police, the effect was to force them into a crime-fighting straitjacket.

There were other, equally significant, unintended consequences. Middle managers – borough commanders and their immediate subordinates – found themselves squeezed between centrally set priorities, on the one hand, and local needs and locally expressed priorities on the other. Meanwhile, managers centrally saw themselves as having to hold the ring between the need for cohesion across the whole of the MPS and accountability for its performance on the one hand, and against the pull towards localisation on the other. Furthermore, boroughs were required to pursue crime-reduction targets that had been arbitrarily set in the absence of any firm knowledge about the means by which they could be achieved.[8]

---

[7] Comparisons will be made between 'families' of BCUs which were originally constructed by the Home Office largely on the basis of 1991 census data. The grouping of London boroughs (Povey *et al* 2001) is in many respects significantly at odds with those in our borough profiles (based on current DETR deprivation scores). It also varies considerably from those used by the MPS as the basis for resource allocation (based on a combination of levels of recorded crime and deprivation scores).

[8] We heard numerous reference to local commanders being called by senior staff at New Scotland Yard to account for week-on-week fluctuations in recorded crime figures.

This gave local managers heavy responsibility but very little power over how they discharged it, and this further undermined them in the eyes of the staff on whom they had to rely for delivering these objectives (see Chapter 9).

Growing public expectations

In addition to the impact of falling police performance in lowering public confidence, however, consideration needs to be given to the likelihood that public expectations of the police have also changed. More specifically, if they have risen at a time when police performance has objectively been falling, this will further exacerbate the loss of confidence.

Since the Scarman report in particular, the MPS had been under pressure to improve the quality of its dealings with the public, and this pressure redoubled with the publication of the Macpherson report. Despite the wide range of initiatives taken by the MPS since 1981 and the further intensification of these efforts since 1999, it is equally plausible that these have been outstripped by the rise in public expectations of the police over the last two decades.

When the Conservative administration came to power in 1979, improving the performance of public services was a priority. The favoured solution was to inject the disciplines of the market place into the public sector, at the same time as increasing choice over the providers of these services.[9] Whilst the primary rationale was that competition would ensure both quality and economy, implicit in the raft of reform policies was the idea that the user of public services was a *consumer* and often the arbiter of public service quality. By the end of the decade, John Major had launched the Citizens' Charter, followed in 1990 by the Victims' Charter. By implication, the public was being encouraged to expect the same responsiveness from public services they could buy from the private sector. And, as Chapter 2 highlighted, the public has, over this period, increasingly opted for services supplied through quasi-private or private arrangements rather than through the traditional public provider. Education and health are obvious examples, but reference has already been made to the growth of private security also.

While it is uncertain that they rate the service they receive from any of these other sources more highly than that of the traditional police, what is clear is that many have a highly visible public presence – whether as security staff in stores and the shopping malls that have sprung up over the period or in policing the night-time economy.[10] This high visibility of alternative sources of policing may strongly reinforce perceptions of the increasing invisibility of the traditional, public service and increase dissatisfaction as a result.

Irrespective of whether and to what extent the fall in confidence in the police reflects rising expectations, it presents a challenge to the service, since confidence in the police, and public satisfaction in their dealings with the police, are the cornerstones of police legitimacy. Without legitimacy the police lose both authority and the

---

[9] This was achieved in a variety of ways from compulsory competitive tendering and market testing to forms of deregulation, fiscal encouragement for private provision and the selling off of parts of some services.
[10] The point is tellingly illustrated by Hobbs *et al* (2001): 'Manchester city centre now attracts an average of 75,000 people on Friday and Saturday evenings. Approximately 30 officers are normally engaged on public order duty at these times, whilst the crowds are simultaneously controlled by almost 1,000 bouncers.'

co-operation of the public in reporting crime and providing the further information on which successful detection and prosecution depend. Without these their job becomes impossible.

Conflicting demands

Finally, there is an argument that there are in-built limits to the extent to which the police can become more responsive. The commonalities of what people wanted from the police were more striking than the differences, as Chapter 3 described. And as Chapter 5 discussed, there is also a substantial overlap between police users and the suspect/offender populations. However, where individuals or groups have conflicting expectations of the police, our research tends to confirm that improving satisfaction can be a 'zero-sum game'.

For example, older people tend to regard groups of youths hanging around on the streets as a threat and a problem, and young people feel needlessly picked on when the police stop and question them or move them on. Within the same local community the former create pressures on the police to take action against the latter. Equally, many of our focus group members in deprived areas thought the lion's share of resources went to more affluent areas; yet – perhaps more plausibly – more affluent respondents thought their areas were stripped of police to cover high-crime areas.

Whatever the reality, the *perception* within our focus groups was widespread that other groups – whether defined by age, geography or ethnicity – were more privileged than their own, and this sense was strongest in relation to ethnicity. Not only did people from minority groups feel the police over-policed visible minority groups, many white respondents thought the reverse.

Not surprisingly, it was in the deprived parts of Boroughs B and C that this sense of other groups benefiting was strongest. Over-stretched response officers were increasingly dealing with crimes and disturbances involving people from different social and ethnic backgrounds in what many saw as a 'no-win' situation. Whatever action they took (or did not take), as Chapter 7 has illustrated, they were seen by one group or the other (and sometimes both) as taking sides against them.

Meanwhile, though, demands on the police from the public and from other local agencies compete for resources with the increasing demands also being made on them by central government and other national bodies. Their impact is described in more detail in the context of the internal organisational issues covered in the next chapter.

Summary of chapter

The reasons why Londoners find their police less responsive, less visible and less accessible than they want include a number of factors that are not directly in the control of the service. These fall broadly under two headings:

An increase in some sorts of demand at a time of falling resources.
Despite the downward trend in crime overall and an apparent fall in public demand, public expectations of the service may have grown. Meanwhile, the demand from other sources has increased, including from other local agencies. At the same time, MPS resources have shrunk slightly in real terms since the mid-1990s and this has been exacerbated by problems of recruitment and retention of police officers, in particular among support staff. These problems were particularly acute at the time of our study.

An increase in the specific demands of central government and other national bodies.
Increased accountability and closer scrutiny of police performance since the early 1980s, while essential, have created their own demands. And the more recent extension of public sector managerialism has added significantly to these demands, along with the requirements of partnership working. These developments have also had important implications for the deployment of the more limited resources available.

Chapter 9: Internal Organisation and Responsive Policing

The previous chapter aimed to analyse how factors *external* to the Metropolitan Police (MPS) have constrained its ability to achieve a more responsive style of policing. This chapter considers a number of additional factors our research identified as undermining officers' performance in their day-to-day delivery of the service Londoners want. They may broadly be described as *internal*, but some are largely determined by the external factors described in the previous chapter. They fall under five headings:

1. Over-centralised decision-making.
2. The impact of quantitative performance management.
3. Increasing specialisation of function and diffusion of responsibility.
4. Poor management.
5. Demoralised staff.

Most of the evidence comes from our fieldwork and, in particular, from interviews and focus groups with police officers and civil staff. Many of the issues this highlighted were also identified in the MPS's own survey of staff in 2000[1] but they have been widely documented elsewhere in research (Fielding 1995; Morgan and Newburn 1997; Reiner 2000; Fielding 2002) and also in the Operational Policing Review mounted collectively by the Association of Chief Police Offices (ACPO), the Police Federation and the Superintendents' Association in 1990 and, most recently, the study *Diary of a Police Officer* (PA Consulting 2001). Importantly, a large number were already described in Smith's original study in the early 1980s.

Centralised decision-making

Irrespective of any differences in their hierarchical structures, the sheer size of the MPS relative to other forces can create a greater sense of distance between those at the top and those in the layers below them. But the MPS tends also to devolve resource management only in a very limited way. At the time of fieldwork, borough commanders managed considerable budgets but the vast majority of this was committed to staffing, and the proportion to be allocated for different purposes was largely established centrally. That is, despite their responsibility, they had direct control of only a small proportion of their budget, although the picture began to change shortly afterwards.[2]

If borough commanders had limited control over their resources, they had even less control over their policing priorities. In the previous chapter we discussed how the Home Secretary's objectives and the Audit Commission's performance indicators (PIs) constrained the Commissioner's own room for manoeuvre. This, in turn, had a knock-on effect to borough commanders. They faced an awesome array of targets and PIs before ever they came to add in the local priorities identified in the context

---

[1] The MPS kindly gave us access to the results of the survey, which replicate quantitatively many of our qualitative findings.
[2] Between the completion of our fieldwork and writing this report, some measures had been taken to devolve more control to boroughs.

of the Crime and Disorder Act 1998 (CDA) (see Chapter 2). In 1999–2000 the tally comprised:

- 9 MPS objectives derived from the Home Secretary's two objectives.

- 9 MPS Charter Targets.

- 29 Public Performance Indicators.

- 38 indicators relating to Best Value, which were due to come into force in April 2000.

In all three areas we studied, the demands of this performance management regime were creating a strong sense of overload among members of senior management teams (henceforth 'senior managers') faced with the number of issues they were supposed to treat as a matter of priority. This was not simply a matter of reconciling national, MPS and local objectives: additional issues would arise *ad hoc* which they were also told to treat as a matter of priority.[3] One described his job as 'Mission Impossible' and another summed up the views of many thus:

> I have to divide up my resources so that I'm able to deliver a service which is all things to all people and yet perform against some really stringent priorities – and the priorities we have are innumerable ... I have no problem with priorities; but the list is endless. You have to prioritise among your priorities and some things just drop off the end.

Borough commanders' limited freedom of action had clear implications for the Crime and Disorder Reduction Partnerships (CDRPs) established by the CDA. In the first place, there was only a very limited amount of money they could actually 'put on the table' in any negotiation between partners. Even more important, they had very little room for manoeuvre in agreeing priorities that deviated from those set centrally. Whilst they and their partners were under a statutory obligation to consult local people about policing priorities, the *key* priorities for borough commanders had been set before any local consultation was under way.[4] These were the criteria against which their performance would be judged within the MPS and on which the MPS would, itself, be judged against other forces. One senior manager vividly summed up some of the tensions this created. In his view, centrally set priorities limited the scope of local consultation from the outset and produced a distorted version of what people actually wanted from the service:

> Consultation consists of sending out a letter which gives them [local people] a list of, maybe ten crimes. We ask them which they think are the most important; and we know in advance what they're going to tell us. So then we say 'We're dealing with this as a priority because that's what the community tells us is important'. But we're not actually giving them much choice.

---

[3] One example early in the fieldwork was the upsurge of concern about an apparent rise in street crime in the capital which all commanders were required to treat as a priority even in areas where street crime was relatively low. Many felt they could not justify using resources for this purpose which were already inadequate to deal with other issues identified as local priorities.

[4] This was true both for the first round of consultation and strategy development in 1998–99 and for the second in 2001–02.

His view of what the public actually wanted corresponded remarkably closely with the views of members of the public presented in Chapter 3:

> They [local people] want community policing where they *know* their officers. They don't expect them to be on the streets 24 hours a day – they're realists – but they want to know and recognise the people that actually serve the community. They want that personal contact. They want to develop relationships. They want officers who know and understand their communities. So that's the first issue.

> They also want police to deal with quality of life issues … It's trivial stuff but it's the sort of thing that affects the quality of their lives; and it's the sort of thing we've had to disengage from. If they call us to an emergency, they want us to respond and respond quickly but we've had to wind down our resources on emergency response to put things in place proactively to deal with 'priority' crime. When they report a crime they don't *necessarily* expect us to solve it – again, they're realists – but they do want to be treated with dignity and respect, to have the time to listen to them. It's about the attitude of the investigator rather than the end result that's important to them.

> If we can achieve on *those* things they're not too worried about the 5 per cent reduction in burglary or robbery. Whereas we can put all our resources into those issues, get massive reductions and lots of Brownie points from those above us …but it doesn't matter a hoot to the community … We're not meeting their demands but we're achieving as far as the Service and the Government are concerned. And *we* have to manage both sets of demands but at the moment we're falling down that big hole in the middle – not satisfying anyone.

In short, senior managers had newly been given responsibility for delivering a police service at borough level to populations that were comparable in size with those of a small shire constabulary.[5] The problems of crime and disorder, though, were more complex than in shire counties and, usually, far more serious.[6] They were expected to deliver in a way that reflected what people locally wanted. So, by implication, priorities might vary from one area to another and, since the framework for delivery was agreed with local partners, this also implied mutual obligations between the police and local agencies. Yet this ran counter to the highly centralised traditions of Scotland Yard already identified in Smith's original report and which, in the intervening period, had been reinforced at the level above by the centralising thrust of central government.

The partnerships were therefore established in the context of a performance culture which judged individual organisations in relation to each other, against critertia which were centrally imposed and which placed a premium on what could be measured in the short term. The partnerships, by contrast, were premised on a collaborative, local approach to tackling problems that were often interrelated. This

---

[5] For example, Lincolnshire's budget for 1999–2000 was £70 million.
[6] The numbers of crimes per thousand population in urban areas tends to be much higher, but there are differences in the patterns within this. Although the rate of burglaries, for example, may be similar, crimes of violence tend to be much higher and so does criminal damage (see tables in *Criminal Statistics, England and Wales*, published annually by the Stationery Office).

was an approach that would pay off in the medium to long term. Meanwhile, though (as the previous chapter highlighted) it would inevitably take a while for the partnerships to bed down and to start to realise this potential.

Impact of quantitative performance management

One particular way in which present forms of performance measurement seemed at odds with the partnership approach was in the assumption that the impact of different initiatives could be measured discretely. For the success of partnership working depended on the effects of a range of approaches to problems that were inter-related and the result of these approaches might not be immediately apparent. This illustrated wider concerns that quantitative performance measurement was narrowing the focus of police activity in ways that might put long-term investment in police–community relations at risk. As one senior manager put it:

> Everything that can be valued can't necessarily be measured but we're now a police service that subscribes to the philosophy that [*only*] what gets counted gets done.

Many of our police respondents – at all ranks – saw this 'philosophy' as increasingly undermining the service's sense of purpose while reinforcing the divisions within it. Effort was increasingly focused on narrow categories of crime at the expense of other functions. Meanwhile the administrative burden it entailed was a further problem in its own right and is probably reflected in the finding from the 2000 staff survey that 70% of respondents agreed with the statement, 'I have to deal with too much bureaucracy to get my job done' (see further below).

Staff in focus groups felt they were being expected to meet a daunting variety of targets, some of which were attached to priorities that changed from one year to another, raising questions for some about the core purpose of policing.[7] Certainly many shared the view of the senior manager reported above that the performance measures by which Scotland Yard and central government judged them were not the criteria by which the public judged them. They did not match the demands placed on the police or what people wanted from the police service as a whole, nor did they reflect the ideals for which many had entered the service.

Specialisation and diffusion of responsibility

Historically, the British police have had a large non-specialist uniformed branch with first one and then two specialist functions – CID and traffic police. The last two decades, and the last five years in particular, have seen a growing tendency towards specialisation within the MPS and the diffusion of responsibility to a proliferation of units to deal with particular areas of work. These developments have been catalysed not only by the need for particular specialist skills (for example, with regard to fraud and computer crime) but also to dedicate effort to issues identified as organisational priorities.

The Community Safety Units (CSUs) described in Chapter 2 are just one example of the move to specialisation in response to political developments and their work is particularly relevant to this study. But our three case-study sites also had specialist units dedicated not only to partnership work but to burglary, robbery and auto crime. Meanwhile, local staff had also to be allocated to the Youth Offending Teams.

---

[7] One respondent referred to a 'crisis of identity'.

The increased investment in local crime analysis was also making demands on the available resources, and the need to strengthen the Area Major Incident Teams (AMITs) also had to be met from the same pool.

Response team officers in all three areas referred to a marked drop in their response capacity which they associated with the move to borough-based policing. Yet personnel figures supplied by Scotland Yard did not show a significant fall in the numbers of officers at borough level 'available for normal duties'. It would appear, therefore, that the move to borough as such was not the main cause but the fact that this coincided with the increased need to staff special posts and units.

Although in theory some of these units were supposed to relieve some of the pressures on response teams, the latter rather than the former provided the pool of resources from which 'abstractions' were made when there were shortages or emergency elsewhere.[8] Many complained of pressure to fill in on rest days (or having rotas changed without notice). Those in the high-crime areas could, to a limited degree, be compensated financially for working overtime[9] but, elsewhere, moral pressure was often the only lever. Ironically – as subsequent focus groups with staff from central units within the MPS brought out – the specialist units themselves often felt similarly stretched and overloaded. And one senior manager reported that his officers were having to deal with cases that should properly have been handled as major incidents but the AMIT had no capacity to deal with them.

Nonetheless, the way this was seen by officers on response teams has contributed significantly to low morale and tended to reinforce divisiveness. As one PC put it:

> Unfortunately, as we all know, we are the ones that make the job work, we are the ones that make a decision in the blink of an eye and will either be praised for it or heavily criticised for it. However, there are a number of people that don't actually respect the work that we do, and if it's not worthy for them to deal with, they'll bounce it back ... [W]e're not supposed to deal with prolonged investigations of crime. However, everyone around this table probably has, in fact, an ongoing investigation that they are dealing with in between dealing with emergency response calls that they shouldn't be dealing with. Because somebody, somewhere has decided: 'I'm not getting into this pile of shit, let him deal with it. *He* reported it: let's bounce it back to him.' And that is the mentality you'll get from divisional CID [and] from the specialist units.

His perception was shared more widely within the service than he and his colleagues seemed to appreciate. One senior manager said:

> They carry huge responsibilities: they're responsible for 60 per cent of all arrests and they're our first point of contact between the police and the public – but they're not treated as adults. They're messed about more than any other officers: they're abstracted to other duties without any choice; they have their leave cancelled at a moment's notice. But the rest

---

8 The first pool of PCs to be plundered were usually community beat officers, but these were far less numerous than officers on response teams.

9 One manager in Borough C, however, said that many of his officers had reached the point where they were no longer prepared to do this because of the strain on their families, adding 'When they won't even work overtime any more, you know it's serious'.

of us are ancillary to the Earlies, Lates and Nights [i.e. officers on the three shifts]. You can't shut down 24 hour response: it's core policing.

The best example of both pros and cons of specialisation is probably provided by CSUs. These achieved rapid success in the sense that, within a year of their formation, they had attracted such a large number of cases that the Her Majesty's Inspectorate of Constabulary (HMIC) report on community and race relations in the MPS was warning of the danger of overload. They probably played a crucial role in improving the MPS's capture of and response to racist incidents in particular, as well as domestic violence and homophobic incidents. However, the same inspection also identified problems arising from this specialisation amongst the non-specialist staff:

> The view was widespread that the rationale behind the definition of racist incidents and the prescriptive approach to their recording was to provide a preferential service to minority ethnic communities thereby prejudicing the policing needs of the rest of society (Home Office 2000).

This meant that response teams had not fully 'bought in' to the new priority attached to the types of crimes and related incidents that were now being handled with greater sensitivity by the CSUs. At the same time, according to CSU officers, they were only too ready to pass racist incidents on to the CSU and to get rid of work which post-Macpherson had become difficult, risky and demanding, for a combination of reasons. These included the sensitivities following the Macpherson report and the MPS policy of enhanced follow-up in racist incident cases.[10]

Although the work of the CSUs was highly regarded by our respondents in relevant local agencies, officers working in them had no illusions about the ambivalence of some colleagues. They understood this but they were also aware of the damage that might already have been done by the initial response to an incident, if only because of the general pressures which produced a poor service for many victims generally. One talked about having to 'brush down' many of the victims they finally got to see: 'It doesn't matter how well we treat the victims subsequently, they won't forget how they were dealt with initially.'

While the fieldwork was underway new instructions were issued to protect the CSUs from their expanding workloads. Henceforth, they were to deal only with the more serious incidents, the less serious being handled by response teams.[11] Officers had just got used to being able to get rid of these incidents to the CSUs and many had been relieved to do so. Now the majority of these cases were being returned to the core teams, adding to their workload, and this did not appear to bode well for the quality of the service's response to racist incidents in the future.

So the case of the CSUs highlights the wider dilemmas in the trade-off between the improvements which can be achieved through specialisation and the potentially

---

[10] The facility to refer incidents to the CSU had effectively removed the disincentive to record incidents as racist. In the wake of Macpherson, some felt it was safer to 'cover their backs' by inferring a racist element in ambiguous cases and, in some instances, it was perceived that officers passed on incidents which were simply interracial. These factors may help to explain the increase of 211% in recorded racist incidents from the beginning of April 1999 to the end of March 2000.
[11] The majority of these will include cases that are better described as racially *aggravated*, rather than racially *motivated* (see FitzGerald and Hale 1996; Clancy *et al* 2001; FitzGerald 2001).

negative consequences for the generality of service delivery. In particular, specialist units inevitably tend to recruit from non-specialist resources, thereby tending to cream off the better or more experienced staff from the pool of generalist officers. At the same time, they also tend to detract from the status of generalist work, which by implication lacks importance relative to work in specific areas of responsibility.[12]

Additionally, as the CSU experience tended to suggest, the approaches developed in these units and some of the skills and knowledge acquired by their staff might be relevant more widely. However, in the absence of any systematic effort to diffuse them throughout the organisation, they were unlikely to impact on the quality of policing as experienced by the public at large. Rather, the additional strains they imposed on generalist staff might actually detract from the service. Meanwhile, these generalist staff retain an important 'gate-keeping' function in determining which members of the public who called on the police for help got the benefit of this improved quality of service.

Poor management

Concerns about management were numerous and many echoed the findings of the PSI study nearly 20 years previously. They often related to issues of career development but it was also apparent that several factors impeded the ability of senior managers in boroughs to provide the style and consistency of leadership they felt was needed.

Career development

A number of criticisms related to the initial training recruits received in terms of how well it equipped them for what they would face on the streets. The service was criticised for failing to value the skills and experience of mature entrants but initial training was also seen as unrealistic in failing to prepare officers in particular for the confrontational situations they would have to deal with:

> *PC 1:*
> Yes, we did role play at Hendon and I can still remember one now. [The instructions to the person playing the suspect were:] 'Don't be rough – and don't be too abusive in what you say.' [But] What you need is … You need somebody who's going to scream and shout at you, eff and blind at you, threaten violence towards you and everything else.

Once officers were qualified, there was considerable further criticism of the provision available for their career development. The abolition of the system of tenure[13] seemed almost universally to be welcomed, but there were some concerns that an alternative was required. Officers wanted to have choices about whether to stay in their jobs or to move, but many would welcome the chance to acquire a range of experience of different types of policing – including (and perhaps especially) those who were not seeking or did not expect promotion.

---

[12] This observation was strongly endorsed in focus groups with central staff from different units, many of whom experienced similar frustrations and pressures as their non-specialist colleagues at borough level. Most, though, acknowledged that their work was still more rewarding because its purpose was clear, it provided more opportunity to get results and it commanded more respect within the service.

[13] The term 'tenure' refers to the bar on officers spending more than a certain length of time in a particular job. Once this point was reached, they had to move into another area of work, regardless of their own preference. Most focus groups contained at least one such officer who had come into post in these circumstances, including one manager in particular who appeared to be seriously distressed and felt quite incapable of meeting his new responsibilities.

More specifically, though, the system of staff appraisal represented a systematic approach to ensuring career development, but it did not appear to function. Civil staff were more likely to go through the regular cycle of staff appraisal than police officers, largely because the former alone were eligible for performance-related pay.[14] Officers, though, did not always get reports on a regular basis but would ask for them if they were applying for promotion. From the accounts they gave, the system even then was less than satisfactory for a number of reasons. Reports were often signed off by a manager who hardly knew the individual and, in any case, the onus was on the individual to provide his or her own 'evidence' of his or her eligibility for promotion. They commonly complained that more weight attached to *what* they had done (commonly described as a 'tick-box' approach) than *how* they had done it. That is, there was little or no informed, independent assessment of their real skills and ability.[15]

At more senior levels, it was pointed out that to be eligible for promotion could require 'evidence' of ability to manage change and this was perceived as creating perverse incentives for more senior officers to generate change for its own sake. More generally, though, officers who did not actively seek promotion felt they were viewed as odd, second rate or, possibly, to some degree insufficiently committed in terms of the cultural norms of the service. This in turn tended further to compound the cynicism of the junior ranks towards senior officers whom many saw as only being interested in 'climbing the greasy pole'.

At the same time, training was often perceived as inadequate to equip officers to meet their responsibilities. They were having to get to grips with an increasing volume of legislation but often had to rely on distance-learning packages, while the need to cover for staff shortages encroached on notional 'training days'. Many felt ill-equipped for the new responsibilities they acquired on promotion – whether for personnel or financial management. And a common complaint was that there was no formal system for familiarising officers with their new environment when they transferred to a different borough. There was a deeply felt need to find out 'how the ground ticks' and, in particular, to be adequately briefed about the different communities in the area.

Constraints on managers
Whether or not as a result of the issues in career development cited above, there appears to be a very high rate of turnover among senior officers. All the three commanders who were in post in our case-study sites at the beginning of the fieldwork period had moved on within the year. In two cases they had initially been seconded to MPS-wide roles and their deputies filled in during months of uncertainty until it was confirmed their predecessors would not return. In the third case, the deputies themselves had already been moved and the commander had chosen to defer a personal opportunity for career development for a year to avoid further disruption yet he, too, was transferred before he could see the year through. The good working relationships such officers had established locally exacerbated the frustration of other local agencies and community representatives with these changes.

---

[14] They complained, however, that in practice almost everyone got the same mark since there was insufficient money for the performance-related pay system to work.
[15] One specific, relevant example was that competence in handling 'diversity' had recently become a criterion for promotion. Several dedicated staff in the CSU had noted an increase in applications from people who appeared to be more interested in ticking the 'diversity' box than in the type of work involved.

A further problem, though, was that borough commanders and other members of borough senior management teams felt especially constrained in the management of their staff for a number of reasons. In part this reflects a common pattern of negative systems of control found in most police forces in the industrialised world (see Wilson 1968, for an early discussion, and Kelling 1999 for a more recent one). In 1983 Smith (Vol. 4: 343) commented that supervision of officers in the MPS tended to be negative:

> There is far more emphasis on criticising officers when things have gone wrong than on encouraging or rewarding officers when they have gone well.

He also referred to an authoritarian style of management in the MPS which was based on a military model. We too were given many examples of this and were conscious that this ethos was at odds with (and, by implication, inimical to) expecting junior officers to avoid taking an authoritarian approach in their own dealings with people in situations where they had a high degree of autonomy and were entrusted with considerable discretion. Ironically, many officers of all ranks resented this tradition, but senior managers we spoke to also felt present circumstances reinforced the problem. They had few rewards to offer. The move to borough-based policing had made them more remote from their staff. And this was compounded by the distractions of the external pressures on them.

One senior officer summed up their frustrations with regard to rewards as follows:

> Sticks are dead easy. Discipline codes and procedures – it's all laid down. Everyone knows a stick when it's thrown at them; but what carrots do I have? Tangible carrots? ... I can say 'Thank you'. I can say 'If you arrest the right people at the right time in the right area, you may get overtime'. (Money talks, there's no doubt about it.) I can employ those officers on overtime to look at particular problems – but that's as against my budget constraints. I can do very little else that makes very much difference to that officer's working life.

His counterpart in another area confided he was trying work out a system to ensure both that he regularly singled out for praise *all* the officers who merited recognition *and* that he could remember (when he met them afterwards) whom he had praised for what. Senior managers no longer knew officers individually. This further limited their ability to supervise them adequately and, at the same time, was bad for staff morale.

Finally, senior managers at borough level were simply very stretched by growing demands on their time. The three main sources have already been discussed in other contexts. They were: factors relating to performance management; the demands of building and maintaining the Crime and Disorder Reduction Partnerships; and the management of human and other resources in the move to borough-based policing.

Staff morale

The issues discussed above were evidently lowering staff morale among senior managers but this was mirrored among more junior staff also in ways that appeared further to reinforce the gulf between the two. And findings from the MPS staff survey conducted in 2000 appeared to confirm this picture. While occupational cynicism is not particular to the police, it is widely viewed as a distinguishing feature of the service,[16] and we had expected to uncover a degree of disaffection *within* the organisation, in addition to the scepticism about the public described in the previous chapter. However, the intensity of these views came as a surprise. Staff in focus groups felt unsupported by their senior managers, under-rewarded and under-resourced.

Amongst our focus groups with officers and sergeants there was little appreciation of the degree to which some of their own managers were concerned about the increasing gulf between them. They simply believed that senior managers – whether at borough level or at Scotland Yard – had lost touch with the real nature of the job and the terms in which this was expressed to us were uncompromising. The following two quotations from constables illustrate the intensity of the feeling that they did not share the same objectives:

> I think in the Met it would be a refreshing change if the senior management and the PCs on the ground all were working towards the same thing.

> …what would make a difference is if actually somebody stuck up for us once in a while. [If] the senior management team said: 'No – my police officers are good (or this person is really good) at their job' and you felt defended and you didn't feel like you were just being … [That] you weren't drowning and they weren't just sticking their foot on your head. What would make it even more rewarding is if the senior management actually turned round and said to the government: 'No. We are not going to do what you want to make you look good. We are going to do what is best for the people of London.'

There was a strong undercurrent of resentment among the junior ranks that senior managers were not only unaware of the pressures they faced: they were seen as *actively* unsupportive and determined to catch people out even in honest mistakes, and some of this feeling was evident at middle-manager level also. The discipline system was also regarded as capriciously draconian.[17] Meanwhile, many sergeants (and some inspectors) appeared to feel unsupported by the ranks above them in general and specifically to feel they could not turn to line managers to discuss any problem in their team.[18] They empathised with junior officers' frustrations and often shared their sense of alienation.

Above all, it was felt that senior managers would not support them even where they were the subject of a malicious complaint. Instead they might, on occasion, reach a

---

[16] See, for example, the discussion in Reiner (2000: 90), who describes police cynicism as 'the Janus face of commitment' (op. cit. p. 90).
[17] During the course of the fieldwork there was considerable publicity about the case of a constable who was dismissed for calling a suspect a 'black bastard'. At the same time, a case came to our attention of a woman officer who had been off work with nervous stress for several months after being sexually assaulted by a colleague who had simply been allowed to resign.
[18] One or two implied that admitting they had a problem at all might be held against them. This was confirmed by a senior officer who thought the response would be: 'It's *your* problem – what are you going to do about it?' He added: 'And that's dangerous. It's terribly dangerous.'

settlement with the complainant in preference to securing justice for the officer accused because the cost of legal action was too high to defend all the defensible cases.

Senior managers' concerns about their inability to reward good work were well placed. Only middle managers or junior officers who personally knew senior managers (possibly because they had worked with them earlier in their careers) seemed to appreciate their concerns, though. For the most part, their sense of alienation from senior managers was such that even the conscious efforts of the latter to bridge the gap might rebound. Thus, one commander tried to attend parades personally to commend people for good work. Yet it became apparent from PCs in a focus group that they saw this as patronising, both because he did not know the individuals concerned and because he was treating as exceptional what most of them did routinely – but without recognition.

In addition to the universal complaint about insufficient staff numbers, there were two other main complaints about the lack of resources. One was that officers, in their view, were required to produce increasing amounts of management information using IT systems with decreasing capacity and reliability. Officers in all three boroughs spontaneously complained about their computer systems. Part of the dissatisfaction related to the technical inadequacy of the IT systems themselves,[19] although a further problem was that staff were often poorly equipped to use them. It also related to the time-consuming business of providing detailed information that was of no obvious relevance to their immediate job:

> *Community PC*:
> I'd love to be able to come on duty and straight away look at a piece of paper that tells me what I need to know and I can walk out on the street. But I can't: I come on duty now – I have to log on to four different computer systems; I have to spend an hour self-tasking, self-briefing…

> *Response team PCs*:
> *PC 1*: The CRIS report … I mean we used to do *a* sheet that you could take out with you on the streets and you could fill it in as you spoke to somebody. And it'd be done certainly, well, as long as you needed to get the information from the person. That's how long it took you to do a crime report 'cause you'd write most of the information out as you had it. Now we come back and it takes half an hour to 45 minutes to put on most CRIS reports I would suggest; and about half of that time is taken up with filling in the statistics sections on it. Which is, to be honest, of no use to us. Mostly it's not even of any use to the police service – it goes away to the Home Office.

> *PC 2*: The problem is the more the job's gone IT mad, it's made it more difficult for officers on teams to do the job. Because you come in, and whereas a simple arrest would only take two hours you're there for like

---

[19] We are obviously not in a position to mount a technical assessment. However, one PC contrasted their system with another urban area where the identity of people coming into custody could be checked within two hours by scanning in their fingerprints. A colleague claimed that in a neighbouring provincial force: 'you put information in [only] once and you can search on: crime, the control room; the local intelligence; everything else. And it all links up!'

four and half hours 'cause you're on the computer, and then the system crashes.

In a different area, another response team PC described eight or nine people queuing up at the end of a shift to enter crime reports on two machines. Another believed that the different systems in use had developed to serve primarily as 'management tools' while a senior officer also suggested that at least part of the problem had arisen because systems that were originally intended for operational purposes were now being used to generate management information. By implication this could contaminate the quality of the crime-related data, since officers knew they were providing information that might be used to measure their own performance.

The other main complaint about resources related to vehicles, and our team had first-hand evidence of the former on several occasions when they had arranged to observe patrols but it was uncertain whether a vehicle would actually be available for them to go out in. One team had only acquired a car by virtue of a successful bid to the Home Office, and many officers complained about the time it took to get problems fixed, as well as the difficulty of getting simple parts (such as light bulbs) and the very variable quality of repairs.[20]

The same old story?

There were a number of specific reasons for the problem of morale at the time of the fieldwork, and some (especially those associated with the immediate aftermath of major organisational change) were likely to resolve themselves in time. Some were amenable to interventions that have been developed since the study was undertaken, although others reflected the external factors described in the previous chapter over which the service itself has little control. Of those internal to the service, though, some appear to be so intractable they might easily be construed as endemic to the culture of the organisation. They were already identified in Smith's study of police–community relations and again at the end of the 1980s in a report specifically on the internal organisation of the service (Wolff Olins 1988). The latter included detailed findings about the interplay between institutional factors, service delivery and public perceptions which echoed Smith and these, in turn, chime with our own observations over 10 years later. Wolff Olins' conclusions included the view that, for the MPS to be more effective, it must:

1. feel more united – be clearer about what it is there for;
2. improve leadership as well as management systems;
3. adopt a positive attitude towards the concept of service;
4. become less defensive and isolated; and
5. improve its communication techniques both internally and to the world outside.

Our study did, however, see significant improvements since the Policy Studies Institute (PSI) study was undertaken. In particular, officers referred to much higher standards of professionalism in the service, and these tend to be borne out independently by our survey findings. Contrary to the norms that prevailed in the 1980s, it was now widely perceived that officers were no longer prepared to cover for colleagues who let them down, as this focus group discussion illustrates:

---

[20] Often they did their own running repairs (as we observed ourselves on one occasion) – sometimes by cannibalising parts from others' vehicles.

Manager 1:

The other change I've noticed since I've been down here is that for the first time in the last ten years … It never happened before.. There used to be a culture, if there was a problem you would *deal* with it: you would never tell your skipper or your inspector … But now it's the opposite way round: people come to you and it's: 'He's not performing properly' … And they *do* … People come to you because they are proud of their own performance and their professional standards; and when [other] people don't come up to it, they'll let you know – but they never used to.

Manager 2:

I have had a few constables come to me and say that they have witnessed someone being assaulted; and that would never have happened twenty years ago – never, ever. They wouldn't report it … Not only that, in fact it would be the opposite: not only would they not report it, but the person would be kind of ostracised for doing it by their peers, but they'd go to some lengths to cover it up so that it wouldn't be discovered. That is not the case now. It's totally the opposite.

One important reflection of this change is that, while Smith found racist attitudes among officers to be widespread and expressed openly, we did not witness any. This is not to say they no longer existed but the contrast was, none the less, marked and must be regarded as significant.

Yet many of the endemic problems identified by Smith remained.[21] And there is still strong resonance in Wolff Olins' (1988) observation that:

> … a profound cultural change … must accompany and reinforce managerial change … Like most large organisations the Met has traditionally tackled change in smallish digestible chunks. Each innovation has been introduced separately. For the most part change in one area and activity has not been overtly linked with change in another. The method has nevertheless brought about a substantial administrative and organisational progress. Over the last few years, of course, the administration and organisational changes have been very big. They have been introduced quickly and over a very short timescale.

> The Met now needs cultural change which will support the recent organisational changes and establish a clear collective vision.

This suggests we were not simply observing the MPS going through a temporary bad patch. Rather, the recommendations of the Wolff Olins' report and, in particular, the Plus programme which developed from it do not appear to have taken root and produced the cultural change and clear collective vision which still appear to elude the service. The reasons for this are likely to be a combination of the external and internal constraints described in this and the previous chapter.

---

[21] For example – observing that these findings are by no means new – he characterises 'the main defects in the present structure as excessive centralisation, a long chain of command, diffusion of responsibility and instability of senior management teams.' (op. cit. p. 352)

Summary of chapter

The service delivered by the MPS is also adversely affected by problems within the organisation. These can be summarised as follows:

- Over-centralisation.

- The demands of meeting quantitative performance management.

- The fragmentation of resources driven by the need to achieve in discrete areas of work.

- Poor management.

- The cumulative impact of all these on the morale of the staff who carry the main burden of responsibility for day-to-day contact with the public.

Many of these result directly from or have been significantly exacerbated by the pressures of managerialism. But many also are deep rooted. They were already identified by Smith's study nearly 20 years ago and have eluded subsequent attempts at reform.

Chapter 10: Conclusions

This report has presented the main findings from the Policing for London Study (PFLS). The aims of the study were to assess what Londoners wanted of their police at the start of the twenty-first century, what their sources of satisfaction and dissatisfaction were, and to consider ways of bridging the gap between expectations and reality. Its frame of reference has been the 20-year period since the Policy Studies Institute (PSI) undertook a similar study in 1981 (Small 1983; Smith 1983a, 1983b; Smith and Gray 1983). Its main focus is the role of the police in the day-to-day lives of the increasingly diverse population of the capital.

The study's central concern with the service's responsiveness to the needs of Londoners rests on the assumption that the police cannot effectively tackle crime without the support of the public. Securing public trust and confidence is undoubtedly more difficult in large urban areas, and this is reflected in the variation in detection rates between forces which consistently tend to be higher in smaller forces away from the main conurbations.[1] The Metropolitan Police (MPS), in particular, faces additional challenges on account of its sheer size and the particular responsibilities of policing the capital. But this makes it no less important to invest in maximising people's willingness to co-operate with the police and to ensure that co-operation is sustained.

This final chapter summarises our conclusions about the picture that emerges from our study, the reasons for the picture, the issues this poses and what will be needed to address them.

Change and continuity over 20 years

The issues then…
The PSI study was undertaken against the backdrop of an intense debate about policing in general and the policing of the increasingly diverse population of London in particular (see, for example, Hall *et al.* 1978). By the time it was published the disturbances of 1981 had further heightened the debate. And issues about the nature of policing were central to the Scarman report (1981), which highlighted the tensions between the police's role in enforcing the law and keeping the peace. In particular, the report (para. 8.14) referred to

> … [the] dilemma [which] is as simple to state as it was, and remains, difficult to resolve: how to cope with a rising level of crime – and particularly of street robbery ('mugging') – while retaining the confidence of all sections of the community, especially the ethnic minority groups.

A recurrent theme in this debate was the demand for greater police accountability, both nationally and locally. A specific demand was that the MPS should no longer be answerable directly to the Home Secretary but, like other forces, be answerable to its own police authority.

---

[1] The average for all forces in England and Wales in the financial year 2000-01 was 24%. This rose to 29% without the main metropolitan forces, and the average for Welsh forces was 41%.

Lord Scarman gave primacy to the police's peace-keeping role as a prerequisite for improving public trust and confidence, and this was accepted at the time by the then Commissioner. There were major changes, which we discussed in Chapter 2, to improve scrutiny of policing, to strengthen accountability and to tackle discrimination. The MPS was in the forefront of many of these initiatives and these efforts had redoubled in the period immediately prior to our research, under the impetus of the Macpherson report of 1999.

... and now

By the time the present study began, crime overall had been falling for several years, although our research coincided with a dramatic rise in recorded street crime and London was at last about to get its own police authority. We found a service that, in the living memory of many officers who had joined at around the time of the previous study, *had* become more professional and more ethical in its methods. One significant reflection of this was that the overt expression of racial prejudice was evidently far less common for, by contrast with the previous study, we ourselves observed none at all.

Yet, despite all these developments, our study paints a picture which in some respects shows no change. Certainly the public appears to have seen no improvement in policing since 1981. Satisfaction amongst victims with the service they receive has fallen. Confidence in the effectiveness of police work has fallen. A smaller proportion believes that the MPS is free of malpractice – even if the proportion thinking malpractice is endemic has also fallen. The process of seeking help from the police itself appears to damage ratings of effectiveness.

Despite the fall in crime, officers responsible for the delivery of day-to-day policing had been increasingly stretched, and many of those we interviewed were seriously demoralised, not least because they believed the standard of service they provide to Londoners is unacceptably low. The detection rate for the MPS in the year 2000–01 was the lowest of any force, at 15%.

Confidence in the police has remained consistently much lower among some groups than others, including young people, those living in high-crime areas and some minority ethnic groups – in particular, black groups, Pakistanis and Bangladeshis. The study highlights the fact that these minority ethnic groups additionally tend to live in deprived high-crime areas and account for a large proportion of the youth population within them. This further compounds long-standing tensions with the black group in particular, while sections of the poorer Asian groups appear now to be expressing similar views about the police as the comparable generation of black young people 20 years earlier.

... and in the future?

The future population of the capital will be an increasingly varied mix of white people with ethnic origins in England, Ireland, Scotland and Wales, along with an increasingly diverse range of minority ethnic groups. In many areas no one group will be 'the majority' population and already much of the work of the police involves incidents within and between members of different minority groups. In these situations, the role of the police as peace-keepers becomes ever more important in securing social cohesion. At the same time the experiences and perceptions of the police which young people from different minorities take with them into adulthood will be critical in determining whether, in the future, the MPS polices London with the consent of the majority of its citizens.

Economic disparities within the London population are also set to become more exaggerated, and the London population may become more divided according to access to education, information technology and knowledge.[2] This poses challenges to the police: both the 'winners' – articulate, affluent, well educated – and the 'losers' in an increasingly competitive society are likely to become more demanding on police resources.

In other words the environment within which the police operate is becoming a more difficult and demanding one. The MPS needs to adapt to the changes if it is to retain the consent of Londoners. In considering what sort of adaptation is needed, we shall first consider what a more responsive style of policing would look like, and then examine what changes in the control of the police and what organisational changes are needed to bring this about.

Delivering more responsive policing: the issues

In arguing that the MPS needs to be more responsive to Londoners we are advocating approaches to policing which are designed to increase users' satisfaction, to reduce suspects' dissatisfaction, and to improve public confidence in police effectiveness and integrity. Steps to achieve this are not an 'optional extra' in policing policy. When several indices of public confidence all point in the same direction, they are essential.

Visible police presence

The one thing almost everyone wants is more bobbies on the beat, despite the evidence this is not an effective way of achieving short-term reductions in crime (see Sherman *et al.* 1997 for a review). There is nothing surprising in our finding that Londoners want visible, accessible foot patrols with a community focus. The PSI study found this in 1983, and many subsequent polls and surveys have pointed in the same direction. Nor is the crime-fighting focus in people's policing priorities unexpected. Policy has resolved the tensions between these two sets of findings in three main ways.

The first is to assume that people are clear about the goals that they want the police to achieve – crime reduction – but ignorant about the best ways of doing this. The policy solution most often chosen over the last two decades has been to give them what they need, rather than what they want – strategies designed to tackle crime, rather than 'bobbies on the beat'. Not surprisingly the call for visible, accessible patrols has continued. Our findings in Chapter 3 suggest that ignoring these calls has a high cost in lack of public confidence.

The second position has been to argue that, regardless of its immediate impact on crime, a visible police presence is necessary to provide public reassurance and to

---

[2] The main reason for thinking this is that the globalised economy creates pressures on governments both to deregulate the labour market and to pare down their welfare provision. It is far from clear whether this process is inexorable and inevitable, though inequality has increased in most industrialised countries over the last two decades (see Giddens 1998 and Hutton and Giddens 2000 for discussions).

reduce fear of crime. This has now become an orthodoxy, and statements of it can be found in the Association of Chief Police Officers (ACPO) policy papers (ACPO 2001), in recent Home Office proposals (Home Office 2001), and in the audits and crime strategies of many Crime and Disorder Reduction Partnerships (CDRPs). There is also some research support for the idea that foot patrols can make people feel safer (see Sherman *et al.* 1997 for a review). However, Chapter 3 casts some doubt on the idea that anxiety about crime is a problem in its own right, in need of urgent action: on most measures, 'fear of crime' has been falling in London.

The third position is that foot patrols provide a good medium through which to deliver responsive policing. Local visible foot patrols are in a good position to find out what local problems are, and they are well placed to find means of solving them. In our view this is probably the best way of conceptualising the patrol function.

It is also consistent with the views of our focus group and survey respondents. When they asked for more bobbies on the beat people in our focus groups did not always find it easy to put into words *why* they wanted an increased police presence. Those who did so made it clear that 'bobbies on the beat' was not an end in itself; nor did they have any illusion these officers would catch criminals red-handed. It was shorthand for articulating a more general demand for the police to *re-engage* with local people in a variety of ways – rather than meeting them *only* in the context of incidents of crime or disorder or of police-initiated consultation.

We have documented in Chapters 7 and 9 the sense of strain amongst response teams at borough levels. Police forces throughout the developed world share this sense of working at breaking point; as we have argued, it is *in part* an inevitable consequence of working in a demand-led service that is free at the point of delivery. However, there are reasons for thinking the MPS was under particular strain at the time our fieldwork was carried out. Its resources had shrunk in real terms. The shortfall in staffing was almost inevitably focused on frontline staff, and especially on uniformed patrol officers. Put simply, there were insufficient numbers of officers to deliver the quality of response that they – and their public – expected.

Reassurance policing?
We have suggested that there is more to a visible police presence than putting officers on the beat so that public anxieties about crime are dampened. Whilst policy statements about 'reassurance policing' emphasise the need to tackle crime and fear of crime in tandem, the implicit justification for it is that 'fear of crime' has become a problem in its own right, needlessly damaging people's quality of life.

If reassurance policing yields reductions in crime and disorder as well as reassurance, it is hard to see how it is differs from effective policing. If it *doesn't* yield these reductions, the case for it needs careful scrutiny. It is difficult to justify devoting limited police resources to policing activity that serves only to give people the *impression* they are safer from crime. If, on the other hand, the aim is to reduce anxiety in ways which are designed at the same time to have a real impact on crime and disorder, then the term sells the concept short: 'reassurance policing' may provide the wrong words for the right solution.

Policing style and deployment

We have suggested that visible patrol presence is not an alternative to targeted approaches to tackling crime and disorder. Rather, providing a more visible and accessible police presence should complement more targeted approaches. However, this must be done *strategically*. By this we mean there should be a clear understanding of the purpose in putting officers on the beat, and clear ways of achieving these ends.

People in our focus groups wanted the police to be more available and accessible in their own environments, for a variety of reasons. Some wanted some protection against threats to personal safety; others wanted the police to deal with less serious problems associated with nuisance and disorder. Others wanted the police to know their communities better, so that the public could keep them properly informed of problems relating to crime and disorder, and so that the police could be more sensitive and more accurate in the way they targeted their suspicion.

Only the first of these depends literally and exclusively on increasing the police presence on the street; there are various ways by which the other functions can be achieved. At the start of the twenty-first century, requiring that officers walk around their beat is not necessarily the best way of increasing accessibility. If there is a real commitment to make beat officers accessible to their local public, they need to be equipped with a mobile phone, a laptop computer and e-mail facilities. There is also a range of natural opportunities for improving information exchange. One senior officer, for example, said he found out far more community intelligence by regular liaison with local tenants groups than from formal police consultation meetings. And a murder inquiry in the course of the study vindicated the importance of investing in good sustained police work in schools (including primary schools). However, the police and public alike complained about cut-backs in this type of activity, but we also came across innovative new approaches that would serve this purpose, including variants on neighbourhood watch[3] and the presence of police officers at drop-in centres or one-stop shops shared with other agencies.[4]

Whether a visible *policing* presence can only be achieved by a visible *police* presence is something we are poorly placed to answer. There is no reason in principle why some of the functions that people expect of visible patrols cannot be discharged by auxiliaries or by staff from other agencies, such as the local council. The challenge will be in ensuring that they command sufficient authority to do their work effectively, and that means their authority needs to be underpinned by power. That in turn requires people of a particular calibre, who can be trusted to use their powers responsibly. The implication is that one cannot extend the 'police family' on the cheap.

Policing incivilities

One of the reasons why visible patrolling enjoys such support amongst the public is, in our view, that it illustrates a particular policing style in which order maintenance, or the policing of incivilities, is given more prominence, and more priority, than at present.

---

[3] One was called 'virtual neighbourhood watch' and was based on community networks which were not necessarily specific to particular physical neighbourhoods. Another was based on electronic networks using systems such as 'Ringmaster'.
[4] This, in turn, is a variation on the concept of 'reporting centres' where the police are available to receive crime reports away from police stations, including in premises used by community groups and organisations.

We saw in Chapter 3 that incivilities did not emerge high on the list of priority problems when 'stacked up' against crimes such as burglary and mugging. However, Londoners clearly did regard problems of rowdyism, vandalism, drug taking and drug selling and other incivilities as significantly more serious problems in 2000 than they did in the mid-1990s. We have argued in Chapters 8 and 9 that there has been a retreat from the policing of incivilities in London over the last decade. The reasons for this are partly to be found in the resource pressures experienced in the late 1990s and partly in the prioritisation of crime that resulted from the process of setting policing targets. The MPS has – perhaps temporarily – lost some of its capacity to respond effectively to low-level crime and disorder. We think there is a strong case for reversing this trend. It is very probably one of the factors leading to the reductions in public confidence that we charted in Chapter 6.

For all that remains to be understood about what drives crime up or down, we do know there is a correlation between low-level disorder and minor anti-social behaviour. And this is part of the reason why they are highly correlated with anxieties about crime as well (see, for example, Skogan 1990). We also know that offenders are, by and large, generalists rather than specialists, with careers that start in the early teens with petty delinquency and offending (Graham 1988; Graham and Bowling 1995; Farrington 1997; Flood-Page *et al* 2000). That is, there are complex inter-relationships between patterns of crime and disorder that mean no one specific type of crime can effectively be tackled in isolation.

Some risks attach to policies which prioritise the policing of incivilities, however. In the first place, some of the evidence in support of the 'Broken Windows' thesis[5] is contested (see Harcourt 2001), and it is not clear that tackling every sort of low-level disorder will inevitably yield a reduction on more serious crime. Secondly, there are serious risks that insensitive policing of incivilities can do more harm than good. One person's definition of an incivility is often another's definition of having fun. The targeting of incivilities inevitably falls hardest on those who spend most time on the streets. It has considerable potential for alienating and criminalising the poor and the socially marginal. We have seen in Chapter 5 that police suspicion is already focused on young, male working-class Londoners. A 'Broken Windows' style of policing could degrade into a 'zero tolerance' approach, whereby police officers exercise minimal discretion in the vigorous policing of minor crimes and disorder. This would bear down heavily on young working-class men and thus – given patterns of wealth and social exclusion in London – on young people from visible minority ethnic groups.

One solution to this dilemma is to plan the policing of incivilities as the *negotiation* of acceptable levels of order, rather than the *imposition* of order at all costs. This implies careful and sensitive consultation. A start has been made with the statutory public consultation required by the Crime and Disorder Act. However, there are also risks here. Unless consultation is done with very great care, the views of the most vocal and articulate will always tend to predominate. We shall return to the issue of consultation later in the chapter.

Do the potential benefits in policing incivilities outweigh the risks in a city as diverse as London? The question is a difficult – and thus a political one – which tends to be

---

[5] The 'Broken Windows' thesis is that if minor disorder is ignored, this brings high long-term costs, as minor incidents cumulatively lead to much larger problems of crime and spirals of social decay (Wilson and Kelling 1982; Skogan, 1990; Kelling and Coles 1996).

submerged in debate about policing. Our answer is that they do, provided that local police have the autonomy and flexibility to respond to problems of disorder as local circumstances require.

Obstacles to consent

Chapter 5 documented some of the sources of friction between police and public. The findings are neither new nor surprising, but they need responding to. Police suspicion bears down most heavily on young, working-class men, who resent being the object of suspicion. Every 'false positive' – where the suspicion proved unfounded – carries a cost. The costs are particularly high if a shared perception in any subgroup of the population emerges that they are treated unfairly. False positives then compound the process, as we have discussed in Chapter 7, triggering spirals of distrust and eroding the consent of the policed.

Policing by consent, in our view, cannot simply involve securing a majority agreement to use their powers of coercion against a minority. For an important part of the role of the police is to protect the rights of minorities, and this study has also highlighted the increasing problems of different groups wanting to co-opt the police against each other.

Policing by consent means the majority of local people – of *all* backgrounds – accepting the police exercising their coercive powers because they trust them to use them effectively, impartially and with restraint for purposes that are seen to be legitimate. More specifically, it means they will not obstruct the police when they need to raid premises in their neighbourhood because they know this is being done with good reason – and that they will accept without protest the arrest and detention of people from within their community when they are reasonably suspected of committing crimes. Policing by consent, in these terms, is essential to securing social cohesion.

In practical terms, this implies sparing use of powers that can intrude into the lives of the innocent. As we saw in Chapter 9, the MPS has taken significant steps to improve officers' professionalism in the use of stop and search powers, ensuring that grounds for suspicion are clearly articulated and recorded. We cannot quantify the losses in terms of detections that might occur if there were still fewer searches than at present. But these losses need to be balanced against the gains that might accrue to community relations. One significant development may be changes in the policing of cannabis. If the offence of possession becomes a non-arrestable offence,[6] patterns of police searches may change substantially. The most likely long-term outcome is a fall in the use of search powers, followed by an improvement in relations between police and young people (see May *et al.* 2002, for a discussion).

One reality that needs to be confronted is that however impartially the police use their powers, some ethnic minority groups are likely to remain over-represented amongst the suspects. Our analysis in Chapter 4 showed that age, sex and class were strong predictors of whom the police target as suspects. This means that even if police decisions relating to stops and searches were completely free of any racial bias, some minority groups would continue to be over-represented in the suspect

---

[6] At the time of writing the Home Secretary was considering whether to reclassify cannabis as a Class C drug under the Misuse of Drugs Act 1971. This would have the effect of removing powers of arrest for the offence.

population. Black, Pakistani and Bangladeshi groups have higher than average proportions of young people, and higher than average people unemployed or in low-paid occupations. Young men from these groups would continue to be over-represented in the stop and search statistics. The temptation for police managers is to ignore this and to continue to focus on the elimination of overt racial bias in street encounters. To do so ignores the sorts of process we have identified in Chapters 4 and 7, whereby vicarious or indirect experience leads to a shared sense of unfair treatment amongst some minority ethnic groups, and a collective belief within these groups that they are over-policed.

Policing diversity

The implications of the previous section need considering in some detail. All local communities are internally diverse to a greater or lesser extent, and we have seen how this diversity can itself create conflict and competing demands on the police, especially in London. Ethnic diversity is one aspect of this but the main lines of stratification between the residents of any area are their age, gender, and socio-economic characteristics. Both ethnic diversity and socio-economic divisions have increased markedly in the capital in recent years, but all these divisions overlay each other along with many other factors – including sexual orientation and lifestyle. They form a kaleidoscope whose patterns change over time and by area, and all individuals are a mix of different characteristics.

In many parts of London, 'the local community' (as administratively defined) consists of a range of communities of interest who are not geographically defined. Although they share the same space, they may compete for physical control of that space or over the distribution of resources within it, including public services. Each of these communities may have its own particular, collective history of relations with the police. The legacy may influence its current perceptions of the service and interactions with them, and it may be mirrored within the service also. What this study has brought out it is the extent to which structural factors that are not particular to any one group may also be important in shaping these collective experiences on an ongoing basis.

The black group of Caribbean origin in particular is the longest established of the visible minority groups in London[7] and its history of tense relations with the police includes experience of overt discrimination. This group – along with other minorities who suffer higher than average levels of economic disadvantage – also tends to live disproportionately in areas where levels of social tension and crime are high. In parts of some boroughs black (Caribbean) or Asian people may now form the longest-established British-born population. Meanwhile new immigrants in turn tend to come to these same areas, including the recent waves of refugees and asylum seekers from countries of eastern Europe as well as Africa and the Middle East. A particular challenge for the police is keeping abreast of these changes and of patterns of social relations *as well as* crime and disorder within and between these different groups – especially when these patterns are differently configured from one area to another.

Importantly, these areas have always been more intensively policed because of their levels of deprivation and the levels of crime and disorder associated with this. Police

---

[7] That is, taking a narrow historical frame of reference and considering only the groups who formed part of the significant immigration from the new Commonwealth countries in the period since the Second World War.

relations with the public have always been more strained here and, in part for these reasons, policing styles have always tended to be more adversarial. In particular, larger sections of people who call on the police for help are also 'known' to them directly or via their family and friends and so fall into the police category of 'roughs' (as opposed to 'respectables') (see Reiner 2000 for a discussion). Particular minority ethnic groups disproportionately occupy this role at present, and the notion of 'police property' has, as a result, become racialised in some areas.

Additionally, the particular attention the police have always paid to young people and the way they approach them also impact disproportionately on minorities. So they will be particularly affected, for example, by policies to crack down on disorderly behaviour associated with young people and the targeting of policing on high crime areas – even though these policies may be race-neutral. There can be no complacency about racism or let-up in attempts to counter the risk of discrimination. Unless steps are taken to improve relations with young people generally, though, and to address the problem of the traditionally more adversarial policing styles in deprived, high-crime areas, little will change in the experience of many black people. Also, this experience will increasingly be replicated among the poorer Asian groups and growing numbers of refugees and asylum seekers.

That is, while the experience of minorities is *particular* to the group and racism is part of this, it may also serve (in Elizabeth Burney's memorable phrase) as a 'barium meal' (Burney 1967) – serving to illuminate wider problems in policing. Minorities are disproportionately affected by factors which also have a negative impact on very much larger numbers of the population more generally – in particular on young people, on those who are on the wrong side of the increasing socioeconomic divide in society and those who live in high-crime areas. Many policing issues that are specifically of concern to minorities – including the question of police searches – cannot effectively be tackled in isolation from the wider issues of which they are part (FitzGerald 1999b). These relate not only to differences in policing style in different areas but also to policing priorities and practice – and to the policy objectives that shape these.

Delivering more responsive policing: the mechanisms

So far we have explored what a more responsive form of policing would look like. We shall now examine what changes are needed in the control and management of the MPS to bring this about. Many of our themes are not new. They have long been identified by police researchers and, more recently, by management consultants. However, the problems have proved remarkably resilient in the face of attempts to overcome them. While the MPS faces particular challenges, many of the core issues are common to other forces.

Performance management and political control

We have argued in Chapters 8 and 9 that the complexities of police work have become forgotten as public sector managerialism has increasingly dominated police administration. The process has to our minds been accidental and unintended. Quantitative targets have been set for the police by successive Home Secretaries and the Audit Commission which have given primacy to narrow crime-fighting objectives. Whilst the process was intended to improve police performance, it has had several perverse effects.

'Producer control' over public services has historically resulted in poor quality. There has been widespread – and welcome – recognition over the last two decades that public services need to be both more financial accountable and more accountable to the public they serve. If they are consuming public money, the argument runs, they should *demonstrate* that they are performing properly. However, the need to secure greater accountability had led politicians, civil servants and senior managers willingly to suspend their disbelief in the value of the performance indicators (PIs) applied to measure the operation of complex institutions. PIs have been oversimplified; unreliable outcome measures have been the rule rather than the exception; and the creation or collation of PI statistics has often fallen within the control of those whose performance is being measured. Targets have been set both nationally and locally in very arbitrary fashion, with little or no idea whether they are within the capacity of those who have to achieve them.

Take targets relating to burglary, for example. At present, our understanding of burglary trends is rudimentary. We know that structural factors such as the state of the economy interact with cultural factors and situational factors[8] and with policing factors to yield a given level of burglary. But we have little idea of the relative effects of each type of factor. No one can definitively explain the rise in domestic burglary until the mid-1990s or its fall since then. Yet, across London, borough commanders and their partners in local authorities regularly set themselves targets for the percentage reduction they will achieve in burglary over the coming three years. They all know that the target is simply a 'shot in the dark'; they do not know the likely impact of various anti-burglary strategies; and yet the imperative to set some target remains overwhelming.

The crudity of performance management regimes of the 1990s has been recognised but accepted as a necessary evil. The general presumption was that PIs would be refined with time, and that in any case the benefits of imposing managerial discipline would outweigh the problems associated with the setting of crude targets. The hope was that the language of targets and performance would ensure that the staff of public services began to think in terms of achievement rather than activity.[9]

To an extent, the agenda to hold the police more firmly to account for their performance has succeeded. Local and senior police managers – and their new partners – are more self-questioning about their achievements and much more committed to the idea that they can do something to affect crime rates. However, the evidence presented in this report suggests there have also been many unintended and perverse consequences.

The perverse effects of quantitative performance management
A recurrent phrase in interviews and focus groups with officers at different levels was: 'What can't be measured doesn't count and what doesn't count doesn't get done.' Organisations certainly respond to target-setting. Thus it is understandable that governments who want to improve public sector performance will use target-setting as a means to do so. However, the bluntness of the instruments means they

---

[8] Levels of household security, levels of household occupancy, the volume of stealable, desirable goods in homes and the market for goods that can be stolen through burglary are all variables that affect burglary rates – in ways that cannot easily be quantified.
[9] In the US, this has been explicitly acknowledged in terminology such as 'aspirational targets' and 'stretch targets' which are intentionally set to be slightly out of reach.

often result not in the desired improvements but in distortions of organisational function.

For example, measuring schools' performance by exam performance may result in a sort of educational equivalent of triage[10] where resources are focused neither on the high-performers nor on those of limited ability, but on those of middling ability whose performance can be raised across a critical threshold. Targets to reduce hospital waiting lists can similarly distort access to treatment, favouring those whose operations can be done quickly rather than those who are in greatest need. Intelligent people when held to account for – and rewarded for – meeting a target will place more importance on hitting the target than meeting the underlying objectives of the target-setter. This is true of policing no less than other public services.

As we have discussed in Chapters 8 and 9, quantitative performance management through target-setting has affected policing at several different levels. At the most general, the targets set by successive Home Secretaries and the Audit Commission have given primacy to crime-fighting objectives at the expense of other police functions such as order maintenance. We think this shift was not fully intended, and was an almost accidental product of the target-setting process that required clear, simple targets that could command a broad consensus. The obvious targets to select were those relating to crime. It could be argued that such a shift was needed. If so, it could – and should – have been publicly debated. Striking the right balance between the various police functions – crime fighting, order maintenance, dealing with emergencies and so on – involves complex, contestable and thus political decision-making. It should not be done 'through the back door' as part of the performance management process. Yet this appears to have happened. In Chapters 8 and 9 we have documented how capacity to respond effectively to the generality of public demand was reduced whilst crime-fighting objectives were prioritised.

Target-setting also has the effect of privileging strategies that yield short-term returns, and marginalising those that are best regarded as long-term investment. The clearest example of this is the way in which less priority has been given to efforts to build up and develop community contact. This could range from spending the time to listen to a victim of crime, to talking to ordinary people in the street, to working on projects with young people – as opposed to encountering them only in potentially confrontational situations. Many officers saw these activities as essential in building trust and thereby both improving the flow of community intelligence and proactively deterring potential young offenders from criminal careers. However, nobody would argue that their benefits accrue in the short term, and few would argue that these benefits can be quantified.[11]

There are more specific perverse effects. Targeting specific categories of crime, such as burglary, necessarily removes priority from other sorts of crime, and encourages

---

[10] A medical term, referring to the practice of grouping of casualties into those who are too seriously injured to benefit from medical help, too lightly injured to warrant immediate attention and those in the middle for whom immediate treatment is essential.

[11] It was of particular interest to discover in the course of the project that the French – whose tradition of policing is very different from the British – have recently begun to invest significantly in the creation of *une police de proximité*. They have recognised that they can only tackle crime effectively by starting to engage the police with their local communities (Monjardet 2000).

'functional displacement' between types of offending. Some of our police respondents thought the rapid increase in robbery could be attributed in part to the focus of policing effort on burglary. Assessing performance in clearing up crime by measuring the volume of judicial disposals[12] removes the incentive from officers to prepare cases to the highest standards in order to ensure conviction when the case goes to court. All they need do is ensure that the offender is charged, regardless of what happens thereafter.

There are also straightforward 'accountancy dodges' where discretion over recording procedure is exploited to improve performance. In focus groups with police officers we were told that the burglary targets meant that theft from garden sheds and outhouses was now being recorded as theft rather than burglary, and attempted burglaries – even where premises were entered but nothing was taken – were entered as 'criminal damage'.

Finally, quantitative performance management can have a corrosive effect on staff morale and vocational commitment. From one perspective, they can be seen as an essential means of raising the performance of public services that have become complacent, self-serving and inefficient. From another, they may appear a distraction imposed on committed professionals who are struggling to meet rising expectations with static or shrinking resources. In Chapter 9 we have discussed how target-setting and performance measurement appeared to have compounded the cynicism which is often found in police organisations. It reinforced divisions between ranks. Sergeants and inspectors found it difficult to motivate junior officers to achieve targets that were set apparently arbitrarily for priorities which might change (equally arbitrarily) from one year to the next. They knew that little *real* change was possible without change in other areas which were either not priorities or not amenable to police intervention. Many shared the view of PCs that senior managers were preoccupied only with hitting targets, regardless of the impact on performance quality.

Despite cynicism amongst the rank-and-file about their bosses' target-chasing, we saw in Chapter 9 that senior managers shared these concerns. They displayed their own scepticism about their managers, and about the political process that imposed simplistic targets on them. Quantitative performance management appeared to be displacing more traditional forms of professional leadership.

An alternative paradigm of performance management?
We are hardly the first to argue that the complexity of the police function cannot be ignored; nor are we the first to criticise crude performance measurement. The last 15 years have seen numerous critiques. The Operational Police Review (Joint Consultative Committee 1990) offered the shared perspective of senior police managers and trades unions. This emphasised how the complexity of the police function ruled out simple performance measurement. A similar research-based analysis was provided by Horton and Smith (1988). More recently, Neyroud and Beckley (2001) dissect the problems of over-reliance on quantitative measures to improve police performance.

A common theme in these critiques is the need to improve performance by developing professional standards and focusing the efforts of managers on ensuring

[12] The current term for clearing up crime. The main forms of judicial disposal are charging offenders or cautioning them.

that their staff maintain these professional standards. Horton and Smith argue for the development of good practice standards; Neyroud and Beckley advocate the development of a 'professional model' of police practice which gives the individual officer greater personal responsibility within an ethical framework. American commentators such as Kelling (1999) have also argued for the development of good practice guidelines. The common theme is that performance management is a two-stage process. Managers need to identify ways of working that achieve policing goals – to develop best practice. This process of development needs to draw on authoritative research to ensure that what is regarded as best practice actually delivers the desired outcomes. Then they need to ensure that their staff meet best practice. What they should *not* do is expect a close-coupled relationship between delivering best practice and reducing crime. According to these perspectives, performance monitoring is not about the setting of targets for goal achievement, but about monitoring policing practice against professional and ethical standards. Whilst policing needs to remain outcome-focused, it does not make sense to deny the complexity of the policing environment and to expect to see a simple relationship between policing effort and the achievement of crime targets. The police cannot be held *directly* responsible for the level of crime.

Performance measurement will always be important, of course, but there is a need for new approaches. These need to capture quality as well as quantity and to strike a better balance between long-term and short-term goals. Simply refining quantitative performance indicators is not the solution. Those who actually deliver the service – and collate the performance statistics – will always be able to subvert the intentions of target-setters if the latter group does not share the former's appreciation of the reality and complexity of police work.

Supervision and support
The development of professional standards creates a critical role for middle and front-line managers. Ensuring the highest standards of behaviour on the streets depends not only on the supervision they receive but also the support available to them. The critical role played by sergeants and inspectors cannot be emphasised too strongly. Their attitudes and style of leadership set the tone for whole teams and carry over into junior officers' largely unsupervised encounters with the public. Where these are going wrong or staff are underperforming it is up to them to challenge. And it falls largely to sergeants and inspectors to motivate the people the service mainly depends on to deliver change and improvement.

Unless sergeants and inspectors themselves are adequately supervised and supported, therefore, progress will be slow and may even be undermined. There are serious dangers if they feel they have no ownership of the changes in policy and practice they are expected to deliver and, in particular, if they are cynical about these changes or feel they place unrealistic demands on the junior staff for whom they are responsible. Particular forms of managerialism can exacerbate these dangers, and consistent efforts are needed to offset the risk of the middle-manager level becoming unnecessarily alienated from senior managers and over-identified with their staff.

This calls for a more systematic approach to staff development that focuses not simply on the needs of individuals but also on relations between them. Effectively this requires changing the internal culture of the organisation along the lines recommended not only by Wolff Olins in 1988 but also the PSI study of the MPS in 1983.

Decentralisation

Problems of overcentralisation were discussed in Chapter 9. One of the biggest challenges faced by MPS is to strike the right balance between meeting London-wide demands and improving standards across the board while supporting the development of local solutions to local problems. Boroughs are often the size of small police forces but the patterns of crime and disorder are far more intense and complex and local commanders are required to work closely with other local agencies in tackling them.

There are considerable risks in decentralising the management of resources to borough level (and more locally) since decentralisation can threaten to compound problems of improving cohesion and consistency in a service that is already under growing pressure to 'put its house in order' by demonstrating that it is using resources efficiently. However, there are more serious risks to police legitimacy if the style, content and quality of the service delivered are not responsive to what local people want, and the aggregated effect of this will militate against the achievement of London-wide objectives.

The MPS needs to continue its policies of devolving power to borough level. For this to be effective, it must also aim to minimise the problem of disruption and discontinuity to local service delivery and the development of relationships which are caused by the 'abstraction' of junior staff to meet London-wide needs and the frequent changes that occur at senior-management level. This will not be easy but it is most likely to be achieved in the context of a coherent London-wide strategy that balances the needs of London as a whole with those of its component boroughs and different communities and neighbourhoods within these. The strategy should ensure the most effective use of resources by facilitating and encouraging partnership both within and between boroughs and between borough and central staff. It should guarantee adequate coverage for the MPS's London-wide functions and its ability to respond rapidly to unexpected events while safeguarding continuity in its day-to-day service to Londoners; and the role of the MPA will be crucial in developing it.

Specialisation

Meeting the need for the police to re-engage strategically with local people raises important issues about the deployment of officers. Clearly, improving the balance between public contact-time and the time officers spend recording these contacts is essential, and this raises wider issues about the rationale for the information required as well as the need for appropriate recording systems and support with inputting data. It also points to a need to improve the balance between staffing specialist units on the one hand and enhancing routine patrol and response teams on the other, as well as ensuring their work is mutually supportive.

Our evidence shows that the costs of specialisation have tended to fall on other organisational functions and, in particular, in cuts on uniformed response teams – not only in terms of numbers but also experience. Increasing the numbers of officers alone will not meet people's need for a more visible and accessible police presence: quality of contact is at least as important. This means the officers involved will need to feel motivated because their role is recognised and valued within the organisation. But they will also need to contain a critical mass of mature, experienced officers whose interpersonal skills should set appropriate standards so that the upcoming generation of officers learns from their example.

This is not to underestimate the stress that already exists within specialist units and their own need for skilled and experienced officers, and we do not suggest there will be easy answers to the problem of reconciling these competing demands. However, it does mean that the work of specialist units cannot be viewed in isolation. Again, a holistic approach is required to look not only at the relation of specialist units to general service provision but also at their relation to each other in order to avoid duplication of effort and maximise the two-way flow of relevant information and experience, including through staffing arrangements. Effectively the role of specialist units must be to ensure that the whole of the organisation adds up to *more* than the sum of its parts rather than less.

Partnership

The increasing recognition over the last 20 that the police alone cannot tackle problems of crime and disorder has identified a wide range of key partners in this, including:

- other agencies of the criminal justice system;

- other statutory agencies;

- the private sector;

- the voluntary sector; and

- individual citizens.

It is not in the scope of this study to comment on partnership with the private sector or with other agencies of the criminal justice system, although these should be central concerns in the systematic overview we believe is needed of the role of the police.

Partnership with the public

Much of this chapter has already focused on the need for the service systematically to re-engage with local communities in order to maximise the partnership potential of individual citizens and the groups they belong to in tackling crime and disorder. A range of institutional opportunities already exists for this – from the important role of the police authorities as the local body to whom forces are accountable, to the role of Police Community Consultative Groups, to lay visitors to police stations and the work of special constables. But there are also many opportunities for voluntary involvement. One traditional route has been through neighbourhood watch schemes, and reference has already been made to innovative variants on these. Other arrangements have continued to develop, including the creation of sector working parties or monitoring groups to consider racist incidents and the use of lay advisers.

At the same time we see re-engaging the police with the public as requiring a strategic programme of school involvement and the development of a youth policy, as well as a systematic approach to further developing proactive contact with existing groups of local citizens – from religious groups to tenants associations and youth centres. This requires the police to harness and develop the support that already exists to help them in this, but this must *not* become a substitute for the more accessible and visible police presence on which the strategy depends and which is what the public wants.

For it also has to be borne in mind that very large numbers of people are not active citizens. They will not be 'represented' in or by local groups and the claims these groups make on the police need to be negotiated with care to avoid any hint of favouritism or discrimination (whether real or simply perceived). Tensions arise in particular with regard to sharing information, for the police cannot share information with members of the public which – if used insensitively or passed on inadvertently to the wrong people – could put individuals or sections of local communities at risk from others. Especially in areas where the population is very diverse, the police constantly have to balance their need for community intelligence against the possibility that this intelligence is consciously biased and/or that acting on it would be discriminatory in effect if not in intention.

Consultation with the public
We have seen that the government has placed great importance on consultation with the public in developing local crime-reduction strategies. Crime-reduction partnerships have a statutory duty to consult locally when auditing local problems of crime and disorder, and when drawing up their three-year crime-reduction strategies. This forms part of a broader government strategy for offsetting the 'democratic deficit' in local authority politics and for reinvigorating local political processes.[13] The Crime and Disorder Act 1998 also placed heavy reliance on consultation both about crime problems and about solutions to crime. However, the extensive use of consultation may have perverse effects. Poorly conducted consultation may:

- fail to represent faithfully people's real views;
- over-represent the views of the vocal and the articulate;
- lead to a sense of 'consultation fatigue';
- fuel unrealistic expectations about responsiveness to consultation; and
- lead to subsequent disillusion and disengagement.

Consulting people about local crime-reduction strategies poses particular challenges. Most people are ill-informed about levels of crime and disorder, and about existing ways of responding to these problems. They have no idea of the relative effectiveness of different strategies. To canvass their unconsidered views is to substitute activity for intelligent action. There is a pressing need to find better ways of mounting local consultation.

Partnership with other statutory agencies
One of the most radical and innovative approaches in recent years to tackling crime and disorder through partnership work was the setting up of the Crime and

[13] For example, the Local Government Act 2000 imposed rather more extensive duties on councils to involve local people in the preparation of a community strategy.

Disorder Reduction Partnerships (CDRPs) under the Crime and Disorder Act of 1998. These were just starting to get established, therefore, at the time of our study.

While multi-agency approaches to tackling specific problems of crime and disorder were increasingly advocated from the 1980s, they took root better in some areas than others. Although their histories were different, two of our boroughs had an established tradition of multi-agency working and this gave them – and other boroughs like them – an important head start in setting up CDRPs and responding to other statutory requirements for police partnership working with other agencies (for example, through the Youth Offending Teams). Even here, though, it was apparent that the CDRPs had numerous and significant obstacles to overcome before they began to reach their potential. The three main areas of difficulty seemed to be as follows.

Each of the individual agencies faced managerialist pressures in its own right. They were accountable to different government departments as well as inspection and regulatory bodies for meeting standards and targets, including demonstrating Best Value. This inevitably constrained their scope for and incentive to pool resources in joint approaches to problems. Where this did happen, further issues could arise about line management responsibilities for and, even, the funding of particular posts. More generally, though, the time and effort of setting up and liaising on partnership issues were a drain on their limited resources for which, as yet, there was little measurable return.

Significant problems also remained to be resolved about sharing information. A recurrent source of frustration for the police was not only other agencies' reluctance to volunteer information which might be essential to the detection and prosecution of crime but also their refusal to respond to requests for information in some very serious cases. The agencies, on the other hand, had important ethical issues to consider – from safeguarding professional relationships based on an undertaking of confidentiality, to protecting vulnerable people and those who might actually be innocent from becoming targets of police suspicion. But similar questions also arose here about what information the police themselves could properly share with others without the danger of it being misused.

Finally, trying to work closely together – whether at committee level or in multi-agency teams – inevitably brought into play cultural differences between the different agencies. Not only was their approach to problems different, but styles of decision-making and expectations about implementation could also produce tensions. And this tended further to be exacerbated by the rapid turnover of police representatives.

These problems will take time to resolve and some partnerships will take much longer to get off the ground than others. The potential of these local partnerships is unique but realising it will take sustained support and encouragement. However, we believe there is no obvious alternative in the medium to long term to developing co-ordinated approaches to crime and disorder by harnessing local resources to tackling local problems.

Conclusion

This study provides a snapshot of policing in London at the turn of a new century. It has found some evidence of falling satisfaction, against the benchmark of the study carried out 20 years ago by the PSI. The reasons for the fall are complex, and may have as much to do with changes in public expectations as with actual quality of service. Even if they do, however, they should command political and managerial attention.

This is because – unlike most public services – the consent and support of the general population are central to the effectiveness of the police. The way in which the police balance competing rights and demands is of critical importance in determining whether they can command consent from the population. There are choices to be made about policing style and policing philosophy. Whilst there is a developing evidence base that can inform such choices, the arguments for and against different policing philosophies are contestable, and involve issues of value as much as fact. In other words, the choice of policing philosophy is a difficult one and thus a political one. The findings of this study are intended to help such choices.

Appendixes

Appendix 1: The Advisory Group

The Advisory Group met six times over the course of the project's life. Its terms of reference were:

> To advise the research team on the design, conduct, analysis and writing up of the study; and on the dissemination and public presentation of the project and its findings.

Membership

Chair
Lord Dholakia

Members
Mr Victor Adebowale, Director, Centrepoint (now Chief Executive, Turning Point)
Mr Godfrey Allen, Chief Executive, Apex Trust
Professor Richard Berthoud, University of Essex
Mr Ian Blair, Deputy Commissioner, Metropolitan Police Service
Ms Sheila Forbes
Professor Roger Graef, Films of Record
Lord Harris of Haringey, The House of Lords
Lord Harris of Greenwich, The House of Lords (until his death in 2001)
Rt Hon Sir Peter Lloyd MP
Professor Robert Reiner, London School of Economics
Mr Gurbuxh Singh, Chief Executive, Haringey Borough Council (now Director of the Commission for Racial Equality)
Professor David Smith, Edinburgh University
Mr Paul Wiles, Director of the Home Office Research Development and Statistics Directorate

Adviser
Ms Lorna Whyte

Observers
Nuffield Foundation ⎫
Paul Hamlyn Foundation ⎬ Funders
Esmée Fairbairn Foundation ⎭

Professor Marian FitzGerald, LSE ⎫
Professor Mike Hough, South Bank University ⎪
Ian Joseph ⎬ Research Team
Tarek Qureshi, South Bank University ⎪
National Centre for Social Research ⎭

Appendix 2: Methodology

The Policing for London Study (PFLS) comprised quantitative and qualitative elements, as follows:

- A survey of Londoners, with a representative sample of people 15 or over.

- Detailed case studies in three London boroughs, involving:
  - focus groups with adults and teenagers;
  - focus groups with constables and sergeants;
  - in-depth interviews with senior officers;
  - interviews with the police's local partners;
  - observation of patrol work and custody suites; and
  - secondary analysis of borough and force-wide statistics.

Survey work

The PFLS was undertaken for us by the National Centre for Social Research. It was designed to random sample about 2,750 people aged 15 or over within the London Metropolitan Police (MPS) area. We needed to be able to analyse the results not only by age, sex, class and geographical area but also by ethnicity. As a simple random sample of the population would yield too few minority respondents to support analysis, the survey design involved the oversampling of the larger minority ethnic groups. The survey results have been weighted in analysis to restore representativeness.

Full details of the survey design are to be found in the survey's technical report (Brown and Whitfield 2002). In summary, addresses were selected for interview using a two-stage stratified sample design:

- Stage 1 – Over-sampling of postcode sectors with a high density of ethnic minority addresses.

- Stage 2 – Selection of addresses within postcode sectors, using the 'focused enumeration' procedure to expand the core sample in order to achieve the required number of interviews within the four ethnic minority groups.

The bulk of fieldwork took place from July to November 2000, with a few interviews in December. In total 2,800 interviews were achieved. From Table A2.1 it can be seen that the number of achieved interviews exceeded that expected from the sample design, but that interviews were not evenly distributed across ethnic groups. The number of interviews in the Asian ethnic groups (particularly Pakistanis) exceeded those expected, but the number in black and white/other groups was lower. This probably reflects changes in the population of London since the sampling estimates were drawn, as well as different levels of response between ethnic groups.

Table A2.1: Achieved sample size

Subgroup	Expected	Achieved
Black	750	621
Indian	400	609
Pakistani	300	361
Bangladeshi	300	325
White/other	1,000	883
Total	**2,750**	**2,799**

Note: Excludes one case where respondent ethnicity was missing.

Calculating response rates for a focused-enumeration sample is complex. Our best estimate is an overall response rate of 49%, with a slightly higher rate for the core sample. This is low against the benchmark of a straightforward national probability sample, where response rates of 65–75% are still achievable.[1] The national British Crime Survey (BCS) focused-enumeration sample achieved a response rate of 58%. London response rates have always been lower than national ones, and focused-enumeration samples pose particular challenges. The BCS focused-enumeration subsample in London is unlikely to have been much higher than ours. The total number of those eligible for interview was 5,680, the non-contact rate was 15% and the refusal rate 34%.

It is not possible to record response rates by ethnicity, as it was often impossible to establish the ethnic group of 'non-responders'. Where such information was available, refusal rates were highest amongst white households and non-contact rates highest amongst black ones. Language problems resulted in unproductive outcomes most frequently in Asian households.

Whilst our response rate is lower than we hoped for, the potential for bias should be assessed against the competing sampling methods. Quota sampling, which is frequently used especially in urban situations where good probability samples are hard to achieve, involves a usually unknown and much higher refusal rate from those approached to participate; the representativeness of quota samples is questionable in social surveys of this sort even when techniques such as 'random walk' selection have been used.[2] As is discussed below, we are able to compare various PFLS estimates with those of the 2000 BCS, which had a higher response rate in London. Most comparisons showed very little difference.

We can only speculate about the nature of sample bias. First of all, the sample was drawn from the Postal Address File. Those living in institutions and those with no permanent home were defined out. Non-contact is likely to be associated with people who live busy social or working lives – amongst whom the affluent and the young are probably over-represented. Refusals are likely to be highest amongst those least sympathetic to, or suspicious about, the enterprise of social research. This may

[1] The Office for National Statistics (ONS) (2001b) provides response rates for major British cross-sectional surveys. Eight out of 20 achieved 65% or less across the country as a whole; three achieved 75% or more.
[2] Quota samples interviewed in the home are more likely than random ones to over-represent those who tend not to go out – whose contact with the police both as victims and as suspects will be more limited than others. This is likely to be the case even when the response rates of random samples are relatively low.

include the busy and the affluent as well as the young, the poor and the socially marginal. Non-contact and refusal are also associated with particular types of dwelling, such as large blocks of flats with entry-phone systems. The sample very probably under-represents those who are routinely the object of police suspicion – young, socially marginal males who spend a lot of their time away from home.

Comparisons with the PSI survey
Like the PFLS, fieldwork for the Policy Studies Institute (PSI) survey was carried out by the National Centre for Social Research (under its previous name, Social and Community Planning Research). Interviewing took place in the second half of 1981. The sample design differed from PFLS in that there was a stratified random sample of 1,411 Londoners, supplemented by a separate ethnic minority sample of 1,009 respondents. This was assembled through a technique of non-focused enumeration in areas selected for the high proportion of minority residents. This means that the PSI sample is likely to have under-represented people from minority groups living in largely white areas. The technique was appropriate to the period, when there were fewer Londoners from minority groups concentrated in fewer areas. The PSI survey differed from PFLS in another respect in that it heavily oversampled people under 25. Although the experience of this age-group is of particular importance, we decided against this, partly because we were able to draw on the 2000 BCS sample (see below), and partly because we did not want to reduce the precision of estimates when the sample was broken down by other variables (obviously ethnicity). Seventeen per cent of our sample is under 25, as against 41% of the PSI sample. The PSI survey achieved a combined response rate of 70% – higher than PFLS's, reflecting the generally higher response rates that could be achieved 20 years ago. As with PFLS, the PSI analysts used weighting to restore representativeness.

Combining the PFLS with the BCS
In designing our survey we took advantage of the fact that we could get access to the 2000 BCS, which had a London subsample of 4,325 people aged 16 or over, of whom 2,943 answered detailed questions on their experience of, and attitudes towards, the police. The BCS sample design was similar to that of PFLS, although differences in over-sampling yielded fewer Asians and more black and white respondents than PFLS. In designing our questionnaire we followed two strategies. First, we recognised that the quality of data could be substantially strengthened by combining the two survey datasets where *precision* was needed. Thus our questionnaire asked exactly the same questions as the BCS on experience of the police, for example, to allow detailed analysis by subgroup. This yielded a combined sample of almost 6,000. (As with analysis of PFLS, we have restored representativeness of the merged sample by weighting the data.) Secondly, we reckoned that for some topics we could rely solely on the BCS, saving space in our questionnaire for other topics, especially those that had been asked in the PSI study. As a result, the two surveys had a shared core of questions, but covered a range of further topics separately, allowing us both a breadth of coverage and depth of precision. The *weighted* demographic breakdown of the two samples is shown in Table A2.2. The *unweighted* number of respondents in the PFLS survey and in the 2000 BCS London subsample who answered questionnaire modules on policing are shown in Table A2.3. Table A2.4 provides *unweighted* breakdowns by ethnicity and other demographic factors of the PFLS and merged datasets.

Table A2.2: Demographic breakdown of PFLS and 2000 BCS subsample: weighted sample (%)

	PFLS	2000 BCS	PFLS/2000 BCS	1999 ONS estimates
Male	44	49	47	49
Female	56	51	54	51
Aged 16–29	23	24	23	26
Aged 30–59	55	54	54	53
Aged 60+	22	22	22	21
Social class: Group 1	10	9	9	n.a
Group 2	37	34	35	n.a
Group 3.1	19	17	18	n.a
Group 3.2	22	24	23	n.a
Group 4	10	12	11	n.a
Group 5	3	5	4	n.a
White	73.8	73.8	73.8	77.8
Black	11.0	11.0	11.0	8.7
Indian	5.0	5.0	5.0	5.4
Pakistani/Bangladeshi	2.5	2.5	2.5	3.2
Other	7.7	7.7	7.7	4.0

Note: The weights have been scaled to yield equal proportions of ethnic minorities in both surveys. The proportions have been drawn from the PFLS. These differ slightly from ONS estimates, which are derived from the Labour Force Survey. It is hard to say which is likely to be more accurate.

Table A2.3: Demographic breakdown of PFLS and 2000 BCS subsample: unweighted numbers

	PFLS	2000 BCS	PFLS/2000 BCS
Male	1,307	1,363	2,670
Female	1,492	1,580	3,072
Aged 16 – 29	815	693	1,508
Aged 30 – 59	1,520	1,734	3,254
Aged 60+	455	513	968
Social class: Group 1	163	160	323
Group 2	724	738	1,462
Group 3.1	474	426	900
Group 3.2	633	527	1,160
Group 4	424	339	763
Group 5	95	120	215
White	692	884	1,576
Black	621	958	1,579
Indian	609	581	1,190
Pakistani/Bangladeshi	686	319	1,005
Other	192	201	393
Total	2,800	2,943	5,743

Note: Missing data for some variables.

Table A2.4: Demographic breakdown of PFLS and merged datasets: unweighted numbers by ethnic group

	White	*Black*	*Indian*	*Pakistani/ Bangladeshi*	*Other*
Merged dataset (PFLS & BCS)					
Male	696	661	603	513	197
Female	880	918	587	492	195
Aged 16 – 29	263	387	329	419	110
Aged 30 – 59	833	986	714	478	243
Aged 60+	479	199	147	107	36
Deprived inner boroughs	183	653	123	493	83
Central London boroughs	155	129	20	33	40
Poor outer London boroughs	331	535	460	236	123
Affluent outer London boroughs	860	261	585	243	147
PFLS dataset					
Male	289	266	309	347	96
Female	403	355	300	339	95
Aged 16 – 29	112	161	184	301	57
Aged 30 – 59	378	370	347	315	110
Aged 60+	201	85	78	69	22
Deprived inner boroughs	110	301	68	349	32
Central London boroughs	86	57	15	25	20
Poor outer London boroughs	155	186	239	166	59
Affluent outer London boroughs	341	77	287	146	81

Note: Missing data for some variables

The case studies

We selected three boroughs as sites for detailed case studies. All our respondents were guaranteed confidentiality and, to safeguard this, we have anonymised the boroughs throughout this report. To provide a range of policing situations, we selected Borough A from the ten most affluent London boroughs, Borough C from the six most highly deprived inner London boroughs, and Borough B from the remaining sixteen boroughs occupying the middle ground. Secondary selection criteria were that the case-study sites should have ethnically diverse populations and that research access was unproblematic.

Our aim in mounting the case studies was to look at issues in police–community relations in each area from the perspectives of:

- the public, including teenagers and young adults;

- the police's local partners in the statutory and voluntary sectors; and

- the police themselves.

The qualitative work involved in-depth interviews with people whose (paid or unpaid) work involved contact with the police, focus groups with the public and with teenagers in schools, and a mix of in-depth interviews and focus groups with police officers.

In-depth interviews (non-police)

In each of the boroughs we interviewed eight respondents from non-statutory organisations who had contact with the police on behalf of particular sections of the local population. It would have been impossible to cover all the relevant agencies in the time available and we make no claims that our sample was representative. However, in each borough we included respondents from organisations concerned with gay people, women, older people, youth, refugees and asylum seekers, and minority ethnic groups.

Other respondents came variously from Victim Support, Neighbourhood Watch, a housing project and umbrella voluntary action organisations. We also interviewed various local authority staff responsible for partnership working in each authority and five of the local MPs – all three from Borough A and one each from Boroughs B and C.

The content and direction of the interviews varied with each respondent but the common core questions concerned their own impressions of the local police, their sense of how the public saw the police and their impression of the police relative to other local agencies.

Public focus groups

In each of the case-study areas, we conducted four public focus groups in the summer of 2000. Respondents were recruited by an agency specialising in this work, but the research team facilitated the groups. They were structured primarily by age but we also aimed to maintain comparability across area in the groups' socioeconomic characteristics. Their ethnic make-up necessarily varied. In all, they included 106 individuals with equal numbers of men and women. Table A2.5 gives a breakdown of the total.

These focus groups all took over an hour, with the longest taking over two. Respondents also completed a short structured questionnaire collecting demographic details and their views about their area. The focus group schedule covered: perceptions and experience of crime; experience of the police; attitudes to the police; police performance; policing priorities; and preparedness to help the police. Respondents were all paid a £10 fee.

Table A2.5: Public focus groups in case-study areas

Age		Gender		Ethnicity		Class	
18–22	21	Male	53	White	55	AB	28
23–30	11	Female	53	Black Caribbean	8	C1	24
30–50	26			Black African	7	D2	1
50-64	25			Indian	8	DE	37
65+	18			Pakistani	0	E1	2
Missing	5			Bangladeshi	9	Missing	14
				Other	5		
				Missing	14		

Schools focus groups

We conducted a total of nine focus groups with Year 11 students (i.e. young people aged 15 and 16) in two schools each in Boroughs A and C and in a single school in Borough B. The size of the groups ranged between 8 and 12 and we left the selection to teachers, having specified that we were looking for single-sex groups that were broadly representative of Year 11 students in terms of their range of ability and ethnic mix. Four were groups of boys and there were five groups of girls. The schedule was similar to that for adults.

Interviews with police

Semi-structured in-depth interviews were conducted with all three local commanders, with their deputies in Boroughs A and C and with several other officers at Chief Inspector level holding general operational or management responsibilities. All heads of Community Safety Units (CSUs) were interviewed, as were heads of Management Information Units and officers with responsibility for partnership working and for schools liaison. Interviews focused on the main issues facing the police, both locally and across the MPS, and possible improvements.

Police focus groups

Nineteen police focus groups were held in all, including three with civil staff. The majority of officers were of constable rank (although the groups included 18 sergeants and inspectors) and the size of the groups ranged from 5 to 12, taking between one and two hours each. In Boroughs A and C, focus groups were also held with community beat officers and with Community Safety Unit personnel in Boroughs A and B.

The focus group discussion schedule was more structured than that for the individual interviews but covered broadly the same ground. All the officers who participated were left with a questionnaire to complete at their discretion and about a third took up this opportunity. Their responses, therefore, cannot be assumed to be representative, but some individual comments highlighted issues that had not been raised either in the focus groups or interviews – and many usefully illustrated those that had been raised.

Observation and other sources of material
We made two sets of direct observations, totalling 20 in all. Most looked at the day-to-day work of local officers in their routine dealings with members of the public, but we also sat in on a number of more formal meetings. In each area, at least one period of observation was undertaken in a custody suite and another of a car patrol. We also accompanied officers on foot patrol in two of our boroughs and the fieldwork offered numerous opportunities for observation of police–public interaction at the front counters of several police stations. Additionally, we took up the invitation to accompany officers on an early-morning drugs raid in Borough C. All these occasions provided the chance to talk informally to officers as well as to observe the interactions between them at parades,[3] on the streets and during breaks.

The formal meetings we observed included those of the Crime and Disorder Reduction Partnership (CDRP)[4] in each area as well as a variety of meetings concerned with community consultation and a day-long multi-agency event to familiarise asylum seekers in Borough C with the responsibilities of the different agencies and, by implication, some of the social and cultural norms on which these are based.

We also accumulated a considerable amount of written material from each area, most of it somewhat *ad hoc* but including the crime and disorder strategies for each and the audits on which these were based.

Analysis of interviews and focus groups
The vast majority of focus groups and interviews were fully transcribed. Analysis of key themes in the focus groups has been done partly using NUD*IST, a computer package for analysing qualitative data, and partly by less formal methods.

---

[3] 'Parades' refer to the start of a shift when officers assemble, are assigned to tasks and provided with briefing material.
[4] These are the interagency groups set up under the Crime and Disorder Act 1998, and include chief officers from the local authority, local police, probation and health services. 157

Appendix 3: Logistic and Ordinal Regression Models

Logistic regression is a well established technique in social research and has been used extensively in other criminological survey analysis (e.g. Mirrlees Black *et al* 1998; Kershaw *et al* 2000; Clancy *et al* 2001). It is a multivariate statistical technique that allows one to determine whether any independent variable (e.g. age or social class) thought to be related to a dependent variable (e.g. experience of the police) is statistically important once possible associations with other variables have been taken into account. For example, income and area of residence are likely to predict experience of crime, but they are also related to each other. Logistic regression means that one can assess whether income has a correlation – and by implication a causal link – with victimisation in its own right and not in a way that is simply explained by its association with area. However, logistic regression can only indicate whether there is a prima facie case that membership of a group has an effect on outcome, taking account of other factors where the survey has information. It does not prove that causal links exist.

As is often the case with survey data, the regression models explain only a small part of the variance in the dependent variables. This is because the dataset captures only a fraction of the relevant information. For example, the models predicting anxiety about crime would obviously be better if the dataset contained information on psychological traits. Where the attribute to be predicted is relatively rare in the population, the model often predicts that *no one* has the attribute. This does not mean the model is valueless, however. It still calculates the extent to which having one attribute (such as living in the inner city) appears to increase the chances of having another attribute (such as being a crime victim).

Ordinal regression is an allied technique, appropriate for predicting who is likely to have had no contact with the police, for example, a little contact or a lot of contact. It is able to take account of the *volume* of contact with the police as well as the *fact* of contact, unlike logistic regression. Finally, linear regression is a similar technique designed to predict values of a continuous, normally distributed, variable.

Table A3.1: Logistic regression model for demographic predictors of police usage

Factor	B	Exp (β)	Significance
Significant			
1. Being middle class	.228	1.25	**
2. Age (entered as continuous variable)	–.011	1.01	**
3. Household has use of car	.334	1.37	**
4. Being inner-city resident	.308	1.36	**
Non-significant			
Income, ethnicity (entered as black, Indian and Pakistani/Bangladeshi), single	–	–	
Weighted data, unweighted *n* = 4,788			

Notes: 1. Variables are ordered according to their order of entry into the stepwise model.
2. Exp (β) rounded to two decimal points. Negative values expressed as the reciprocal of their own value.
3. ** Indicates statistical significance at the 1% level, *indicates significance at the 5% level.
Source: PFLS and 2000 BCS.

Table A3.2: Logistic regression model for demographic and experiential predictors of police usage

Factor	B	Exp (β)	Significance
Significant			
1. Being the victim of crime	.964	2.62	**
2. Being stopped in a car	.671	1.96	**
3. Being middle class	.225	1.25	**
4. Being young	–.006	1.01	**
5. Being inner city resident	.381	1.46	**
6. Household has use of car	.250	1.28	**
7. Being stopped on foot	.671	1.64	*
Non-significant			
Income, ethnicity (entered as black, Indian and Pakistani/Bangladeshi), single	–	–	
Weighted data, unweighted *n* = 4,788			

Notes: 1. Variables are ordered according to their order of entry into the stepwise model.
2. Exp (β) rounded to two decimal points. Negative values expressed as the reciprocal of their own value.
3. ** Indicates statistical significance at the 1% level, *indicates significance at the 5% level.
Source: PFLS and 2000 BCS.

Table A3.3: Ordinal regression model for predictors of being stopped in cars

Factor	Estimate	Significance
Significant		
1. Household has use of car	1.48	**
2. Being black	.70	**
3. Being male	.63	**
4. Being young	.63	**
5. Being single	.33	**
6. Social class (continuous variable, manual more at risk)	.10	*
Non-significant		
Income, being Indian or Pakistani/Bangladeshi, living in inner city	–	–
Weighted data, unweighted $n = 4,794$		

Notes: 1. Variables are ordered according to their estimate size.
2. ** Indicates statistical significance at the 1% level, *indicates significance at the 5% level.
3. Categories: Not stopped, stopped once, stopped two or three times, stopped more.
Source: PFLS and 2000 BCS.

Table A3.4 Ordinal regression model for predictors of being stopped on foot

Factor	Estimate	Significance
Significant		
1. Being aged under 30	1.84	**
2 Being male	1.25	**
3 Being black	.75	**
4. Being from manual household	.65	**
Non-significant		
Income, being Indian or Pakistani/Bangladeshi, living in inner city, car-ownership	–	–
Weighted data, unweighted $n = 4,795$		

Notes: 1. Variables are ordered according to their estimate size.
2. ** Indicates statistical significance at the 1% level, *indicates significance at the 5% level.
3. Categories: Not stopped, stopped once, stopped twice or more.
Source: PFLS and 2000 BCS.

Table A3.5: Logistic regression model for demographic predictors of annoyance with the police in the last five years

Factor	B	Exp (β)	Significance
Significant			
1. Age (entered as continuous variable) class	−.026	1.02	**
2. Being black	.690	1.99	**
3. Income over £15,000	.265	1.30	**
4. Living in a poor borough	.312	1.37	**
5. Coming from non-manual background	.203	1.23	*
6. Household has use of car	.224	1.25	*
Non-significant			
Being Asian, being single	–	–	
Weighted data, unweighted *n* = 4,226			

Notes: 1. Variables are ordered according to their order of entry into the stepwise model.
2. Exp (β) rounded to two decimal points. Negative values expressed as the reciprocal of their own value.
3. ** Indicates statistical significance at the 1% level, *indicates significance at the 5% level.
Source: PFLS and 2000 BCS.

Table A3.6: Logistic regression model for demographic predictors of thinking the police do a bad job

Factor	B	Exp (β)	Significance
Significant			
1. Living in a poor borough	.380	1.46	**
2. Age (entered as continuous variable)	.013	1.01	**
3. Low income	.153	1.14	**
Non-significant			
Being from an ethnic minority, class, being single, gender	–	–	
Weighted data, unweighted *n* = 5,013			

Notes: 1. Variables are ordered according to their order of entry into the stepwise model.
2. Exp (β) rounded to two decimal points. Negative values expressed as the reciprocal of their own value.
3. ** Indicates statistical significance at the 1% level, *indicates significance at the 5% level.
Source: PFLS and 2000 BCS.

Table A3.7: Logistic regression model for demographic and experiential predictors of thinking the police do a bad job

Factor	B	Exp (β)	Significance
Significant			
1. Being searched on foot	1.180	3.25	**
2. Seeking police help	.525	1.69	**
3. Living in a poor borough	.374	1.45	**
4. Age (entered as continuous variable)	−.009	1.01	**
3. Below average income	−.164	1.18	**
Non-significant			
Being from an ethnic minority, class, being single, gender	–	–	

Weighted data, unweighted *n* = 4,975

Notes: 1. Variables are ordered according to their order of entry into the stepwise model.
2. Exp (β) rounded to two decimal points. Negative values expressed as the reciprocal of their own value.
3. ** Indicates statistical significance at the 1% level, *indicates significance at the 5% level.
Source: PFLS and 2000 BCS.

References

ACPO (2001) *Blue Print for Policing in the 21st Century*. Association of Chief Police Officers. www.acpo.police.uk

Audit Commission (1993) *Helping with Inquiries: Tackling Crime Effectively*. London: Audit Commission.

Audit Commission (1996) *Streetwise: Effective Police Patrol*. London: Audit Commission.

Aye Maung, N. (2001) *2000 British Crime Survey: Findings for London*. London: Regional Crime Reduction Director's Office, Government Office for London.

Banton, M. (1973) 'The Sociology of the Police II', *Police Journal, 46*, 341–362.

Bennett, T. (2000) *Drugs and Crime: the Results of the Second Development Stage of the NEW-ADAM Programme* (HORS 205). London: Home Office.

Berthoud, R. (1998) *The Incomes of Ethnic Minorities*. ISER Report 98–1. Colchester: Institute for Social and Economic Research.

Bittner, E. (1970) *The Functions of the Police in Modern Society*. Chevy Chase, MD: National Institute of Mental Health.

Bowling, B. and Phillips, C. (2002) *Racism, Crime and Justice*. London: Longman.

Brown, J. and Whitfield, G. (2002) *Policing for London. Technical Report*. London: National Centre for Social Research.

Burney, E. (1967) *Housing on Trial: A Study of Immigrants and Local Government*. Oxford: Oxford University Press.

Cabinet Office (2001) *Satisfaction with Public Services: A Discussion Paper*. London: Cabinet Office Performance and Innovation Unit.

Childs, P., Marsden, J., Boys, A. and Strang, J. (2000) *London Strategic Needs Assessment for Drug Misuse*. Paper prepared for the Pan-London Drug Commissioners' group (unpublished).

Clancy, A., Hough, M., Aust, R. and Kershaw, K. (2001) *Crime, Policing and Justice: findings from the 2000 British Crime Survey*. Home Office Research Study No. 223. London: Home Office.

Clarke, R. V. (1999) *Hot Products: Understanding, Anticipating and Reducing Demand for Stolen Goods. Police Research Series* Paper 112. London: Home Office.

Department for Education and Skills http://www.dfes.gov.uk/statistics

Dorn, N., Murji, K. and South, N. (1992) *Traffickers: Drug Markets and Law Enforcement*. London: Routledge.

Edmunds, M., Hough, M., Turnbull, P.J. and May, T. (1999) *Doing Justice to Treatment: Referring Offenders to Drug Services. DPAS Paper* 2. London: Home Office.

Edmunds, M., May, T., Hough, M. and Hearnden, I. (1998) *Arrest Referral: Emerging Lessons from Research. Drugs Prevention Initiative Paper* 23. London: Home Office.

Farrall, S., Bannister, J., Ditton, J. and Gilchrist, E. (1997) Measuring crime and the fear of crime. *British Journal of Criminology 37*: 657–678.

Farrall, S., Bannister, J., Ditton, J. and Gilchrist, E. (2000) Social psychology and the fear of crime. *British Journal of Criminology, 40*: 399–413.

Farrington, D. (1997) Human development and criminal careers. In M. Maguire *et al* (eds.) *The Oxford Handbook of Criminology (2nd edn)*. Oxford: Clarendon Press.

Felson, M. (1998) *Crime and Everyday Life* (2nd edn). Thousand Oaks, CA: Pine Forge Press.

Fielding N. (1995) *Community Policing*. Oxford: Clarendon.

Fielding, N. (2002) 'Theorising Community Policing', *British Journal of Criminology*, 42, 147–163.

FitzGerald, M. (1997) Minorities, crime and criminal justice in Britain. In I. H. Marshall (ed.) *Minorities, Migrants and Crime: Diversity and Similarity across Europe and the United States*. California: Sage.

FitzGerald, M. (1999) *Stop and Search: Final Report*. London: Metropolitan Police (available: http://www.met.police.uk/)

FitzGerald, M. (2000) *Young People and Street Crime in London: a Preliminary Analysis of Recent Statistical Trends*. Unpublished report to Youth Justice Board.

FitzGerald, M. (2001) Ethnic minorities and community safety. In R. Matthews and J. Pitts (eds.) *Crime, Disorder and Community Safety* London: Routledge.

FitzGerald, M. and Hale, C. (1996) *Ethnic Minorities: Victimisation and Racial Harassment: Findings from the 1988 and 1992 British Crime Surveys*. London: Home Office.

FitzGerald, M. and Stockdale J. (forthcoming) *Young People's Involvement in Street Crime*.

Flood Page, C., Campbell, S., Harrington, V. and Miller, J. (2000) *Youth Crime: Findings from the 1998/1999 Youth Lifestyles Survey*. Home Office Research Study 209. London: Home Office.

Giddens, A. (1998) *The Third Way: The Renewal of Social Democracy*. Cambridge: Polity Press.

Graham, J. (1988) *Schools, Disruptive Behaviour and Delinquency. Home Office Research Study*, 96. London: Home Office.

Graham, J. and Bowling, B. (1995) *Young People and Crime*. Home Office Research Study, 145. London: HMSO.

Hale, C. (1993) *Fear of Crime: A Review of the Literature*. London: Metropolitan Police Service Working Party on the Fear of Crime.

Hale, C. (1996) Fear of Crime: a Review of the Literature. *International Review of Victimology, 4*, 79–150.

Hall, S. *et al* (1978) *Policing the Crisis*. London: Macmillan.

Harcourt, B. E. (2001) *Illusion of Order: The False Promise of Broken Windows Policing*. Cambridge, MA: Harvard University Press.

Harrington, V. and Mayhew, P. (2001) *Mobile Phone Theft*. Home Office Research Study 235. London: Home Office.

Her Majesty's Inspectorate of Constabulary (1997) *Winning the Race: Policing Plural Communities*. London: Home Office.

Her Majesty's Inspectorate of Constabulary (2000) *Policing in London: 'Winning Consent' – a Review of Murder Investigation and Community and Race Relations Issues in the Metropolitan Police Service*. London; Home Office.

Hobbs *et al* (forthcoming) Door Lore: the Art and Economics of Intimidation. In *British Journal of Criminology*.

Home Office (1993) *Police Reform: A Police Service for the 21st Century* (Cm 2281). London: HMSO.

Home Office (1994) *Review of Police Core and Ancillary Tasks. Interim Report*. London: Home Office.

Home Office (1999) *The Police Grant Report (England and Wales) 1999/2000*. Report by the Secretary of State for the Home Department under Section 46 of the Police Act. London: House of Commons.

Home Office (1999) *Recorded Crime Statistics England and Wales April 1998 to March 1999*. Home Office Statistical Bulletin 18/99. London: Home Office.

Home Office (2001) *Policing a New Century: a Blueprint for Reform. CM 5326.* London: Stationery Office.

Home Office (2001a) *Motoring Offences and Breath Test Statistics.* Home Office Statistical Bulletin 24/01. London: Home Office.

Home Office (2001b) *Control of Immigration Statistics: United Kingdom 2000.* Home Office Statistical Bulletin 14/01. London: Home Office.

Horton, C. and Smith, D. (1988) *Evaluating Police Work.* London: Policy Studies Institute.

Hough, M. (1995) *Anxiety about Crime: Findings from the 1994 British Crime Survey. Home Office Research Study* 147. London: Home Office.

Hough, M., Turnbull, P. and McSweeney, T. (2001) *Drugs and Crime: What are the Links? Paper submitted by Drugscope to the Home Affairs Committee of Inquiry into the Drug Legislation.* London: Drugscope.

Humphry, D. (1972) *Police Power and Black People.* London: Panther.

Hutton, W. and Giddens, A. (2000) *On the Edge: Living with Global Capitalism.* London: Jonathan Cape.

Johnston, L. (2000) 'Private Policing: Problems and Prospects'. In *Core Issues in Policing* (eds.) Lieshman, F., Loveday, B. and Savage, S. Harlow: Longman.

Joint Consultative Committee (1990) *Operational Policing Review.* Report published by ACPO, Superintendents' Association and Police Federation.

Kelling, G. L. (1999) *'Broken Windows' and Police Discretion.* NCJ 178259. Washington: National Institute of Justice. (http://www.ojp.usdoj.gov/nij).

Kelling, G. L. and Coles, C. M. (1996) *Fixing Broken Windows: Restoring Law and Order in our Communities.* New York: Free Press.

Kershaw, C., Budd, T., Kinshott, G., Mattinson, J., Mayhew, P. and Myhill, A. (2000) *The 2000 British Crime Survey.* Home Office Statistical Bulletin 18/00. London: Home Office.

Matheson, J. and Edwards, G. (eds.) (2000) *Focus on London 2000.* London: HMSO.

May, T., Warburton, H., Turnbull, P. and Hough, M. (2002) *Times they are a-changing: policing of cannabis.* York: Joseph Rowntree Foundation.

Mirrlees-Black, C., Budd, T., Partridge, S., and Mayhew, P. (1998) *The 1998 British Crime Survey.* Home Office Statistical Bulletin, 21/98. London: Home Office.

Modood, T. *et al* (1997) *Ethnic Minorities in Britain: Diversity and Disadvantage.* London: Policy Studies Institute.

Montjardet, D. (2000) Unpublished paper delivered to the Franco-British Council seminar, 'Policing in France and Britain'. London, 7 November.

Morgan, R. and Newburn, T. (1998) *The Future of Policing.* Oxford: Clarendon Press.

Morgan Report (1991) *Safer Communities: the Local Delivery of Crime Prevention through the Partnership Approach.* London: Home Office.

MORI (2000) *British Public Opinion. Vol. XXIII.* No. 2. London: MORI.

MPS (1984) *The Policing Principles of the Metropolitan Police.* London: Metropolitan Police.

Neyroud, P. and Beckley, A. (2001) *Policing, Ethics and Human Rights.* Cullompton: Willan Publishing.

ONS (Office for National Statistics) (2001a) *Mid-2000 Population Estimates.* (http://statistics.gov.uk/popest_mid00.asp).

ONS (2001b) *Social Trends 31.* London: Office for National Statistics.

PA Consulting (2001) *Diary of a Police Officer.* Police Research Series paper 149. London: Home Office.

Povey, D. *et al* (2001) *Recorded Crime (England and Wales, 12 Months to March 2001)*. Home Office Statistical Bulletin 12/01. London: Home Office.

Reiner, R. (1978) *The Blue Coated Worker.* Cambridge: Cambridge University Press.
Reiner, R. (2000) *The Politics of the Police.* Oxford: Oxford University Press.
Reiner, R., Livingstone, S. and Allen, J. (2000) *No More Happy Endings? The Media and Popular Concern about Crime since the Second World War* in Crime, Risk and Insecurity (eds. Hope, T. and Sparks, R.) London: Routledge.
Reiss, A. J. (1971) *The Police and Public.* New Haven: Yale University Press.
Roberts, J., Stalans, L., Indermaur, D. and Hough, M. (in press), *Penal Populism and Public Opinion.* Oxford: Oxford University Press.
Rose E. J. B. *et al* (1969) *Colour and Citizenship: A Report on British Race Relations.* Oxford: Oxford University Press.

Scarman, Lord (1981) *The Brixton Disorders: Report of an Inquiry by the Rt. Hon. Lord Scarman OBE.* London: HMSO.
Sheehy Report (1993) *Report of the Inquiry into Police Rewards and Responsibilities.* (Cm 2280). London: HMSO.
Sherman, L., Gottfredson, D., MacKenzie, D., Eck, J., Reuter, P., and Bushway, S. (1997) *Preventing Crime: What Works, What Doesn't, What's Promising: a Report to the United States Congress* (available: http\\www.ncjrs.org).
Skogan, W. (1990) *Spirals of Decline: Crime and the Spiral of Decay in American Neighbourhoods.* New York: Free Press.
Skolnick, J. (1966) *Justice without Trial: Law Enforcement in a Democratic Society.* New York: Wiley.
Small, S. (1983) *Police and People in London. II. A Group of Young Black People.* London: Policy Studies Institute.
Smith, D. J. (1983a) *Police and People in London. I. A Survey of Londoners.* London: Policy Studies Institute.
Smith, D. J. (1983b) *Police and People in London. III. A Survey of Police Officers.* London: Policy Studies Institute.
Smith, D. J. and Gray, J. (1983) *Police and People in London. IV. The Police in Action.* London: Policy Studies Institute.
Storkey, M, and Bardsley, M. (1999) Estimating the numbers of refugees and asylum seekers in London. In *Refugee Health in London.* London: The Health of Londoners Project.

Willis, C. (1983) *The Use, Effectiveness and Impact of Police Stop and Search Powers.* Research and Planning Unit Paper 15. London: Home Office.
Wilson, J.Q. (1968) *Varieties of Police Behaviour.* Cambridge, MA: Harvard University Press.
Wilson, J. and Kelling, G. (1982) Broken Windows: the police and community safety. *Atlantic Monthly* March: 29–38.
Wolff Olins (1998) *The Corporate Identity of the Metropolitan Police.* London: Wolff Olins.